THANKS,
DANIEL & JANE

MAY THIS BOOK
ENCOURAGE YOU THRU
HEROES WHO HAVE
GONE BEFORE

Fallible Heroes

Fallible Heroes

Inside the Protestant Reformation

Stephen Fortosis
and
Harley T. Atkinson

Foreword by Donald T. Williams

RESOURCE *Publications* · Eugene, Oregon

FALLIBLE HEROES
Inside the Protestant Reformation

Wipf & Stock
An Imprint of Wipf and Stock Publishers
199 W. 8th Ave., Suite 3
Eugene, OR 97401

www.wipfandstock.com

PAPERBACK ISBN: 978-1-6667-4550-4
HARDCOVER ISBN: 978-1-6667-4551-1
EBOOK ISBN: 978-1-6667-4552-8

JULY 28, 2022 3:48 PM

Scripture quotations taken from the HOLY BIBLE, NEW INTERNATIONAL
VERSION, Copyright © 1973, 1978, 1984 by International Bible Society.

Contents

Foreword

THE REFORMERS—LUTHER, CALVIN, ZWINGLI, and others—were flawed men who made many mistakes. But I am convinced that they were essentially right about their main premise: "salvation by grace alone through faith alone in Christ alone, revealed in a Bible that stands alone as the only inspired and infallible authority about that Gospel." So I wrote in *Ninety-Five Theses for a New Reformation*.[1] Evangelicalism has been that movement which transmitted the spiritual gains of the Sixteenth-Century Protestant Reformation to the present, mediated through the Puritans of the Seventeenth Century and the Revivalists of the First Great Awakening in the Eighteenth. If we lose touch with our historical roots in those movements, we will be in danger of letting the doctrinal and spiritual legacy they entrusted to us slip through our fingers. And that is just where I think we are as an Evangelical movement.

I was therefore trying in that opening quotation to characterize the historic Reformation of the sixteenth century in one sentence as context for understanding the new Reformation that I think the church needs in the twenty-first. That sentence could very profitably be expanded into a book of its own; and such a book would serve a critical need in getting us back in touch with our spiritual roots. That is exactly what Harley Atkinson and Stephen Fortosis have given us in *Fallible Heroes: Inside the Protestant Reformation*.

Books on the Reformation and the reformers are legion. This one is a worthwhile addition to that number in that it does two things that none of the others have done quite so well. First, it gives equal attention to many of the minor figures that most of us know less about but

---

1. Williams, *Ninety-Five Theses*, 24.

who were important to the ways the contributions of major players like Luther, Zwingli, and Calvin were received and worked out. Melanchthon, Bullinger, Farel, Bucer, Beza, Tyndale, and others deserve to be better known, and this book will give you enough information about them to whet your appetite for more.

Even more importantly, *Fallible Heroes* looks at this critical period from the standpoint of the thesis that God always works through flawed human beings because in a fallen world flawed human beings are the only ones available for Him to work with. Redemption effects a real transformation in them, but it does not make them perfect. Here both of the temptations that beset many Protestants writing about the Reformation are avoided—the men and women of the Reformation are neither put on a pedestal nor are they debunked. We get neither hero worship nor cynicism. We meet them as real human beings that we can relate to in such a way that we can learn from their flaws as well as their virtues, their mistakes as well as their triumphs.

Atkinson and Fortosis hope that their book "will spark interest and further discussion regarding what the Christian church can learn from the character, ideals, and inter-relationships" of the reformers. They want their writing to be an "impetus toward constructive personal reflection and dialogue" about these matters. Their hope was fulfilled in my reading of *Fallible Heroes*. I believe it will be fulfilled in yours as well.

DONALD T. WILLIAMS
Toccoa, Georgia

Preface

THERE IS NO SHORTAGE of books penned concerning individual Protestant reformers and there is also an abundance of accounts of the Protestant Reformation as a movement. Why this particular book? As I (Steven) read works on the Reformation, it appeared that there were individual works that attempted to cover the vast Reformation landscape from the 1300s through the 1700s. Other books dug deep into the theological debate between Roman Catholicism and Protestantism. Others featured only the most prominent or well-known reformers, such as Erasmus, Martin Luther, John Calvin, Huldrych Zwingli, and Philip Melanchthon. One book might focus on the Lutheran Church while another focused primarily upon the Counter-Reformation. One might emphasize the peasant revolution while another concentrated on the Anabaptist movement.

As I continued to read works on the subject, I found the names of notable characters who were fortunate to receive only a passing glance. Among these were Johann von Staupitz, Martin Bucer, Andreas Karlstadt, Wolfgang Capito, Matthew and Katharina Zell, Conrad Grebel, Felix Manz, Wilhelm Reublin, Balthazar Hubmaier, Oecolampadius, Katie Luther, and Heinrich Bullinger. A few books focused on some of these lesser-known individuals, but they were disengaged—each reformer was doled out a four or five-page summary. What I did not find was a work dedicated primarily to these individuals' interpersonal relationships, not only with their constituents but also with fellow leaders. There may be those readers who do not realize that significant relationships existed throughout much of the sixteenth century, and vigorous dialogue existed between these individuals. They visited in one another's homes, churches,

and universities, wrote thousands of letters, met one another at colloquies and councils, learned from one another, and debated. Bitterness
and harsh language entered relationships at times.

Many questions emerge. In what ways did the relationships of these
leaders prove constructive? Destructive? Was it necessary to some extent that there be vigorous and sometimes fiery debate to keep the Reformation doctrines from becoming insipid tenets of uncertainty? Were
reformers tougher on each other and on enemies than are Christian
leaders today? What can we learn, both positive and negative, from their
leadership? What might they have done differently or better? In what aspects of leadership have we improved, and in what ways have we perhaps
regressed? What principles can we take away with us? Based upon the
Reformation, what does the evangelical Church need most in our era and
how can leaders reach these objectives? These are some of the questions
about which the authors hope this book can stimulate constructive discussion and action.

STEPHEN FORTOSIS

Introduction

Moral Decline of the Behemoth

"If Christianity had remained what its founder made it, things would have gone differently, and mankind would have been far happier; but there is no plainer proof that this religion is falling to pieces than the fact that the people who live nearest to Rome are the least pious of any." [1]

— MACHIAVELLI

EVERY GENERATION FACES ITS peculiar crises, but the Middle Ages in Western Europe were perhaps one of the bleaker, more brutal periods in recorded history. During the first few decades of the fourteenth century, a series of cold, wet, growing seasons led to a continent-wide famine and widespread death and malnutrition. By 1320, between ten and twenty-five percent of the population perished. Then came the Bubonic Plague, commonly known as Black Death. Though it reached its peak between 1347 and 1350, with an estimated 23,840,000 casualties, periodic outbreaks continued to occur during the following 120 years. By 1450 the dreadful disease depopulated Western Europe by 60 to 75 percent. [2] The Hundred Years War (1337-1453) also wreaked devastation on the masses and took many thousands of lives.

With the shortage of workforce, many peasants revolted against their lords, seeking better treatment or pay. Attacks led to repression.

1. Quoted by Spitz, *The Protestant,* 50.
2. Payton, *Getting,* 26.

1

When the dust settled, a vast host of lives had been lost and the workforce had taken an almost irrecoverable hit. Undoubtedly, one could sense the underlying terror as life became more and more tenuous. Pessimism and cynicism spread far and wide, and if there was any humor remaining at all, it tended to be a dark and bitter variety, with a heavy dose of vulgarity thrown in.

We should acknowledge from the outset that the remaining masses in Europe were not overwhelmingly Catholic. Some scholars believe that a large portion of the Middle Ages population may have been semi-pagan rustics and spirit worshippers: "in many parts of Europe and on all levels of society of a persistence of paganism, the survival of Germanic folklore, an inclination toward superstition, the practice of witchcraft, a substratum of materialism, and a failure to understand or appreciate the transcendent and otherworldly dimensions of their faith."[3] Though many of these unsophisticated peasants were somewhat familiar with Catholicism, some had conveniently sought to merge it with their deep-seated traditions and folklore. Divine portents were seen in the birth of deformed animals or humans, unusual dreams, the passage of a comet, and the display of northern lights. Thunder and poltergeists were warded off with special prayers, magick, or consecrated herbs. For some, amulets and spells were not considered incongruent with anointed water, miraculous prayers to saints, or holy candles.[4]

A Splintered Papacy

In the early years, the Roman Church and the pope were considered unassailable, almost perfect overlords in religious matters. However, after Pope Innocent III (1198–1216), the papacy began losing a bit of its prestige and power. There were occasional good men who served during the following centuries, but the seeds of corruption were being sown. Certain popes were assassinated or died under suspicious circumstances. Then came the Avignon papacy (1309–1378), during which seven French popes ruled in succession from Avignon, France. These popes multiplied the ways the Church extracted money from kings, clergy, and the general populace—even the papacy was considered up for sale. Sexual appetites had free rein and violation of canon law, protocol, and morality became

3. Spitz, *The Protestant*, 54.
4. Ozment, *Protestants*, 96–7, 196.

common. Then, for about forty years (1378–1423), the Church voted in one pope for Rome and another for Avignon. Now the Church had two and sometimes three popes simultaneously, all battling for dominance with no holds barred. The Roman Church had hammered home the fact that there was one pope ordained explicitly by God and perfect in all matters *ex-cathedra*. Suddenly there were several popes, each claiming to be God's ideal choice.

Well before the mid-1500s, the Church was in decline. The ordinary citizen was being taxed to death by fees for indulgences, for hearing confessions, for performing requiem masses, baptisms, marriages, burials, and other rites. Monasteries and convents were becoming known in some areas as increasingly corrupt, hornet nests of sin rather than havens of righteousness. Princes began rebelling against the fact that clergy were free from prosecution under state law because the Church had its own courts. Perhaps the Church had done her perceived job of heaping on guilt too well. Even if citizens repented, who knew if the repentance was acceptable and genuine? Many sinners were so desperate to make their peace with God, they were willing to look beyond a Church that could make one weep in penitence yet could offer no hope of forgiveness or peace.

Then came the Renaissance, and instead of pursuing church reform papal leadership tended to seek greater pomp and circumstance by using great artists, sculptors, and authors to beautify the Vatican and massive cathedrals, perhaps hoping to blind the populace in its glory. The low watermark of the Renaissance papacy involved Pope Alexander VI (1492–1503), perhaps the most debased and unpopular pope. He unabashedly promoted his illegitimate children by different mistresses to prominent positions, including a cardinalship to his nine-year-old son.

Julius II only reigned as pope from 1503 to 1513 but brought force back into the papacy. More of a warrior than a pope, he was impetuous, untrustworthy, vulgar, and rude. Nevertheless, his administrative ability, his use of violence, and his threats of ex-communication allowed him both to intimidate and extort money from the masses. Leo X followed him, accomplishing by shrewdness and sleight of hand what Julius had accomplished by brutality. Though this work will encompass the period of later popes, Leo was tested by the first tremors of church reform, and it was Leo who failed that test.

In Germany, as well as surrounding nations, Rome was said to traffic in church benefices, not for citizens of that nation or the most qualified churchman, but to the highest bidders. The Church often snatched the first year's income of a new parish office. Along with the preachers of indulgences came Rome's legions of mendicant friars, relic hawkers, and miracle workers, profiting enormously at the expense of both rich and poor. Laypeople struggled under weekly tributes by monasteries and convents and were often forced to stand trial in Church courts and pay expensive reparations. Some priests ran gaming parlors on their properties, and shamelessly claimed the winnings as their own. It was a relatively common practice for parish priests to whore or even live openly with mistresses.

Moreover, the trump card the Church held over the heads of the people was always ex-communication. This threat struck fear in many hearts because it meant a complete cutting off, that is, certain damnation and destruction for all of eternity. Germans especially became increasingly cynical and alienated from the Church because of practices such as these.

Mini-Reformations

James Payton believes that the mounting anti-clericalism in Western Christendom during this period indicated an evident yearning for *better* Christianity and *clearer* theology, not less of it.[5] Reformation flames had been lit in various places and by various individuals, but the Church had so far been able to extinguish them before becoming conflagrations. In the early 1300s, Walter Burley of Merton College had the nerve to dispute the scholastic approach and recommend returning to the direct study of the Scriptures. He was decades ahead of his time, but when John Wycliffe became a don at Oxford in 1360, he took Burley literally and eventually provided England with its first translation of the Bible in everyday English, though his translation was not from the Greek but from the Latin. As he saw faults in the Roman Church, Wycliffe also wrote a book entitled *Divine Dominion*, challenging the supremacy of the Catholic Church. He taught that the relationship of humans to God was direct and did not require intermediaries, good works did not win salvation, the pope was not to be worshipped, auricular confession was not necessary, simony was unjust, monasteries were often dens of thieves, many priests were

5. Payton, *Getting*, 43, 50.

lecherous, indulgences were not a teaching of Christ, and priests could not change the bread and wine into the physical body and blood of Christ.

Wycliffe became a highly respected Doctor of Theology and taught at Oxford for decades. Enemies contemptuously called his followers "Poor Preaching Priests," or Lollards—in other words, mumblers who spoke nonsense. The Lollards eventually retreated from the mainstream of political power as well as from the universities. Printing did not yet exist, so they did not have access to the means by which Luther used to the maximum. Another useful weapon of the sixteenth century Reformation—popular music and hymn writing—went ignored by Wycliffe's followers.

Wycliffe's writings spread to the Bohemian capital of Prague and Jan of Husinetz (John Huss), priest and dean of the philosophical faculty at Prague University, took them to heart. Wycliffe voiced some reasons for Huss's growing dissatisfaction with existing Church institutions. His sermons about church reform became hugely popular in Prague. Huss's movement also became a clear statement of Czech identity against German influence in the Bohemian Church and commonwealth.

When Huss was summoned to the Church's general council in Konstanz in 1414 to explain his acts of rebellion, it was under a safe-conduct from Holy Roman Emperor Sigismund. However, the council reneged and put him on trial for heresy. He was burned at the stake in 1415 by the decision of the council and the emperor. It caused an explosion of fury in Bohemia, and within five years, a Czech rebellion established a Hussite church in Bohemia independent of Rome.[6]

There were two branches of Hussites: 1) the Ultraquists, whose primary differences from Catholicism were insistence that attendees receive both bread and wine at the Eucharist and that the Mass be conducted in the Czech language, 2) and the Taborites or *Unitas Fratrum*, who condemned political repression, capital punishment, military service, the swearing of oaths, a separate priesthood, and transubstantiation.[7] Thus, in eastern Bohemia and Moravia, a new Christian sect was formed called the Church of the Brotherhood, dedicated to a simple agricultural life. By 1500 it claimed 100,000 members. These Moravian Brethren, known for their religious toleration, unassuming piety, peaceful fidelity, and missionary zeal, were almost exterminated during the Thirty Years' War.

---

6. Durant and Durant, *The Reformation*, 165–7.

7. Durant and Durant, *The Reformation*, 168–9.

Peter Waldo, a wealthy merchant, abandoned that life to follow Christ into poverty. The group that grew around him became known as the Waldensians. Concentrated at first in the remote mountainous regions of southeastern France, they took an interest in Huss, translating some of his writings into Provencal. Many of their evolving tenets coincided with the spirit of Lollard and Hussite beliefs: Holy Scriptures alone are sufficient to guide to salvation, repentance is imperative for all, Catholic priests and the pope have no authority over the masses, everyone has the right to proclaim the Word of God publicly, oaths constitute a mortal sin, purgatory is an invention of the sixth century, blessings and consecrations by the Church do not confer sanctity, the invocation of Saints cannot be admitted, images of paintings and relics of Saints should not receive honor or worship, and, besides Sunday, no fast or supposed holy day can be commanded, the Church and State should remain as separate authorities, and the Eucharist is to be viewed as a memorial, not as a sacrifice. The Waldensians went to Rome at different times and appealed to both Pope Alexander III and later Pope Lucius III, for permission to preach but were denied by each. In 1211, they were declared heretics. More than eighty were burned at the stake in Strassburg, touching off several centuries of sporadic persecution.

During this period, other mini reformations occurred within the Roman Church through such entities as the Theatines, Girolamo Savonarola, and others like him. However, the poison had oozed too deep and too broad. As Derek Wilson writes, "After fifteen hundred years of exercising spiritual power, developing the doctrines and disciplinary procedures to buttress that power, and suppressing radicals, mystics, and zealots who posed inconvenient questions, nothing less than a complete shake-up would do."[8]

When Savonarola became a Dominican priest in 1475, he was already making noises regarding corruption in the Church with his poem *De Ruina Ecclesiae* (*On the Downfall of the Church*). He immersed himself in theological studies for about seven years then was dispatched to Florence, where he made absolutely no impression during the next five years. He returned to Bologna and more study. When he reappeared in Florence in 1490, his preaching had turned fiery and apocalyptic. The rich and powerful Medici family was declining, a syphilis plague was spreading, and, with the year 1500 approaching, the minds of the public

8. Wilson, *Out of the Storm*, 36.

had turned millennial. His Church of San Marco became crowded to overflowing. He preached that the Christian life involved being good from the heart, practicing Christ-like virtues, and minimizing Church displays of excessive pomp and ceremony. At first, the preaching resulted in a wide turning to devotional books, sacrifices by the wealthy, and a considerable drop in cheating, usury, and other such crimes. However, it did not last. Interlopers convinced the Holy See that Savonarola must be cut down to size, and he was summoned to Rome and instructed not to continue such preaching. In great anguish, the Dominican refused, and his words became harsher against Church leaders: "They speak against pride and ambition but they are immersed in it up to the eyes. They preach chastity but they keep concubines. They recommend fasting but they live luxuriously. It is the Pharisaic spirit come to life in the rulers of Christ's Church."[9] On April 8, 1498, a mob stormed his convent, dragged him out, tortured him beyond belief, and brought in papal judges to conduct a mock trial. On May 23, he was hanged, then burned in the Piazza della Signoria.[10]

A Reformation that Should Not Have Happened

Nevertheless, despite such mini reformations, there are many reasons why the Protestant Reformation should theoretically have never occurred. The Roman Catholic Church was still massive, wealthy, and quite overpowering. Even Lorenzo Valla's exposure of the Donation of Constantine as a forgery in 1440 did little to damage the papacy's fearsome prestige. Besides wealth, the Roman Church also had on their side the reverence for traditions long established, a dread of touching the Sacred and the Holy See, the consciences of millions, the passions of the fanatical, the self-interested alarm of princes and politicians, and fear of shaking beliefs that had formed the cement of human society for centuries.

Nonetheless, diverse explanations have arisen as to why the Reformation succeeded to the extent that it did: the greed of monarchs for church wealth, the Renaissance and its individualist quest of humanism, the corruption of Catholicism, a desire for religious self-expression, hunger for the Word of God. These are all vital factors, but Augustine of Hippo must also be given the lion's share of the credit for the seeds

---

9. Quoted by Clark, *Savonarola*, 153.

10. Heraud, *The Life and Times*, 349, 371.

of revolution that, at long last, burst into full bloom. Both the Roman Church and the Protestants used Augustine as a reference point but for opposite reasons. The Church latched onto his vital teachings regarding the Catholic Church and strict obedience to it; the Protestants proclaimed his discussion of human depravity and salvation of the elect by grace through faith in Christ.

This encapsulated summary sets the stage for uniting one of the most unique groups in history. We may hear primarily about Luther, Calvin, Melanchthon, and Zwingli, but the Protestant Reformation was not about a few leading individuals who independently changed the minds and hearts of hundreds of thousands of people. It involved a considerable number of reformers, especially throughout much of the sixteenth century. As noted in the Preface noteworthy relationships existed between these individuals, and spirited conversation was exchanged repeatedly—in homes, churches, universities, and councils. They clashed, collaborated, schemed, encouraged, and oft times celebrated one another. This is their story, up close and personal.

1

Desiderius Erasmus

Reluctant Initiator

> *"I would have the weakest woman read the Gospels and the Epistles of St. Paul. . . . I long for the plowboy to sing them to himself as he follows the plow, the weaver to hum them to the tune of his shuttle. . . . Other studies we may regret having undertaken, but happy is the man upon whom death comes when he is engaged in these."*[1]
>
> —ERASMUS

THE YEAR WAS 1511, and in a Europe that seemed to have precious little to laugh about, there was a small volume released that would provide wickedly spiced mirth to thousands for decades to come. Titled *Encomium Moria* (*Praise of Folly*), it was arguably the most popular book written by the humanist Desiderius Erasmus (1466–1536). Allegedly, Erasmus penned it in 1509 during one week at Thomas More's estate and then dedicated it to the Saint. When the book was released in 1511, readers found *Folly* personified, as she both scorned and praised self-deception and madness and then moved to a satirical examination of pious but superstitious abuses of Catholic doctrine and corrupt practices within the Roman Church. These were not the first published barbs against the Church by humanists, but they achieved a much higher circulation.

1. Quoted by Durant and Durant, *Story of Civilization*, 285.

Erasmus: Holy Catholic Jester

Erasmus's true feelings regarding the Roman Church were that its theologians' "brains are the rottenest, intellects the dullest, doctrines the thorniest, manners the brutalest, life the foulest, speech the spitefulest, hearts the blackest that I have ever encountered in the world."[2] The only way Erasmus saw of shaming a corrupt Church without losing his head was to jest at the enormity of the fiasco. As noted by J. A. Froude, "The condition of the Church was a comedy, as well as a tragedy, a thing for laughter, and a thing for tears."[3] He trusted that a light satire of the secular, as well as the sacred, would protect him from Church retribution.

A brief, representative sample reads: "They [churchmen] call it a sign of holiness to be unable to read. To work miracles is old and antiquated, and not in fashion now; to instruct the people, troublesome; to interpret the Scripture, pedantic; to pray, a sign one has little else to do; to shed tears, silly and womanish; to be poor, base; to be vanquished, dishonorable and little becoming him that scarce admits even kings to kiss his slipper; and lastly, to die, uncouth; and to be stretched on a cross, infamous."[4] He concluded that the Church scatters her enemies, "as if the Church had any enemies more pestilential than impious pontiffs who by their silence allow Christ to be forgotten, who enchain Him by mercenary rules, adulterate His teaching by forced interpretations, and crucify Him afresh by their scandalous life."[5] In the grim world of the plague, frequent famines, vast poverty, and almost no means of entertainment, this was high humor. Perhaps the most surprising thing about this satirical work is that Pope Leo did not rush to condemn it. How long would it take the pope to retaliate against such bold mockery?

Erasmus' Beggarly Beginnings

To say that Gerrit Gerritszoon—later to be known as Desiderius Erasmus—was reared under unfortunate circumstances would be a significant understatement. He was born in Rotterdam, Netherlands, the illegitimate son of a Robert Gerard and a woman named Marguarit. Though it is up

2. Quoted by Froude, *Life and Letters,* 75.

3. Froude, *Life and Letters,* 135.

4. Erasmus, *In Praise of Folly,* 42.

5. Erasmus, *In Praise of Folly,* 42.

to debate, his birthdate is thought to have been October 28, 1466. It is possible Gerard's parents did not approve of the relationship, and it was not until Gerard was deceived into thinking that Marguarit was deceased that he entered the priesthood. If this is true, technically, Gerrit was not born of a priest.

Gerrit had an older brother named Peter, but the younger son demonstrated more promise as a student. At age nine, he was enrolled in a school in Deventer, Holland. An exceptionally inquisitive child, Gerrit consumed books like one would devour bread. When he was in his adolescence, his parents died, victims of the plague, and the brothers were placed under the guardianship of three of their father's associates. Gerrit sharply accused the guardians of negligence, believing they did not have the best interests of the boys in mind. After much of the inheritance was exhausted, they tried to pack their charges off to a monastery to be done with them, after which the boys were reared in *Devotio Moderna* schools, most notably a school run by the Brethren of the Common Life, a Roman Catholic religious community which typically prepared young men for monastic life.[6] Gerrit spent two years here; years he later considered thoroughly wasted. According to Froude, Erasmus "knew more than his teachers of the special subjects in which the instructors tried to teach him, and found them to be models of conceit and ignorance."[7]

In 1491, Peter was intimidated into taking monastic vows, but later ran away and gave himself up to debauchery. Already disenchanted with the abuses he saw in monastic life, Gerrit strenuously fought against being placed in a monastery. However, he was forced by his poverty into spending some years in a house of Augustinian canons. With threats from his guardian that his inheritance was exhausted, he agreed to try the novitiate, specifically in a canon at Steyn. In 1492 he was ordained a priest at Utrecht. Throughout this period, he was not only reading but also beginning to write and circulate his publications. Finally, the prior at the monastery noticed how bright a young man was Gerrit and advised him to throw himself upon the protection of the Bishop of Cambray. The bishop had the pope's ear at the time, and he reported that he had need of

6. Collationary Fathers were men employed by Franciscans and Dominicans to do the work of instructing young boys. They were apparently of dubious character, however, whose "business was to catch in some way superior lads, threaten them, frighten them, beat them, crush their spirits, tame them, as the process was called, and break them in for the cloister." [Froude, *Life and Letters,* 9].

7. Froude, *Life and Letters,* 9.

a secretary, and there was an exceptional youth in a Holland monastery who would fit the bill exactly. The request was granted.

Although the young man was grateful, he was a restless soul and, within a few years, talked his master into allowing him to study in Paris with a modest stipend. Surprisingly, some individuals at the University of Paris already knew of his poems and admired them. He took on private pupils of wealth and, with the income, attended plays and parties. His tastes did not lie in excesses, so he had a clear mind with which to impress others with sharp wit and deep thought.[8] At some point, Gerrit changed his name to Desiderius Erasmus, which combines the Latin and Greek terms, meaning "beloved" or "desired." At age thirty, he returned to Holland to see if there was anything left of his inheritance—however the money was long gone. In this embryonic age of publishing, writing was expensive and rarely lucrative for even the most talented authors. However, he made the acquaintance of a wealthy lady, Anna Bersala, marchioness of Vere, who then lived in the Castle of Tornhoens. For a while he tutored her son, Adolphus. Erasmus had begun realizing the potential of winning wealthy sponsors, and he latched onto her. However, she eventually married a middle-class fellow, and the free ride ended. To continue a comfortable lifestyle, Erasmus next located a wealthy canon of Orléans who took a liking to him and treated him generously. Nevertheless, Erasmus grew tired of the dissipated banquets, sordid and rude people, and the contempt and jealousy with which some people treated the learned.

Erasmus: Famed Writer's Beginnings

Erasmus also developed a close friendship with John Colet, the Oxford scholar who was among the first to dare to lecture directly from Paul's epistles. In the years to follow, Erasmus crisscrossed the continent many times, and he found ways to charm and cajole money from his many admirers, thus living a comfortable existence for most of that time. It would be impossible to trace his journeys; suffice it to say that he traveled between England, Holland, France, Italy, Switzerland, and perhaps a few other nations.

Almost on a whim, Erasmus collected a witty array of sayings, which he called *Adagia*, and sold a great many copies (eventually twenty-six

8. Durant and Durant, *The Reformation*, 271–2.

editions with 4,251 entries), especially to those who wished to sound well-read by spouting off adages from books they had never read. In Erasmus' 1504 bestseller, *Enchiridion Militis Christiani* (*Dagger for a Christian Soldier[9]*) he set out his vision of a return to a purified, Christ-centered faith—something to appeal to pious readers who chased after the rare devotional literature of the time. Outward rituals and ceremonies mattered much less than quiet, austere devotion springing from an abundant inner life. He did not support ecstatic mysticism, nor did he delight in ancient Cabalism (magical variants of Plato's thought). Erasmus wished for a disciplined, biblically-based Christianity cast in a humanist mold—the learned wisdom of Christ. Among many other writings, a sample printed prayer by Erasmus appears to reflect a genuine faith that went beyond the superficial or merely philosophical: "Sever me from myself that I may be grateful to you; may I perish to myself that I may be safe in you; may I die to myself that I may live in you; may I be emptied of myself that I may abound in you; may I be nothing to myself that I may be all to you."[10]

Colet should likely receive significant credit for inspiring this spirit in Erasmus. One day Erasmus praised Thomas Aquinas as the ablest of the teachers. Colet gave him a stern glance and snapped, "Why do you praise to me a man who, had he not had so much arrogance, would never have defined everything in such a rash and supercilious way, and who, had he not had a worldly spirit, would never have contaminated the teaching of Christ with his profane philosophy?"[11] We can only imagine the shock Erasmus must have felt at this remark. There is also evidence that Colet, at some point, wrote Erasmus a letter, essentially challenging him to put up theologically or shut up. Perhaps knowing that Colet's very friendship may depend upon his response, Erasmus turned his powerful mind toward the Scriptures.

Colet knew a little Greek and taught the Bible in a style more akin to the church fathers than the philosophy-minded scholastics. However, English humanists such as William Grocyn, Thomas Linacre, and possibly William Latimer also knew Greek well. There was a new spirit growing among scholars to use the original languages to *ad fontes,* that is, get back to "the sources" and their true meaning. When Erasmus left England, he began the challenging process of fully mastering the language.

---

9. Dagger, in the sense of an all-purpose tool.

10. Quoted by Pollock and Pollock, *Book of Uncommon Prayer,* 66.

11. Quoted by Harbison, *The Christian Scholar,* 75.

Between 1501 and 1505, Erasmus developed in the Netherlands a close relationship with a combative, reform-minded Franciscan friar named Jean Vitrier. This man's inner spiritual devotion and ideas may have had a significant impact on Erasmus's developing critique of the Roman Church. In 1511, Erasmus went to Cambridge to lecture in Greek. He detested living in England, but he avidly began laboring to compile his Greek New Testament and remained in England for three years. Above all, Erasmus would protect his independence of body and mind. He eventually accepted a pension from Charles V and received gifts from Archbishop Warham, Lord Mountjoy, Jean Sauvage (Chancellor of Burgundy), and others. However, with flowered courtesy, he refused the court of France, a possible bishopric at Courtrai, and professorships at the universities of both Leipzig and Ingolstadt. He would not be labeled and would not write in the interest of any one party or religious group.

Northern European Humanists and the Influence of Erasmus

The effects of the European Renaissance or "rebirth" had now spread far and wide, and whole societies seemed to be waking out of a long and troubled slumber. Those who claim that the Renaissance was the secular answer to issues the Church could not solve are mistaken. A humanist was not an individual who wished to build a secular world; humanists simply emphasized humanities—the liberal arts—to prepare students to become capable, efficient members of society, no matter their chosen profession. Most Renaissance scholars were intellectually eclectic, sharing a hodgepodge of philosophical loyalties. Renaissance figures produced a panoply of devotional literature.

By now an influential thinker and theologian, Erasmus was known as the "prince of the humanists." He used his broad scholarship to develop a text of the New Testament in Greek, based on four Greek manuscripts available to him, a pursuit which would eventually result in his translation of a new edition of Jerome's Latin Bible translation based on the original Greek and with added interpretative notes. Pope Leo X's endorsement of the work was surprising, considering it spoke, in places, against Catholic text corruption. The pope's endorsement of the work is even more remarkable when we realize that the Greek Testament provided excellent fuel for church reformers' minds. Despite his criticisms,

Erasmus was faithful to the Roman Church, and he may have eventually regretted the uproar set off by his direct interpretation from the original Greek.

Northern Christian humanists flocked to Erasmus, who furnished more than enough ammunition to shake up a decadent and complacent Catholic behemoth. The majority of what became "Protestant" leaders ended up being northern Christian humanists, though Luther himself was a product of a scholastic education and not a humanist in the truest sense. Moreover, none of the "former" northern Renaissance humanists who became Protestant leaders ever denounced, repudiated, or otherwise distanced themselves from the humanism in which they had been trained and to which they had been devoted. The result of this emphasis was an interest in a return to the Scriptures, restoration of primitive Christianity, and a direct relationship with God, eschewing the evils in the Church of their day and calling for internal reform. Meister Eckhart also impacted what some call the Rhineland mystics—individuals such as Johannes Tauler, Geert Groote, Henry Suso, and Thomas á Kempis. In addition, there were preachers to the common peasant, such as Vincent Ferrer and John Capistrano. However, these were still Roman Catholics with a sometimes-evangelical edge.

Renaissance scholars north of the Alps shared many of the same interests—a love for ancient sources, an emphasis on the human being as an individual, and a belief in the rational abilities of the human mind. These northern Christian humanists, however, had more significant interest in the Christian past than in the classical past. They applied the techniques and methods of Renaissance humanism to the study of the Scriptures in their original languages, as well as the study of church fathers such as Augustine. Their chief concern for human beings was for their souls. Their emphasis was ethical and religious rather than aesthetic and secular. Unlike the Scholastics, humanists wished to appeal winsomely and convincingly to the truth, rather than bludgeon their audiences into submission.[12] While Erasmus was the prince of humanists, other northern Christian humanists included Philip Melanchthon, John Calvin, Ulrich Zwingli, and Martin Bucer.[13] The great reformer Martin Luther was not technically a humanist, in that he was more restrained in

---

12. Payton, *Getting*, 70-1.

13. Since these scholars will be given full attention in subsequent chapters, they will only be briefly introduced regarding their humanism and relationship to Erasmus.

embracing secular (humanistic) works than his Reformation brethren. With that said, humanistic thought indeed influenced him.

Martin Luther

No man did more to "prepare the way for Luther or was more fitted at first sight to co-operate with him"[14] than the great humanist Erasmus himself. However, Erasmus modified the connection between the two reformers when he remarked, "I laid a hen's egg: Luther hatched a bird of quite a different breed."[15] V. H. H. Green describes the two scholars as fundamentally dissimilar in character and purpose: "Erasmus was the true scholar, the great Latin stylist, the friend of the great world, averse to enthusiasm and extremism, cool, almost skeptical in his attitude, tending to conceal the under-current of genuine spirituality, which gave life to his personality. Whereas Luther, with a longer, richer and ultimately more fruitful experience of monastic life than Erasmus, was almost exclusively concerned with religion, Erasmus' interests were very much wider. Erasmus was never a true monk, but Luther in a certain fashion never escaped the impress of his monastic training."[16]

On Erasmus' part, he rejected Luther's dogmatic Augustinianism and the threat of violence and, overall, believed his teaching was not in accord with orthodox Christianity. From Luther's perspective, Erasmus emphasized the human over the divine, depended too much on the classics, and neglected the text's religious significance. The strife turned the men into incompatible foes and "showed that there was a real difficulty in reconciling genuine humanism with dogmatic Protestantism."[17]

Philip Melanchthon

Next to Luther, the most significant German reformer was Philip Melanchthon. As a co-worker of Luther, he was an expert in the Greek language and a skilled grammarian. Introduced to humanism and Erasmus's writings at the university at Tübingen, he was ultimately included

14. Green, *Luther*, 164

15. Quoted by Green, *Luther*, 164.

16. Green, *Luther*, 164–5.

17. Green, *Luther*, 167.

in Erasmus' circle of scholars.[18] He admired and respected Erasmus but loved Luther, his friend. As such, he sometimes served as a mediator between the rival theologians and eventual bitter enemies. For example, in a dispute over the doctrine of the will of man, Melanchthon attempted to "restrain the contestants from violence."[19] In 1524 Erasmus published a book on the freedom of the will, titled *De Libero Arbitrio Diatribe sive Collatio*, in which he argued against Luther's doctrine of the bondage of the will. Melanchthon had already anticipated a bitter controversy and sought in vain to restrain the opponents from mutual aggression. In 1525 Luther responded with his book *On the Bondage of the Will—De Servo Arbitrio* in such a polemic manner that Erasmus complained, in the words of James Richard, "that he was treated worse than a Turk."[20] Displeased with both Luther and Erasmus, he wrote to Joachim Camerarius, "Did you ever read anything more bitter than Erasmus's *Hyperaspistes*? It is almost venomous. How Luther takes it, I do not know. But I have again besought him by all that is sacred, if he replies, to do so briefly simply, and without abuse. At once after Luther published his book, I said this controversy would end in the most cruel alienation. . . . Oh that Luther would keep silent! I did hope that with age, experience, and so many troubles, he would grow more moderate; but I see he becomes the more violent as the contests and the opponents exhibit the same characteristics. This matter grievously vexes my soul."[21] Melanchthon remained loyal to his friend Luther, but his friendship with Erasmus was extinguished, and they only exchanged occasional letters, refraining from discussing theological issues.[22]

John Calvin

After Luther, no man was more influential in the evangelical movement than the humanist and reformer John Calvin. Born in the French town of Noyon in 1509, a generation after Luther, he commenced training for the priesthood at the University of Paris before his father sent him to Orléans to study law. He also attended Bourges, where he studied under

18. Schnucker, "Melanchthon, Philip," 702.

19. Richard, *Philip Melanchthon,* 119.

20. Richard, *Philip Melanchthon,* 120.

21. Quoted by Richard, *Philip Melanchthon,* 120–1.

22. Manschreck, *Melanchthon,* 121.

the humanist Andrea Alciati and probably became a Protestant.[23] The decadence of the Church, suggests Quirinus Breen, no doubt contributed to the development of Calvin's humanistic thinking, and consequently, "Young Calvin found truth far beyond the confines of the church, a fact which lay at the heart of his work as a reformer."[24] The impact of Erasmus on Calvin is not without significance. Unlike other reformers, however, Calvin never met Erasmus in person, and because of the age discrepancy did not likely exchange letters with him. Nonetheless, "the influence of Erasmus on Calvin would not have been slight."[25] Quirinus Breen writes, "Not only had he absorbed much information about the classics from Erasmus, but also much of the old humanist's thought. . . . The spiritual authority of Erasmus lent weight to his position in letters. The evidence present is conclusive that Calvin was one of his followers. The elegant words of praise he gives the old humanist in the Commentaries were no extravagance. After his conversion to Protestantism, he would withhold such encomiums, as 'Erasmus is the chief ornament of letters, none having greater charm.'"[26] Furthermore, Erasmus's inspiration came through "his membership in a community of Protestant exegetes, all indebted to Erasmus."[27] These included other reformers such as Luther, Bucer, Zwingli, and Melanchthon.

Ulrich Zwingli

A key Protestant reformer after Luther and Calvin was the Swiss scholar, Zwingli, who was born in 1484 in Wildhaus, Switzerland. Zwingli's introduction to humanism came early in his life when at ten years of age was sent to St. Theodores in Basel for three years to learn Latin. From Basel, he went to the humanist school at Berne (1496 or 1497), where he came under the influence of the teacher and exponent of Renaissance ideas and methods, Henry Wolfflin (Lupulus). He then studied at the University of Vienna briefly before graduating from the University of Basil with a Master of Arts Degree (1506). It was here that he became impressed

---

23. Reid, "Calvin, John," 185.

24. Breen, *John Calvin*, 8–9.

25. Breen, *John Calvin*, 78.

26. Breen, *John Calvin*, 78–9.

27. Bouwsma, *John Calvin*, 119.

and captivated by humanistic thought.[28] In November of 1505, Thomas Wyttenbach arrived to teach at Basel, and many young men, including Zwingli, flocked to him to learn the Scriptures. Ahead of his times, Wyttenbach stated, "The hour is not far distant in which the scholastic theology will be set aside and the old doctrines of the Church revived. For Christ's death is the only ransom for our souls."[29] This was a period of time when humanistic studies were replacing scholasticism of the Middle Ages, and Zwingli hurried into this new course.

In 1514, Erasmus arrived in Basel. By this time, Zwingli had made friends with three men who would figure powerfully in the Swiss Reformation: Wolfgang Capito, Oswald Myconius, and John Hausschein (Oecolampadius). Myconius was the rector of the school of Basel, and Oecolampadius had been appointed preacher in Basel through the influence of Capito. Zwingli himself was the priest at Einsiedeln. All of these young men exulted in the presence of Erasmus and at Einsiedeln Zwingli continued to be influenced by the great humanist. It was here that he studied the Greek New Testament edition of Erasmus, had any new publication of Erasmus sent to him immediately, and from here followed the successes of Erasmus and his ever-widening movement. It was also at Einsiedeln that he "studied with unceasing vigour day and night, the Greek and Latin philosophers and theologians."[30]

Martin Bucer and Wolfgang Capito

In 1507, neither 16-year-old Bucer nor his family or friends had the slightest hint that a religious revolution would take place less than ten years hence or that he would eventually appear as a noteworthy contributor to the dialogue of a Reformation Church. It was at this early age that he was admitted into the Dominican Order, a situation he would later claim was engineered by his grandfather, who thought it the only hope for an education for one of the poorer class. His father, Claus, was a cooper and seemed to support young Martin in his education, which was taken in Selestat, south Germany, not far from Strassburg, a German city on the Upper Rhine where he was later to spend twenty-five years in

---

28. Noll, "Zwingli, Ulrich," 1203; Bromily, *Zwingli and Bullinger*, 14; Farner, *Zwingli the Reformer*, 14–16.

29. Quoted by d'Aubigné, *For God and His People*, 6.

30. Farner, *Zwingli*, 27.

ministry. After a year as a novice Dominican, he was consecrated as an acolyte in the Strassburg church and in 1508 took vows to become a full Dominican monk. By 1510 he was consecrated as a deacon.

Bucer was commissioned to study at Heidelberg, where, by 1517, he was well on his way to a doctorate in theology, which could open all sorts of doors, including a professorship at a university. He loved reading and became a dogged collector of books. He collected everything of Aquinas and became extremely well acquainted with the writings of Erasmus and Luther. At Heidelberg, he was expected to attend classes, take part in disputations, and lecture on 160 chapters of the Old and New Testaments within two years.

Bucer became friends with Capito, and they would later work for years together as close colleagues. There is not a great deal known about Capito before 1515 when he was appointed to Basel's cathedral preacher. It was here that he met Erasmus, and by the time Erasmus left Basel, he would call young Capito a better Hebraist than Reuchlin himself, and a man "so very upright: in morals, so holy that I have never seen anyone more unspoiled." Moreover, Capito would write to Erasmus, "I live right well, most excellent Erasmus, if living well is suffering sadly a sense of loss for the most desirable Desiderius."[31] Capito was so loyal that when Edward Lee attacked one of Erasmus' writings with his own book, he wrote Erasmus: "the poor little thing thirsts for fame. If you would be open to advice from Capito to Erasmus (this is a pig teaching Minerva), it would seem better to overlook everything and to smile unconcernedly. . . . [Nothing] would harm your reputation with influential and learned men."[32]

Conclusion

Erasmus, the leading Christian humanist of the Reformation era, was compelled to cleanse and sanitize the Church through the application of humanistic thinking to Christian thought. As such, he impacted many of the reformers and even could be credited with sparking the Reformation movement, though he never broke with the Roman Catholic Church. However, his relationships with many of the reformers through his writings, letters, and conversations are significant. This chapter introduced

31. Kittelson, *Wolfgang Capito*, 26.
32. Kittelson, *Wolfgang Capito*, 28.

Erasmus to the reader and highlighted the influence on and relations with some of the reformers, including Luther, Melanchthon, Calvin, Zwingli, Bucer, and Capito. Unfortunately for Erasmus history passed him by in a sense and in the words of R. G. Clouse, left "him to defend his position against reformers and Counter-reformers."[33] In chapter two, we turn our attention to the first of the great reformers—Martin Luther.

33. Clouse, "Erasmus, Desiderius," 361.

2

Martin Luther

The First Reformer

"It can hardly be denied that the men who have most changed history have been the great religious leaders. . . . Among the great prophets, and, with the possible exception of Calvin, the last of world-wide importance, Martin Luther has taken his place. His career marks the beginning of the present epoch, for it is safe to say that every man in Western Europe and in America is leading a different life today from what he would have led, and is another person altogether from what he would have been, had Martin Luther not lived."[1]

—PRESERVED SMITH

WHILE DESIDERIUS ERASMUS MAY have triggered an inevitable and necessary Church reform, it was Martin Luther who ignited the flames of the Protestant Reformation with the publication of his *Ninety-five Theses* in 1517. However, Luther's eventual impact on the event that not only transformed the Church but Western society as well came, to coin a contemporary phrase, with a strong supporting cast. In addition to the patronage of Prince Fredrick, Luther gained the support of distinguished scholars such as Andreas Carlstadt, George Spalatin, John Staupitz, and Philip Melanchthon. Several chapters of this book are dedicated to Luther, the chief reformer. In this chapter we introduce

1. Smith and Backhouse, *The Life and Letters*, 9.

the reader to Luther the person, including his early years, his brief time as a monk, his visit to Rome, his struggles with the Catholic view of salvation, and finally, his conversion.

Luther's Early Years

Luther (Luder or Lueder) was born near midnight on November 10, 1483, approximately seventeen years after Erasmus, who would eventually play both positive and negative roles in the young man's life. He was the second son of Hans Luther and Hanna Lindemann, and by 1505, when Luther entered an Augustinian monastery, he had four sisters and three brothers. His father once alienated Martin with a full-on beating, and his mother thrashed him one day until blood flowed—for taking a walnut. Nonetheless, Luther generally spoke positively of his parents though he later surmised that a reason he took refuge in a cloister and became a monk was because of the "severe and harsh life I led with them [his parents]."[2]

Historically, this was a ruthless and harsh period for most people. Fortunately for Luther, his parents chose for him the relatively softer road of formal education while his brother, Hans Jr., lived the more severe life of a common peasant. Though young Martin excelled in educational endeavors, schools still could be a harsh place as well. A schoolmaster once gave him fifteen lashes for, among a week's trespasses, incorrectly declining a noun. The child Luther went from Mansfeld *Grundschule* (grade school) to an institution of the Brethren of the Common Life.[3] He attended school in Magdeburg for a year, then to St. George's parish church at Eisenach, where he found a friend in John Trebonius, a rare instructor who treated his students with integrity and respect. It was there that he contracted a raging fever which might have killed him had he not drunk some water against doctor's orders.[4]

In Magdeburg, Martin spied the prince of Anhalt, who had forsaken his wealth and begged bread on the highway. He was so emaciated that

2. Quoted by Beard, *Martin Luther,* 121.

3. The Brethren of the Common Life was a Roman Catholic pietistic religious group founded in the 14th century by Gerard Groote in the Netherlands. Members modeled and taught a simple community lifestyle and established schools in which they emphasized scholarship.

4. See Beard, *Martin Luther,* 126–30 for expanded details of his school years.

his head looked like a death's head; indeed, he died soon after.[5] Incidents such as these seemed to have a profound impact upon the young Luther. A master at the University of Erfurt heard a speech Luther gave at St. George's and was so impressed that he told Trebonius to prepare him for an education at Erfurt. So, in April 1501, he matriculated to the University of Erfurt, where he stood out as an exemplary student and became known by fellow students as "the philosopher." Erfurt was an important religious center containing twenty cloisters, thirty-six chapels, and twenty-three churches. There had only been about 2,000 residents in all of Eisenach, so it was somewhat of a shock for Luther to find that the University of Erfurt alone had 2,000 students. The regimen here was even more severe. Students were wakened at 4:00 a.m. each morning for a day of rote learning and spiritual exercises, and Luther rose steadily toward the top in his classes.

He achieved his bachelor's degree in one year, and in the fall of 1502, he headed home, a proud graduate. On the way home, he tripped, and the sword he manfully carried sliced an artery in his leg. Carried back to the city, he almost bled to death before receiving the care he needed. He was so weak that it took weeks to fully recover. Then a close friend died unexpectedly when a plague swept through Erfurt. Thus, Luther was glimpsing the more foreboding side of life, and he was impressed, not just regarding how transitory life could be, but how much he feared death and feared facing God after death. Luther's near-death experiences, the encounter with the pauper prince, and his perception of a cruel and raging God all contributed to this trepidation.

At age twenty, Luther happened to locate his first Bible, chained in place at the university library. He began stealing hours alone with the volume—he read it through once and then reread it several times, seeking to sate his thirst. Though he reported little understanding of it at the time, it sparked a quest for answers. At the same time, seeds for his future skepticism about accepting the thoughts of men without question were sown by two of his tutors—Bartholomaus Arnoldi von Usingen and Jodocus Trutfetter. They taught him to be suspicious of even the greatest thinkers and test everything by knowledge and experience.[6]

Luther graduated on January 7, 1505, with his M.A., second in his class of seventeen. His father bought him an expensive copy of the *Corpus*

---

5. Luther, *Table Talk: Conversations*, 10.

6. Marty, *Martin Luther*, 5–6.

Juris body of law. Luther tried to apply himself toward a law degree, but he gave it up within two months. When Martin told his father, the man was furious. He had his son's career all planned out—even the woman he was to marry—and now the upwardly mobile young man was about to cast it all away. Hans commanded him to go back to law school, and an angry, confused Martin left that evening for Erfurt.

Given its familiarity, it is possibly not necessary to dramatize his vow to become a monk. That night, July 2, 1505, as he traveled, a blasting thunderstorm broke above him. Lightning struck a massive tree trunk in his path and left it split and smoking. In his fright, Luther made a terrifying commitment to St. Anna that he would be a monk. Fifteen days later, he made good on his pledge.

Luther Chooses the Cloister

Luther held a farewell meal and invited his student friends for beer, song, and lute playing. He told them, "Today you see me; henceforth never more."[7] The next day Luther sold his *Corpus Juris* and left law school behind, entering a closed Augustinian friary in Erfurt on July 17, 1505, just before his 22nd birthday. He could not tell his father face to face; instead, he sent a letter explaining his decision.

Luther survived his first two months at the monastery and was thus accepted as a novice in September 1506. He would have another year to decide for sure if this life was his calling. It was evident to all who observed that the young man had not fled to the monastery to drone out his years lazily impersonating a rapt worshipper. He became a tortured confessor, occasionally boring his mentors to tears with six-hour confession sessions. Finally, Johann von Staupitz, his confessor, surely out of exasperation and partly in jest, exclaimed: "Look here, if you expect Christ to forgive you, come in with something to forgive—parricide, blasphemy, adultery—instead of all these peccadilloes."[8]

Luther later declared: "I often repeated my confession and sedulously performed my allotted penance. And yet my conscience could never give me certainty: 'You were not contrite enough. You left this or that out of your confession.'"[9] He tortured himself almost to death with

7. Spitz, *The Rise*, 61.

8. Quoted by Bainton, *Here I Stand*, 41.

9. Quoted by Rupp, *The Righteousness of God*, 104.

fasting, scourging, and other self-abuses in an effort to earn his salvation. His fellow priests broke into his small cell and found him lying senseless on the ground. He would backlog his prayer times for a week, or even longer; then he would take off a Sunday or a whole weekend without food or drink and devote the entire time to intense marathon praying spells. After one such ordeal, he could not sleep for five days and lay in bed like a zombie until the doctor gave him a sedative. During convalescence, the prayer book revolted him, and he fell in arrears about a quarter of a year.[10] He eventually confessed that "I was a pious monk and followed the rules of my order so faithfully that I may say, if ever a man could have entered heaven through monkery it would have been I. All my comrades in the monastery who knew me would testify to that. And if I had kept on any longer I would have martyred myself with vigils, prayers, readings, and other works."[11]

Staupitz, theologian and vicar general of German Augustinians, was determined to reform the Augustinian monasteries under his charge, and he apparently saw in the young monk Luther, the sincerity, intensity, and intellect that he wanted in his houses. He made sure that Luther was chosen for the priesthood, not the ponderous repetitions of monkhood. The two built a deep friendship that seemed, at least for a time, to replace the relationship Luther undoubtedly longed for in his father. Indeed, Luther stated, "If it had not been for Dr. Staupitz, I should have sunk into hell."[12] Though Staupitz accepted the penitential system that caused Luther so much personal anguish, he was somewhat of a mystic.[13] In humanity's weakness, the mystic believed, he must cease from the rabid, incessant striving for holiness and sink into the goodness of God, and in that compassionate abyss, find a sense of inner peace.

Luther was terrified of God, not only for what God could do to him but to all of humanity. He cried to Staupitz, "Dear Doctor, our Lord God treats people too horribly. Who can serve Him as long as He strikes people down right and left . . . ? Why does God seem so unjust?" Staupitz answered, "Dear fellow, learn to think of God differently. If He did not treat

---

10. Luther, *Table Talk: Conversations*, 13.

11. Quoted by Bainton, *Here I Stand*, 45.

12. Quoted by Bainton, *Here I Stand*, 53.

13. In contrast to the academic scholasticism of the Middle Ages that incorporated a systematic and analytical knowledge of the Divine, mysticism emphasized a more intuitive knowledge of and personal relationship with God. Christian mystics of the Middle Ages include Teresa of Avila, John of the Cross, and Thomas à Kempis.

them [humans] this way, how could God restrain the blockheads? God strikes us for our own good, in order that He might free us who otherwise would be crushed."[14] Staupitz did not know that as he sought to nurture this intensely suffering young thinker, he was lighting a spiritual powder keg that would shake Germany, then the rest of Europe and beyond.

Staupitz put him on a fast track, and Luther was priested on April 3, 1507, conducting his first mass on May 2. Staupitz realized that Luther was much troubled by spiritual questions, but he thought that total immersion in theological study would distract him from his murky depressions. During the next ten years, Luther would move gradually, almost inexorably into direct opposition to the Roman Church, though that was not his original intent. Significant pressures from several different directions would squeeze him to a bursting point: the demands of his Augustinian order, a compulsion to intellectual dissent, and a spiritual battle to find forgiveness and an authentic relationship with Christ.

In the fall of 1508, Staupitz appointed Luther temporarily to teach Aristotle's *Ethics* at the University of Wittenberg. While teaching there, Luther earned his bachelor's degree in biblical studies on March 9, 1509. He was unhappy teaching philosophy, and seven months later, he was called back to Erfurt to teach theology, where he taught for the next two years. He also possessed various other skills (including administration) as evidenced in his eventual letter to Prior Lang in 1516:

> I require two scribes or secretaries. I spend almost all my time writing letters, so that I am not sure whether I am repeating what I have said before. I am lecturer at the convent, reader during meals. I am also called from day to day to preach in the parish church, act as regent of studies at the convent and subvicar, which means prior of eleven convents, have to gather the fish at Leitzkau, administer the affairs of Herzberg at Torgau, lecture on Paul, edit my lectures on the Psalms, and besides I am burdened with writing letters which, as I have said, takes up much the greater part of my time. I have insufficient time for the prayers in the breviary or for saying Mass. [15]

Clearly, Luther's devotion to the Church and monasticism was absolute, and his eventual disillusionment would be equally complete.

---

14. Luther, *Table Talk: Conversations,* 14.

15. Quoted by Green, *Luther,* 45.

Rome Darkly Disillusions Luther

In 1510 Luther was teaching at Erfurt when his work was interrupted by one of the most significant events in his life. No doubt, the nailing of his ninety-five theses to the church door in 1517 would not have occurred without his trip to Rome. The cause of the visit was related to a dispute in the Augustinian order calling for a resolution by the pope. Staupitz chose Luther, along with another by the name of John von Mecheln, to represent the cloister at Erfurt. The 850-mile journey began in blustery November and took an exhausting forty days to complete. Filled with naive anticipation, Luther was shocked at the things he saw. The seven-hilled city welcomed him and his brother with immorality, disorder, and a high crime rate. He observed that the nearer one approached Rome, the less Christian spirit was found. Nonetheless, the monk stated that he would not trade his visit to Rome for a hundred thousand gulden.[16] He later wrote,

> Rome is a harlot. . . . I never would have believed the true state
> of affairs from what other people had told me, had I not seen
> it myself. The Italians mocked us for being pious monks, for
> they hold us Christians fools. They say six or seven masses in
> the time it takes me to say one, for they take money for it and
> I do not. The only crime in Italy is poverty. They still punish
> homicide and theft a little, for they have to, but no other sin
> is too great for them. . . . So great and bold is Roman impiety
> that neither God nor man, neither sin nor shame, is feared. All
> good men who have seen Rome bear witness to this; all bad ones
> come back worse than before.[17]

Nevertheless, at the time, the shocking revelations and things he saw did not shake his faith or his allegiance to the pope—that breach came sometime later. Rather he diligently practiced all the observances, believed the misrepresentations told to him, visited churches and chapels, and performed with devotion all the required observances.[18] He went so far as to regret that his father and mother were still alive in that he would miss the opportunity to engage in some of the observances: "What a

---

16. Smith and Backhouse, *The Life and Letters*, 36.

17. Quoted by Smith and Backhouse, *The Life and Letters*, 36.

18. d'Aubigné, *History Vol. III*, 193.

pleasure I should have in delivering them from the fire of purgatory by my masses, my prayers, and by so many other admirable works."[19]

Luther: Prized Scholar

One hundred miles northeast of Erfurt, Wittenberg was little more than a postage stamp of a village compared to Erfurt, with several hundred lowly homes, a church, and a town hall. However, Frederick, the elector of Saxony, desired to put Wittenberg on the map as a cultural center rivaling his cousin's Albertine Saxony. He had two great loves: his collection of religious relics and icons, which grew eventually to over 19,013 items by 1520, and the new school he had founded, the University of Wittenberg. He could take little pride yet in the school, but he gloated over his collection, which allegedly included a piece from Moses' burning bush, hay from the Bethlehem manger, a strand of hair from Christ's beard, a piece of His swaddling clothes, and one of the nails driven into His hand on the cross. Just one reverential visit to all these relics, along with the stipulated contributions, could enable a sinner to reduce purgatory for himself or others to the extent of 1,902,202 years and 270 days.[20]

It is not certain whether Luther ever had a prolonged meeting of any sort with Frederick, but the wise man became Luther's sometimes silent benefactor, most likely because Luther had been highly recommended for a professorship at Frederick's university. George Spalatin (George Burkhardt of Spalt) became the intermediary between Frederick and Luther. Spalatin was a Bavarian scholar and humanist thinker highly enamored with Erasmus and his writings. He was eventually appointed tutor, chaplain, secretary, and councilor for Frederick's brother, Prince George. In this role, he met the young monk who was rapidly gaining a name for theological brilliance. He found that he liked and respected Luther and soon became an ally and confidante. Though hard to believe, he would eventually persuade Frederick to approve an overhaul of the Wittenberg curriculum in accordance with Luther's ideas.[21]

In the early summer of 1511, Staupitz helped get Luther elected sub-prior of the Wittenberg monastery. Most of his brothers at Erfurt were furious that Luther would forsake them and place himself under

19. Quoted by d'Aubigné, *History Vol. III,* 193.
20. Bainton, *Here I Stand,* 53.
21. Gritsch, *Martin: God's Court Jester,* 21.

the authority of Staupitz. At age twenty-seven, he was one of the young-
est sub-priors ever to serve. One afternoon, under a lone pear tree in a
garden on the north side of the Wittenberg cloister, Staupitz challenged
Luther to study for a doctor's degree in theology. J. H. Merle d'Aubigné
summarizes the conversation between the mentor and reluctant priest:

> "My friend, you must now become Doctor of the Holy Scrip-
> tures." Luther shrunk at the very thought: this eminent honor
> startled him. "Seek a more worthy person," replied he. "As for
> me, I cannot consent to it." The vicar-general persisted: "Our
> Lord God has much to do in the Church: he has need at this
> time of young and vigorous doctors." . . . "But I am weak and
> sickly," replied Luther. "I have not long to live. Look out for
> some strong man."—"The Lord has work in heaven as well as
> on earth," replied the vicar-general: "dead or alive, He has need
> of you in his council." . . . "I have no means of defraying the
> expenses incidental to such a promotion."—"Do not be uneasy
> about that," replied his friend: "the prince has done you the fa-
> vour to take all the charges upon himself."[22]

Luther finally relented and felt it his duty to give in to the persuasive
Staupitz. He proved himself an outstanding student—indeed, he thrived
on the scholarship. By October 4, 1512, a twenty-eight-year-old Luther
passed all the exams for the doctorate, and Elector Frederick paid the
fifty-guilder fee for him. Soon after this, Staupitz retired from his chair
as professor of the Bible at Wittenberg University and named Luther to
take his place.

At first, Luther lectured very hesitantly, asking how he could instruct fellow monks who had been his equal for years. However, the doctorate seemed to empower Luther in the momentous crusade he would
soon touch off. D'Aubigné suggests that a personal oath to preach the
Scriptures "faithfully, to teach them with purity, to study them all his life,
and to defend them, both in disputation and in writing against all false
teachers, so far as God should give him the ability. . . . was Luther's call to
the Reformation."[23]

Luther was now studying the Scriptures in Hebrew and Greek, and
he shared in his sermons the remarkable things that were coming to light.
Soon the small chapel on monastery grounds was overflowing, and he was
asked to preach in the larger St. Mary's sanctuary in town. Elevation to a

---

22. Quoted by d'Aubigné, *History Vol. I*, 201–2.

23. d'Aubigné, *History Vol. I*, 203.

doctorate should only have occurred after Luther had ten years' teaching to his credit, but Wittenberg was a new university in a great hurry, and Luther was a bright intellectual mind that Frederick wanted on his faculty. Though Erfurt's director Johannes Nathin and other jealous brothers in Erfurt wrote letters of protest demanding Luther's demotion, he was not easily rid. They protested that he had promised to study for further degrees in Erfurt, not Wittenberg, so his defection was a violation of Roman Catholic law. Luther eventually became very incensed at these stubborn men and preached a fiery sermon against evil gossip, sending them a copy of the message. He did not begin classroom teaching in earnest for a year. Then for the next thirty years, except for brief absences, he would deliver his twice-weekly lectures on the Bible to generations of students.[24]

Aristotle Demoted

For centuries, Aristotle had been considered the great philosophical master by many professors, and Thomas Aquinas had scholasticized Catholic doctrine based on Aristotle's approach. However, as Luther delved deeper into the study of theology, he realized that Aristotle was certainly not the be-all and end-all of a sound education. Luther wrote in *Against Latomus,* "Thomas wrote a great deal of heresy and is responsible for the reign of Aristotle, the destroyer of godly doctrine."[25] Calling Aristotle "the Greek buffoon," he added from Wittenberg: "Our theology and St. Augustine are progressing well, and with God's help, rule at our University. Aristotle is gradually falling from his throne, and his final doom is only a matter of time. . . . Indeed no one can expect to have any students [here] if he does not want to teach theology, that is, lecture on the Bible or on St. Augustine or another teacher of ecclesiastical eminence."[26]

As Melanchthon began turning his incisive intellect more toward theology, he also declared in 1521 to theologians in Paris, "Evidently a profane scholasticism has hatched at Paris. The Gospel is obscured; faith is extinguished; and a doctrine of works based on Aristotle prevails. Should we hold Aristotle higher than Christ?"[27] Not only was Luther debunking Aristotle as the philosophical genius through which the

24. Collinson, *The Reformation,* 53.

25. Quoted by Payton, *Selected Writings,* 196.

26. Luther, *Luther's Works Vol. 48,* 42.

27. Quoted by Manschreck, *Melanchthon,* 67.

Scriptures must be interpreted, but he also began tossing out some critical questions about the infallibility of the Church's interpretational methods. In a library situated in the tower latrine above the Wittenberg monastery sewer, Luther prepared his daily lectures almost as if he were unaware of the growing buzz his questions might be causing. He struggled with Paul's explanation of the phrase from Habakkuk 2:4: "the just shall live by faith." Of Romans 1:17 the apostle wrote, "In the Gospel the righteousness of God is revealed, a righteousness by faith from first to last, as it is written, 'the just will live by faith.'" The verse either made no sense, or it made a terrible sense. If God is perfect justice and absolute righteousness, Luther mused, and treats humanity according to that standard, then all is doomed.

Luther's Mighty Wrestlings

Like Jacob's famous Old Testament affray with God, Luther had been wrestling mightily with the means of salvation for years, even as he taught Psalms (1513–1515), Romans (1515–1516), Galatians (1516–1517), and Hebrews (1517–1518). He later seemed to claim his spiritual breakthrough to be as late as 1518, but it is apparent that he had been moving gradually toward the pure Gospel throughout this period. We may observe this evolution clearly in Luther's teachings from 1513 to 1519, in his understanding of theology, and especially salvation by grace through faith. In 1513, he taught that the psalmist in Psalm 4:1 "lays claim to no righteousness, he boasts of no merit, he displays no worth, but that he praises the pure and exclusive grace and free kindness to God."[28] In 1515, from the Epistle to the Romans, he taught against the terror of God's Law: "But how are we discharged from the Law? Doubtless because through faith in Christ we satisfy the demands of the Law and through grace we are freed and voluntarily perform the works of the Law. But those who do not have this faith are active in works unwillingly and almost in fear or in a desire for their own convenience."[29] In 1517, while teaching the book of Hebrews, Luther stated, "God does not compel believers to salvation by force and fear, but by this pleasing spectacle of His mercy and love He moves and draws through love all those whom He will save."[30]

28. Luther, *Luther's Works Vol. 10*, 46.
29. Luther, *Luther's Works Vol. 25*, 59–60.
30. Luther, *Luther's Works Vol. 29*, 132

During this period, Luther was also digesting what he found palatable in the Catholic mystics. He spent much of 1515 and 1516 reading and annotating John Tauler, the leader of the school of German mystics. Though he rejected Tauler's basic ontological and anthropological presuppositions, he treasured his description of spiritual torments, soul struggle, and surrender. What Luther was attracted to in Tauler and the other mystics, "was their doctrine of the necessity of a spiritual rebirth of anguish and despair before a man could approach the felicity of union with God."[31] He further embraced from them an emphasis upon the pervasive presence of God in all matters, great and small, majestic and lowly—the indwelling of Christ in the heart, the personal involvement of the individual in faith and, in producing the fruits of faith, the birthing of social compassion.[32]

At the Heidelberg Disputation in 1518, Luther reflected his growing freedom: "through the cross works are dethroned and the old Adam, who is especially edified by works, is crucified. It is impossible for believers not to be puffed up by their good works unless they have first been deflated and destroyed by suffering and evil until they know that they are worthless and that their works are not theirs but God's."[33] By 1519, Luther was delivering sermons that proclaimed grace and mercy: "Grace and mercy are there where Christ on the cross takes your sin from you, bears it for you, and destroys it. Likewise, he also takes your sins upon Himself and overcomes them with his righteousness out of sheer mercy, and if you believe that, your sins will never work you harm."[34]

A "Perfect" Monk Converted

Luther boasted as living as a monk without reproach—but outraged at God. He wrote, "I felt that I was a sinner before God with an extremely disturbed conscience. I could not believe that he was placated by my satisfaction. I did not love, yes, I hated the righteous God who punishes sinners, and secretly, if not blasphemously, certainly murmuring greatly, I was angry with God and said, 'As if, indeed, it is not enough that miserable sinners, eternally lost through original sin, are crushed by every

31. Smith and Backhouse, *The Life and Letters*, 45.

32. Spitz, *The Rise of Modern Europe*, 79.

33. Luther, *Luther's Works Vol. 31*, 53.

34. Luther, *Luther's Works Vol. 42*, 104–6.

kind of calamity by the law of the Decalogue, without having God add pain to pain by the gospel—a gospel threatening us with his righteousness and wrath."[35] If this raging deity was the true God, Luther could not force himself to love such a God. Indeed, he wrote, "When I looked for Christ it seemed to me as if I saw the devil."[36] When it finally dawned on him that justification was secured simply by faith and not by the volume of works, he was never the same again: "I felt that I was altogether born again and had entered paradise itself through open gates."[37] As he threaded Scriptures through his mind, this was everywhere confirmed.

As a monk, he had struggled for peace and salvation for twelve long years, and now in an explosion of grace, it had come. Like Blaise Pascal, Luther claimed his free surrender a joyful bet on God's yet unfelt, untried goodness. Thus, in contrast to the then-current teaching that the righteous acts of believers are performed in cooperation with God toward human justification, Luther came to understand justification as entirely God's work. He began teaching that Christians receive such righteousness entirely from outside themselves—that righteousness not only comes from Christ but is the righteousness of Christ imputed to believers through faith, not gradually infused into them. Now instead of detesting God and His pitiless brutality, Luther realized God was love.

However, Luther also came to understand that there is something within us humans that incessantly wrestles against a pure gospel of grace. He called this struggle *Anfechtungen*, or "delicious despair" because God ever pushed him toward a humble, selfless surrender to the omnipotent wrestler, Christ Himself. Though Christians may surrender to Christ's sacrifice for sin, deep in the heart, there is a whisper we may never verbalize that continues to repeat that we can gain a corner on God's favor through our spirituality or unselfish service. Like some other giants of Christian leadership, Luther would continue to war against this tendency in later times.

> [an individual] shall at length find how grievous and hard a thing it is for a man that hath been occupied all his lifetime in the works of his own holiness to escape out of it and with all his heart by faith cleave to this one Mediator. I myself have preached the gospel almost twenty years and have been exercised in the same daily, by reading and writing, so that I may

35. Luther, *Luther's Works Vol. 34*, 336–7.
36. Quoted by Smith and Backhouse, *The Life and Letters*, 30.
37. Luther, *Luther's Works Vol. 34*, 337.

well seem to be rid of this wicked opinion; notwithstanding I yet now and then feel the same old filth cleave to my heart. I wish to bring *something with myself,* because of which He should for my holiness' sake give me His grace. And I can scarcely be brought to commit myself with all confidence to mere grace . . . for we ought to fly only to the mercy seat, forasmuch as God hath set it before us as a sanctuary, which must be the refuge of all them that shall be saved.[38]

In the years to follow, one of the toughest questions Catholics could muster was one that has been asked *ad infinitum* since Paul answered it in Romans. They railed at Luther—*if salvation is by grace alone through faith and good deeds are worthless in God's sight, why try to be good? Why not be as evil as humanly possible?* Luther believed that the freedom of the Christian was the beautiful paradox that made this question moot. The Christian realizes that no commandments can be kept perfectly or even properly but that God does not condemn us for that—indeed, He has come to die in anguish to save our anguish. Therefore, "A Christian is a perfectly free lord of all, subject to none. A Christian is [at the same time] a perfectly dutiful servant of all, subject to all." [39] Consequently, good works come naturally to the saved believer as an expression of love and gratitude for God's saving and loving nature. Luther went on to state, "If we believe Christ to have redeemed man by his blood, we are obliged to confess that that the whole man was undone; else we should make Christ either superfluous, or the redeemer in the vilest part in man: which is blasphemous and sacrilegious."[40] Luther sets forth his views on works most clearly in his popular pamphlet *On the Freedom of the Christian Man:* "Good works do not make a good man, but a good man does good works. . . . Unless a man is already a believer and a Christian, his works have no value at all. They are foolish, idle, damnable sins, because when good works are brought forward as ground for justification, they are no longer good."[41]

The other chief reformers also emphasized clearly the importance of good works as evidence of true salvation. Melanchthon wrote, "Trust in the good will or mercy of God first calms our hearts and then inflames us to give thanks to God for his mercy and we thus keep the law gladly

38. Quoted by Bonar, *Words Old and New,* 69.
39. Luther, *Luther's Works Vol. 31,* 344.
40. Luther. *The Bondage,* 467.
41. Quoted by Bainton, *Here I Stand,* 178

and willingly."[42] Zwingli proposed, "We must add at once that the pious will not cease from good works simply because it is impossible to gain any merit by them. Rather, the greater our faith, the more and greater our works."[43] Bucer emphasized the importance of works as summarized by David Steinmetz: "The man who is justified *sola fide* and given the gift of the Holy Spirit is enabled to perform works of love. These works do not justify him, though they are the fruit of his justification."[44] John Calvin later added in his incisive manner: "Those who boast of having the faith of Christ and are completely destitute of sanctification by his Spirit deceive themselves. For the Scripture teaches that Christ has been made for us not only righteousness but sanctification."[45]

Conclusion

We began the chapter with a quote by Preserved Smith who proposed that "the men who have most changed history have been the great religious leaders."[46] And few would argue that Martin Luther has taken his place among the greatest. The historian Merle d'Aubigné argues that "The first period in man's life—that in which he is formed and molded under the hand of God—is always important."[47] And it is exceptionally so in the life of Luther. Thus, in this chapter we have introduced the reader to the great reformer from his early years, to his struggles as a monk, and to his conversion. The next chapter addresses Luther's attack on the sale of indulgences, the subsequent publication of his *Ninety-five Theses,* and the confrontation with Rome at Augsburg.

42. Melanchthon, *Commonplaces,* 92
43. Bromiley, *Zwingli and Bullinger,* 272.
44. Steinmetz, *Reformers,* 124.
45. Calvin, *Instruction,* 17.
46. Smith and Backhouse, *The Life and Letters,* 9.
47. d'Aubigné, *History Vol. I,* 143.

3

The Sale of Indulgences

Seed of the Reformation

"The preaching, selling, and buying of indulgences were a central part of late medieval practice, even as revival meetings are a familiar feature of today's religious scene. Indulgences also had a perfectly legitimate standing in the doctrine of the church. Theologians agreed that while baptism had washed away the penalties for original sin, Christians still had 'to do what was in them' in order to be saved. According to this view death brought believers to purgatory. The stain of sins that remained on their records—particularly those that were unacknowledged and therefore unconfessed—was purged from them there before they were presented to St. Peter and Christ at the gates of heaven. To be 'indulged' a sin before death meant simply to have its penalties pardoned by the church and therefore to be released from paying for it in purgatory. As with confession and penance, all that was required was some evidence of a sinner's sincerity."[1]

—JAMES KITTELSON

"A great agitation prevailed at that time among the German people. The Church had opened a vast market upon earth. From the crowds of purchasers, and the shouts and jokes of the sellers, it might have been called a fair, but a fair conducted by monks. The merchandise that they were extolling, and which they offered at a reduced price, was, said they, the salvation of souls."[2]

—MERLE D'AUBIGNÉ

1. Kittelson, *Luther*, 101.
2. d'Aubigné, *History Vol. I*, 239.

IN THE YEAR 1516, the noble family of the Brandenburgs made a bid for control of the Roman Church in Germany by getting twenty-three-year-old Albert of Brandenburg appointed to three high offices in the Church. Already Archbishop of Magdeburg and administrator of the Diocese of Halberstadt, the young humanist wished to add to his clerical duties through the acquisition of the Archbishopric of Mainz. Unfortunately, Albert lacked the fees necessary for the purchase of the pallium[3]—21,000 ducats for the Archbishopric itself and 10,000 additional ducats for the papal permission to hold multiple sees. This practice was not exactly legitimate, but the family knew that often money was counted weightier than principle in the Holy See. While Albert required currency to advance his ecclesiastical pursuits, Pope Leo X was also in need of financial help to cover his considerable expenses. Among other things, the disintegrating bones of Peter, Paul, and innumerable martyrs were now subject to the destructive elements of the weather and who knew what else. Thus St. Peter's Cathedral was urgently needed to shelter these Holy relics. Subsequently, Archbishop Albert proposed using the indulgence scheme to raise funds, and Leo agreed that the Brandenburgs could sell indulgences to collect the money if a hefty portion of it would go toward finishing the construction of St. Peter's Basilica in Rome. The German banking House of Fugger was the loaning agent for this massive undertaking; in return, they would receive a revenue share. Three parties benefited—Albert, Pope Leo, and the House of Fugger.

The Practice of Indulgences

Purchasers of indulgences would enjoy a plenary or full and perfect remission of all sins. They would be restored to the state of innocence, which they enjoyed in baptism and would be relieved of purgatory pains, including those incurred by an offense to the Divine Majesty. As a bonus, those securing indulgences on behalf of the dead already in purgatory need not themselves even be contrite or confess their sins. V. H. H Green provides a most helpful explanation of indulgences as a by-product of

---

3. A pallium is an ecclesiastical vestment of the Roman Catholic Church initially reserved for the pope but by the 16th century was also conferred by the Holy See on bishops and archbishops as a symbol and thereby giving them jurisdiction over a particular territory.

the medieval notion of penance, which includes three parts of contrition, confession, and satisfaction: "The Church, so it was taught, through the existence of a treasury of merit, accrued by the infinite merits of Christ and the saints, had the right to distribute the benefit of these merits in consideration of the prayers or pious works undertaken by the faithful. . . . An indulgence implied therefore the communication of the act of satisfaction, but it did not eliminate the need of either contrition or confession."[4]

The practice of indulgences proliferated after 1095 when popes began promising Crusade combatants paradise if they participated in the military reclamation of lands that were once Christian. Eventually a pardon was offered to those who contributed enough money to equip one soldier to go on crusade. In 1300 Pope Boniface VIII offered a plenary indulgence to all who made a pilgrimage to Rome. Later, Boniface IX announced a complete remission of both guilt and penalty to purchasers of his letters. From that point, it was but baby steps for popes to proclaim their power to deliver the souls of the dead from purgatory for the right price. Indulgences eventually became so embedded and intertwined in the Medieval Church's economic and financial system that none of the other church taxes or levies brought in comparable sums of income. The European banks were eventually drawn into the indulgence business, and kings and princes followed suit so that the pope might count only a third to a half of the takings. Such was the impact indulgences had on the Western European societies of the Middle Ages, specifically the world of professor Martin Luther.[5]

The Fundraising Scheme Unfolds

Albert selected a Dominican friar, papal commissioner, and salesman extraordinaire named Johann Tetzel to direct the sale of the indulgences, and Albert confirmed instructions regarding the process. Tetzel would enter a city in great pomp, with robed acolytes, a cross and standard bearing the papal arms, Leo X's bull or decree, and a pulpit from which he dispensed on impressive parchment certificated indulgences signed by the pope himself for those who were willing to shell out sufficient money. An indulgence theoretically constituted a remission by the Church of

4. Green, *Luther*, 65.
5. Friedenthal, *Luther*, 134.

temporal punishment for sin already confessed and forgiven. As mentioned earlier, the indulgence extended merit to a sinner from its "Treasure House of Merit," an accumulation of merits supposedly amassed based on the good deeds of Christ and the saints. It seemed only natural to church leaders that church members should show gratitude for indulgences by paying money.

In April 1517, Tetzel approached the borders of Ernestine Saxony, proclaiming, "Will not you part with a farthing to buy this letter? It won't bring you money but rather a divine and immortal soul, whole and secure in the Kingdom of Heaven. Can you not hear your dead relatives screaming out in pain in Purgatory while you fiddle away your money?"[6] Luther was particularly troubled by a jingle Tetzel used among the peasants to garner monies: "As soon as the coin in the coffer rings, the soul from purgatory springs."[7] As noted earlier, these indulgences promised pardon not only to the payee but also to friends and relatives—living or dead—whether they had ever repented or done penance of any kind. Tetzel did not encroach on the town of Wittenberg because of Frederick the Wise's restrictions, but he operated just over the border—close enough for the parishioners of Luther to make the short excursion and return with their pardons. This abusive routine was all too much for Luther to take.

The "Little" Treatise that Exploded

By this time, Luther had, for the most part, won the Wittenberg faculty to his Scriptural view of the practice of indulgences. The professors he won over included Johann Lang, Andreas Carlstadt, Nicolaus von Amsdorf in theology, and Jerome Schurff in law. Luther sent a brief treatise to Archbishop Albrecht, Albert of Brandenburg, and others, suggesting in a humble tone that they rein in Tetzel and company a bit. Then, about noon on October 31, 1517, he posted on the door of the Castle Church—in accord with the current custom—ninety-five theses (or principles) in Latin, not German, on such matters for public discussion. For two weeks, an eerie silence greeted his letters and theses. Not one person showed up for his academic disputation regarding the theses. However, these days

---

6. Naphy, *Documents*, 11–12.

7. While Tetzel may have used the jingle, the phrase often credited to him had been used by the German Catholic Church prior to his time.

of silence became alarmingly similar to the seconds before a fuse burns down to the gunpowder. Many people had been thinking what Luther alone was unabashed to say, and almost everyone seemed to detonate in either praise or bitter opposition. Such were the beginnings of his works, and "The germs of the Reformation were contained in these propositions of Luther's."[8]

Luther was not only upset regarding the unscriptural practice of indulgences but also disgusted by the exploitation of the poor. One of the *Ninety-five Theses* reads: "Why, say they, does not the pope, who is richer than the richest Croesus, build the mother-church of St. Peter with his own money, rather than that of poor Christians."[9] The monk believed indulgences were spiritually worthless, that they were positively harmful to the giver by diverting charity, and they induced a false sense of spiritual security. He declared that indulgences did not represent the actual "merits of Christ and the saints because, even apart from the Pope, these merits are always working grace in the inner person and working the cross, death, and hell in the outer. Moreover, any true Christian, living or dead, participates in all the benefits of Christ and the Church, and this is granted to him by God without letters of indulgence."[10]

Luther did not realize that his brief theses were destined to become public knowledge far and wide. Though he made efforts to prevent dissemination, his students and others had them printed in both Latin and German in Nuremberg by the hundreds, and the demand quickly spread, as d'Aubigné puts it, "with the rapidity of lightning."[11] A Church revolution had been sparked, successful to a considerable extent due to the invention of movable type—the printing press. No man before Luther would make such prolific use of the press, and, in time, his books and leaflets flew across Europe as in a whirlwind, for there was a great famine for written materials for the masses.

The usually jovial Tetzel now bared fangs of fury, calling Luther a bald heretic and bragging that he would see the monk burn at the stake within weeks. As outraged as he was about being contradicted, he may have been angrier at the potential loss of a salary twenty times that of a

8. d'Aubigné, *History Vol. I,* 273.

9. Quoted by d'Aubigné, *History Vol. I,* 272.

10. Quoted by Kittelson, *Luther,* 107.

11. d'Aubigné, *History Vol. I,* 278.

professor, plus expenses.[12] The Dominican had a series of counter-theses printed in January 1518, and about 800 copies reached Wittenberg in March. Luther's students gleefully converged on the bookseller shop, bought up the entire stock, and made of them a raging bonfire.

However, Luther placed himself in submission to Leo X on May 13, 1518, and wrote very humbly, as if it was not the pope but his predecessors who had erred and led scandalous lives:

> For if I were such as they say and had not held a public discussion on the subject . . . then assuredly his Serene Highness Fredrick, Elector of Saxony, who is an ardent lover of Christian and apostolic truth, would not have suffered such a dangerous person in his University of Wittenberg. Also, the beloved and learned doctors and magisters of our University, who cleave firmly to our religion, would certainly have expelled me from their midst . . . therefore, most holy father, I prostrate myself at your feet, placing myself and all I am and have at your disposal, to be dealt with as you see fit. My cause hangs on the will of your Holiness, by whose verdict I shall either save or lose my life. Come what may, I shall recognize the voice of your Holiness to be that of Christ, speaking through you. If I merit death, I do not refuse to die, for "the earth is the Lord's," and all that is therein, to whom be praise to all eternity! Amen. May He preserve your Holiness to life eternal.[13]

Just a month earlier on February 3, 1518, Leo X had sent a brief to Gabriel della Volta, the Augustinian prefect, ordering him to "quiet that man," who was introducing novel doctrines to the populace.[14] The first opportunity to quench the monk came shortly, as Luther was invited to defend the theology of St. Augustine on the depravity of man during a meeting in April and May of the general chapter of Augustinians' order in Heidelberg. Warnings of danger came from many sources, and his enemies boasted that they would burn him within a month.[15] The issue of indulgences was not on the docket. It generally turned into a disputation in which the Wittenberg monk denied free will and man's capacity to satisfy God, presented a theology of the cross, and proclaimed salvation by faith in Christ alone. A vigorous discussion followed during which

12. Collinson, *The Reformation*, 55.

13. Luther, *Letters*, 30–1.

14. Quoted by Smith and Backhouse, *Life and Letters*, 67.

15. Bainton, *Here I Stand*, 65.

one doctor declared, "If the peasants heard you they would stone you to death."[16] At this, the audience burst into laughter.

A young twenty-seven-year-old Dominican by the name of Martin Bucer was permitted to attend the session and was among the converts won by Luther. He would eventually become the third most prominent German reformer after Luther and Melanchthon. Bucer claimed that Luther spoke with "a marvelous graciousness in response and unconquerable patience in listening. In argument he shows the acumen of the apostle Paul. That which Erasmus insinuates, he speaks open and freely."[17] No one suspected at this point that Bucer would figure prominently in the Reformation to come, though he would end up a somewhat unsung hero.

The Augsburg Confrontation by Cardinal Cajetan

The general chapter of the Saxon province challenged Luther to recant his beliefs in May of 1518, which he refused to do, though he did resign his office as district vicar. In that same month, Luther learned of a brutal critique of his teachings penned by a Dominican Thomist named Sylvester Mazzolini in which he superciliously proclaimed Luther to have a brain of brass and a nose of iron. In early August, he received a personal copy of the critique. That summer, he also learned from Count Albrecht of Mansfeld that several prominent and influential individuals had sworn to seize him and hang or drown him. Then on August 7, 1518, Girolamo Ghinnucci, supreme justice of Leo's curia, summoned Luther to appear in Rome within sixty days to answer for the declarations he had made regarding indulgences and papal authority. Upon negotiations, Luther's trial was transferred from Rome to Germany.[18]

On August 23, the pope decided to send an envoy named Cardinal Cajetan (Thomas de Vio of Gaeta), a leader in the Catholic reform movement, to either talk some sense into this upstart or bring him back in chains to Rome. In actuality, this meeting in Augsburg represented a far greater potential danger to Luther's survival than three years later when he would be summoned to Worms as the champion of an aroused German populace. At this point, Luther was only an obscure religious recluse accused of gross heresy. Luther had no death wish, but he was willing to

---

16. Bainton, *Here I Stand*, 66.

17. Quoted by Bainton, *Here I Stand*, 66.

18. Green, *Luther*, 72.

face a cross if God placed it on his shoulders. He would later state: "No man ought to lay a cross upon himself or to adopt tribulation, as is done in popedom. But if a cross or tribulation come upon him then let him suffer it patiently and know that it is good and profitable for him."[19] Many of his friends warned against making the journey to Augsburg; indeed, they believed he was signing his death warrant. Nonetheless, he set out for Augsburg and arrived on October 7, tired, and of a weakened body.

When Luther and Cajetan met at the Fugger estate on October 12, Staupitz was also present with the monk, as well as Wenceslaus Link. There was to be no discussion or debate (this expectation fell short, to say the least), and three interviews took place on Tuesday, Wednesday, and Thursday—October 12 through 14, 1518. Luther prostrated himself before the father on the first day, then rose to his knees, but only stood when beckoned to do so. He was graciously received, but Cajetan came quickly to the point with three demands: first, Luther must recant his errors; second, he must give assurance that he would not continue such teaching, and third, he must agree to not disturb the peace of the Church again. Where, Luther queried, lie the content of his heresy for which he was charged? The Cardinal replied that, among other things, he had denied the legitimacy of the doctrine of "the treasury of merit" upon which the practice of indulgences existed. Things promptly heated up when neither seemed especially attentive to the other. Cajetan was the first to lose his cool when Luther began showing more considerable skill in arguing Scripture, and he proceeded to try everything including, but not limited to, ranting, threatening, holding private talks with Luther's friends, and offering to drop some charges. Poor Staupitz and Spalatin, caught in the crossfire and at the request of Cajetan, begged Luther to modify his language and withdraw from the entire fiasco, but the young monk was unwilling to recant. Cajetan shouted again, "Recant. Acknowledge your errors; this and nothing else is what the Pope desires you to do."[20] Luther answered, "I am not so audacious that for the sake of a single obscure and ambiguous decretal of a human pope I would recede from so many and such clear testimonies of divine Scripture. For, as one of the canon lawyers said, 'In a matter of faith not only is a council above a pope, but any one of the faithful, if armed with better authority and reason.'"[21]

19. Putnam, *Anecdotes*, 99.

20. Quoted by Friedenthal, *Luther*, 180.

21. Quoted by Bainton, *Here I Stand*, 73.

Luther said he tried to speak nine or ten times that first day but Cajetan kept interrupting. The argument degenerated until Cajetan said to Staupitz, "I am not going to talk with him anymore. His eyes are as deep as a lake, and there are amazing speculations in his head."[22] Luther replied privately in a letter home that the Cardinal was about as fit to judge in spiritual matters, as "an ass to play on a harp."[23] At the conclusion of the third interview Cajetan, now clearly abandoning any attempt at goodwill, shouted, "Go! Do not let me see you again unless it is to recant."[24] "This moment," suggests Richard Friedenthal, "marked Luther's break with the Church and the Church's break with Luther,"[25] though no one present grasped that reality, he goes on to say.

On October 17, Luther wrote a statement to the Church official regarding his stand and why he could not violate it. Both sides denied defeat, and likely the only reason Cajetan did not arrest Luther was because of the monk's ties to Elector Frederick. A saddened Staupitz left Augsburg, but not before secretly releasing Luther from his vow of obedience to the Augustinian order, realizing that in such a crisis, the priest may not be able to keep the vow. Their relationship would never be as close again. After three days of tense silence from Cajetan, Luther was smuggled out of the city on October 22 for a most uncomfortable horseback ride of some eighty kilometers. He rode a hard-trotting nag in his knee britches and without spurs; when he dismounted a few hours later, he could barely waddle. He arrived back in Wittenberg almost one year after he had nailed the *Ninety-five Theses* to the Castle Church door. The Augsburg conference ended in a stalemate—neither side would admit to defeat.

By December, it was evident that Rome wanted the monk silenced by whatever means. In December 1518, Staupitz wrote to Luther from retirement in Austria, "You have few friends, and would that they were not hidden for fear of the adversary. Leave Wittenberg and come to me that we may live and die together. The prince [Fredrick] is in accord. Deserted let us follow the deserted Christ."[26] Luther offered to leave the city, and Frederick agreed that it might be best. However, during the priest's

---

22. Quoted by Bainton, *Here I Stand,* 74.

23. Bainton, *Here I Stand,* 73.

24. Quoted by Friedenthal, *Luther,* 183.

25. Friedenthal, *Luther,* 183.

26. Quoted by Bainton, *Here I Stand,* 77.

farewell dinner, a message arrived from Spalatin, indicating that the prince wished him to stay. Perhaps the prince suddenly realized that Luther had placed his little university on the map, and it might be a mistake to fire his increasingly famous and popular professor. The elector wrote Cajetan that he would not deliver Luther to Rome nor evict him from his territories until he was officially convicted of manifest heresy. There are reasons why Luther was not arrested and dragged to Rome for trial as a heretic. Luther was Frederick's prize professor at Wittenberg, Frederick was Germany's most powerful prince, and the empire needed German money and soldiers to fight the Turkish invasion. As Maximilian I aged, Frederick's vote for his successor was also crucial.[27]

The von Miltitz Intervention

On January 6, 1519, Karl von Miltitz, an envoy from the pope, arrived weeks after the Cajetan affair, carrying an anointed Golden Rose[28] to Frederick from the pope himself. He decided to make a scapegoat of Tetzel in order to gain the confidence of Luther. He also believed that the problem would die down if Tetzel were eliminated. He did this by discrediting him morally, charging him with embezzlement and extravagant traveling, and accusing him of having two illegitimate children An aging Tetzel retired to a convent and died shortly after, but not before Luther tried to console him by saying, "Don't take it too hard. You didn't start this racket. The [illegitimate] child had another father."[29]

Von Miltitz also was not above using flattery, cajolery, and skillfully obscured threats—actually telling Luther point-blank of the widespread polarization he was beginning to arouse within Germany. Realizing he was being pushed into a corner by the publicity, Luther backed off a bit. The monk agreed to drop the indulgences controversy if his enemies would do likewise, but he added that antagonistic debate had spread so far so fast that he was not in a position to revoke his convictions publicly. Miltitz was also able to procure from Luther a promise that if his opponents abstained from debate and publication, he would do the same.

27. Gritsch, *Martin: God's Court Jester*, 24.

28. The Golden Rose is an ornament blessed by popes and presented to men, women, shrines, or churches as a symbol or token of reverence or appreciation. It is unsure precisely when the practice began but dates back at least to the eighth century. The custom has continued to the present.

29. Quoted by Bainton, *Here I Stand*, 81.

Luther promised, and Miltitz was so thrilled he wept. "Crocodile tears," Luther commented, as he was not fooled.[30] Miltitz reported the good news to the pope in bubbly terms that so pleased Leo that he sent a friendly missive to Luther, inviting him to Rome to make his confession and even offering him money for the journey. When Luther received the friendly letter on March 29, Leo did not realize that the monk was far from being gagged.

Eck Enters the Fray

A period of relative quiet followed Luther's conference at Augsburg and subsequent encounter with von Miltitz. However, Luther's battle with Rome was picked up by fellow German Johann Eck, who was not about to be left out of the ecclesiastical dispute. Eck, a one-time friend of Luther, was a Roman Catholic Doctor of Theology, chancellor of the University of Ingolstadt, canon of Eichstatt, preacher at Augsburg, and famous author. In furious opposition to Luther's *Ninety-five Theses*, he penned a document he titled *Obelisks* in which he opposed Luther's teachings on indulgences. Andreas Carlstadt, a colleague of Luther at Wittenberg, was also involved in the dispute though Eck was more concerned with targeting Luther. Luther and Carlstadt both wrote counter pamphlets in response to Eck's attacks to which an enraged Eck challenged his foes to a public debate. Nevertheless, before the debate was scheduled, personal correspondence was already taking place. In a letter to Eck on February 18, 1519, Luther wrote, "I regret, Eck, to find so many reasons to believe that your professed friendship for me is hypocritical. You boast that you seek God's glory, the truth, the salvation of souls. . . . You have such a thick head and cloudy brain that, as the apostle says, 'you know not what you say.'"[31] To a friend in Zwickau, Luther stated, "What cuts me most is that we [Luther and Eck] had recently formed a great friendship. Did I not already know the machinations of Satan, I should be astonished at the fury with which Eck has broken that sweet amity without warning or letter of farewell. In his *Obelisks* he calls me a fanatic Hussite, heretical, seditious, insolent and rash, not to mention such slight abuse as that I am dreaming, clumsy, unlearned, and a despiser of the Pope."[32]

30. Quoted by Bainton, *Here I Stand*, 81.
31. Quoted by Smith and Backhouse, *The Life and Letters*, 82.
32. Quoted by Smith and Backhouse, *The Life and Letters*, 81.

The deliberations were scheduled for the summer of 1519 at the Pleissenburg Castle in Leipzig. Initially, it was recognized as a disputation between Eck and Carlstadt, but Luther eventually involved himself—to the encouragement and satisfaction of Eck. Before the official disputation began, Eck visited Luther and asked of him, "What is this? I am told that you refuse to dispute with me." To this, Luther responded, "How can I, since the duke has forbidden me?" Eck exclaimed, "If I cannot dispute with you, I care little about meeting Carlstadt. It was on your account I came here. . . . If I can procure you the duke's permission, will you enter the lists with me?" "Procure it for me," responded Luther, "and we will fight."[33] Duke George granted the necessary permission for Luther to debate.

The debate began on June 27 and lasted until July 15, and Luther entered the discussion on July 4. The topics of debate were expanded to include the existence of purgatory, apostolic succession and papal authority, abuses of Rome, and penance. On July 11, they finally addressed indulgences. "It was a mere joke, the dispute was ridiculous. The indulgences fell outright and Eck was nearly of my opinion."[34] Eck himself admitted, "If I had not disputed with Doctor Martin on the papal supremacy, I should almost have agreed with him."[35] The topic of indulgences became a relatively minor issue. While Luther initially had attacked the sale of indulgences, the question of such became peripheral to the issues dividing the reformers and the Catholic Church. The primary result of the Leipzig debate was that Luther recognized no longer the authority of the pope and the Church in matters of faith.[36]

Conclusion

Neither Cajetan nor von Miltitz were able to contain Luther. The conference between the Cardinal and Luther at Augsburg ended in a draw, with neither party willing to admit defeat. In a second effort to control the monk, von Miltitz thought he had muzzled Luther, but that pact lasted only two months. At Leipzig, Luther went far beyond the issue of

33. Quoted by d'Aubigné, *History Vol. II*, 37.

34. Quoted by d'Aubigné, *History Vol. II*, 62.

35. Quoted by d'Aubigné, *History Vol. II*, 62.

36. The Roman Catholic Church eventually addressed the abuses of indulgences; however, they continue to play a role in contemporary Catholic religiosity.

indulgences, addressing other theological issues such as justification by faith, purgatory, and penance, as well as attacking Rome and the Pope himself. The Church was not yet finished with Luther, however, and with more debates yet to come, none of the parties involved could anticipate what the future held for the Church and Western Europe. The following chapter describes the Leipzig Debate, a disputation convened to address Luther's teachings, including those on indulgences, and describes the aftermath of the debate.

4

The Debate that Set Europe Abuzz

"On June 24th, 1519, a motley band of Wittenbergers, Luther, Carl-stadt, the rector of the University, Duke Barnim of Pomerania, Mel-anchthon and a dozen or so professors and jurists in wagons (the one in which Carlstadt was travelling lost its wheel outside St. Paul's Church and threw the theologian), with a number of students armed with halberds and spears running beside their leaders, entered the Grimma gate of Leipzig. Eck, together with the Duke of Bavaria and representatives of the wealthy banking house of Fugger, had already arrived."[1]

Cajetan and Karl von Miltitz failed to rein Martin Luther in, so the German Johann Eck took it upon himself to challenge Luther and did so by recommending the Leipzig debate. The streets of Leipzig, Germany, sizzled with tension. People gathered in clusters on street corners, and arguments bubbled and burst into strife. The time had come for the much-awaited disputation.

The Pivotal Debate

Prior to the debate Andreas von Carlstadt, a Doctor of Theology, doctor of secular and canon law, and a professor at Wittenberg had been the first to respond to Eck's *Obeliskian* attack on Luther's theses. He wrote 380 theses, which later he expanded to 405, perhaps hoping to bury Eck in

1. Green, *Luther,* 84–5.

sheer apologetic paperwork. Eck did not respond right away, preferring to wait for Luther's reply. This rejoinder came in a rather mild extended letter entitled *Asterisks*, which seemed more conciliatory than harsh. However, by this time, Eck was spoiling for head-to-head conflict— which, of course, he got.

Carlstadt got first dibs on Eck, and they met on June 27 in the great hall of Duke George's Castle. The day before, the Wittenbergers had entered the city in wagons with two hundred students waving battle-axes and shouting slogans with great vehemence. Eck appeared with a body-guard of seventy-six men. The spectacle was spoiled to some extent when a wheel caromed off one of the wagons, ejecting Carlstadt and his books onto the street.

Preliminary arguments continued for days regarding whether the debates should be recorded and who the judges should be. Finally, tired of the incessant bickering, Luther gave in to most of the opposition's preferences. In the richly decorated hall of the Pleissenburg, Carlstadt and Eck sparred vigorously for ten days, but it was Eck and Luther that people wanted most to see. Moreover, Luther had spent the past six months in preparation for this crucial joust. They got their wish on July 4.

As the arguments began, supporters cheered and jeered, much as one would at a sporting event. Luther's collaborator, the mellow Philip Melanchthon, was there teaming powerfully with Luther and irritating Eck to no end with his quiet spirit and whispered suggestions to the monk. "I have been born to war and fight with factions and devils," Luther once stated. "Therefore my books are stormy and warlike. I must root out the stumps and stocks, cut away the thorns and hedges . . . as the rough forester to . . . make things ready. But Master Philipp walks softly and silently, tills and plants, sows and waters with pleasure, as God has gifted him freely."[2]

The debate ranged between many topics, including purgatory, penance, and indulgences, but Eck kept doggedly bringing it back to church authority. Eck said, "I see that you are following the damned and pestiferous errors of John Wycliffe, who said, 'It is not necessary for salvation to believe that the Roman Church is above all others.' And you are espousing the pestilent errors of John Huss, who claimed that Peter neither was nor is the head of the Holy Catholic Church." "I repulse the charge of Bohemianism," responded Luther. "I have never approved of their schism.

---

2. Ledderhose, *Life of Melanchthon*, 38.

Even though they had divine right on their side, they ought not to have withdrawn from the Church, because the highest divine right is unity and charity."[3]

Thus, at first, Luther denied any connection to Hussite beliefs. Finally, however, Eck managed to force Luther to admit that, though he was against the Hussites as a movement he would admit, "I am sure on this, that many of Huss' beliefs were completely evangelical and Christian."[4] Luther went on to affirm that he did not believe that it was necessary for salvation, to believe the Roman Church superior to all others. He reminded the diet that innumerable Greeks had been saved, though they knew nothing of this superior Roman Church. It was not within the power of the Roman pontiff or the Inquisition to construct new articles of faith or coerce individuals beyond holy writ.

Luther was taking a courageous stand on issues the Church officially condemned as heretical. Many years earlier, Luther had read one of Huss's writings while still in the cloister and wondered how a heretic could speak so Christianly. By the time he prepared for the Leipzig debate, he had come to believe that many of Huss's propositions were orthodox. Indeed, later, in a 1520 letter, Luther wrote, "I have hitherto taught and held all the opinions of John Huss unawares; so did Johann Staupitz; in short, we are all Hussites without knowing it. Paul and Augustine are Hussites to a word."[5]

When Eck felt he had attached Luther to Huss, "the reptile swelled up, painted Luther's 'crime' in the darkest colors, and almost drove the audience wild with his rhetoric."[6] Eck sneered, "Do you really think you are the only one who knows anything? Except for you, is all the Church in error?" "I answer that God once spoke through the mouth of an ass," replied Luther. "I will tell you straight what I think. I am a Christian theologian; and I am bound, not only to assert but to defend the truth with my blood and death. I want to believe freely and be a slave to the authority of no one, whether council, university, or pope. I will confidently confess what appears to me to be true, whether it has been asserted by a Catholic or a heretic, whether it has been approved or reproved by a council."[7]

3. Bainton, *Here I Stand*, 89.

4. Quoted by Naphy, *Documents*, 18.

5. Smith, *Life and Letters*, 72.

6. Smith, *Life and Letters*, 89.

7. Quoted by Benson, *A Man Called*, 73.

This was unprecedented—the peoples' priest, a Doctor of Theology, and an esteemed professor at the University of Wittenberg was placing himself under fierce attack from the Roman Catholic behemoth. Driven by a vision of pure, unexploited Christianity, this brilliant, pious, intolerantly willful man had done something considered the zenith of reckless audacity—he had defied the Catholic See. When Pope Leo had first read Luther's theses, he thought they were witty, though motivated by envy, and he claimed they had been composed by a drunken German who would see the error of his ways when sober once again. However, the Leipzig Luther/Eck debate of 1519 was a turning point for Luther. The monk surely realized then that reconciliation with the Church was no longer possible.

Petrus Mosellanus, the humanist scholar who gave the opening Latin oration at the 1519 Leipzig disputation, stated, "Luther is extraordinarily learned. Above all, he possesses such an astonishing knowledge of the Bible that he knows almost all of it by heart. He understands enough Greek and Hebrew to be able to give an independent judgment of the value of the translations. He is never at a loss in speaking, such an immense stock of ideas and words does he have at his command."[8]

According to some historians the debate was a draw. For example, Merle d'Aubigné notes that no decision had come to the disputation, and everyone "commented on it according to his own feelings."[9] Luther concluded that "there was great loss of time, but no seeking of truth."[10] Following the debate, Eck raced to Rome to secure a papal bull[11] from the pope, excommunicating Luther. However, the debate was not to be dismissed as inconsequential. Indeed it was a turning point for Luther and the beginning of the Reformation. "Luther's words," concludes d'Aubigné, "had sunk with irresistible power into the minds of his hearers."[12] The students, in particular, were impacted by the "spirit and energy of the Wittenberg doctor," and the student numbers at the university at Wittenberg soon doubled.[13] It was here too that Melanchthon received his call.

8. Quoted by Boemer, *Road to Reformation*, 288.

9. d'Aubigné, *History Vol. II*, 63.

10. Quoted by d'Aubigné, *History Vol. II*, 63.

11. A papal bull is an official document (a letter or a decree) issued by a pope of the Roman Catholic Church. The name is derived from the lead seal—*bulla*—affixed to the documents.

12. d'Aubigné, *History Vol. II*, 65.

13. d'Aubigné, *History Vol. II*, 66.

Heretofore he had been a student of literature, but the Leipzig conference launched him into a religious profession focused on God's Word.

The Papal Bull and Aftermath

Even before Eck arrived at Rome, Pope Leo and company were beside themselves the more they heard about Luther. The monk must receive a final terrible warning before complete excommunication. The pope's first commission was disbanded because their statement condemned Luther without substance. The second commission more cautiously wrote up a list of propositions as partly heretical, partly scandalous, and partly offensive to pious ears—thus, they may have thought that a peaceful solution was still possible. At this time, Eck arrived in Rome from Worms breathing fire, with brimstone smoking from his ears. Leo was moved by Eck's rage and appointed a third commission to demand full recantation within sixty days. This process had occupied five months.

The third bull against the monk was willingly approved and issued on June 15, 1520. Its words began: "Arise, O Lord, and judge thy cause. A wild boar has invaded thy vineyard."[14] The pope also cited forty-one heresies and ordered Luther's writings burned. Now Luther found himself on Church's most wanted list and to be treated like a fugitive. Luther was given sixty days to recant, and anyone who presumed to infringe on the excommunication would stand "under the wrath of Almighty God and of the apostles Peter and Paul."[15] In August Luther appealed to the Emperor stating,

> I have published certain books, which I have kindled the hatred and indignation of great men against me, but I ought to be protected by you for two reasons: first, because I come unwillingly before the public, and only wrote when provoked by the violence and fraud of others, seeking nothing more earnestly than to hide in a corner, and secondly, because, as my conscience and the judgment of excellent men will testify, I studied only to proclaim the gospel truth against the superstitious traditions of men. Almost three years have elapsed, during which I have suffered infinite wrath, contumely, danger and whatever injuries they can contrive of me.[16]

14. Quoted by Bainton, *Here I Stand*, 114.
15. Quoted by Bainton, *Here I Stand*, 114.
16. Quoted by Smith, *The Life and Letters*, 99.

The Elector of Saxony ignored the papal bull but traveled to Cologne to ask for advice on the matter from Desiderius Erasmus. When asked if Luther had erred, Erasmus answered, "Yes, he has erred in two points, in attacking the crown of the Pope and the bellies of the monks."[17] Erasmus drew up twenty-two propositions or axioms, suggesting to the Emperor that the Pope put the decision into the hands of a "tribunal of learned and impartial men."[18]

By November, Luther's time to recant had expired and, rather than doing so, fought back against his oppressors. On December 10, 1520, Melanchthon summoned a crowd of Luther's followers with the words, "Come, pious and zealous youth, to this pious and religious spectacle, for perchance now is the time when the Antichrist must be revealed."[19] A large crowd met Luther near the Black Cloister at the Gate Elster, near the city dump. Luther laid the pope's writings on a wood fire. He then placed the papal bull in the flames declaring, "Because thou hast brought down the truth of God, he also brings thee down unto this fire today. Amen."[20] Students kept the bonfire burning until late afternoon, torching other Catholic writings. The professors went home, but the students continued to parade about the town, raucously singing funeral songs. Now Luther's manifest heroism displayed itself, and excitement swept through Europe when it learned that a relatively unfamiliar monk from Germany had burned a papal bull. Knowing daily that genuine danger loomed everywhere, he went quietly about his business, teaching, preaching, and doing his duties. He was now determined to examine everything about the Church by the measuring sticks of *sola fide* and *sola scriptura*.

One should not imagine that Luther was speaking against the tenets of either the Church fathers or the great Church councils. Luther himself drew many of his central teachings from Augustine—his favorite—and freely quoted others such as Ambrose, Hilary, Cyprian, and John Chrysostom. Moreover, Melanchthon underlined the fact that "he has done nothing else than call us back to Scripture and also to the fathers who came the closest to the meaning of Scripture." He went on to assert to the

---

17. Quoted by Smith, *The Life and Letters,* 100.

18. Smith, *The Life and Letters,* 100.

19. Quoted by Smith, *The Life and Letters* 101.

20. Quoted by Smith, *The Life and Letters* 101.

Sorbonne faculty, "It is your theology, my masters, and not Luther's that disagrees with the fathers."[21]

Luther also reflected great respect for church councils. He summarized the four principal councils and the reasons they were held. The first, in Nicaea (A.D. 325), defended the divinity of Christ against Arius; the second, in Constantinople (A.D. 381), defended the divinity of the Holy Spirit against Macedonius; the third, in Ephesus (A.D. 431), defended the one person of Christ against Nestorius, the fourth, in Chalcedon (A.D. 451), defended the two natures in Christ against Eutyches. Nevertheless, no new articles of faith were thereby established. Luther believed that the councils focused on defending the historic Christian faith as presented in scripture, proclaimed in the Gospel, and handed down faithfully as the tradition from Christ and the apostles. These councils also defended Christian doctrine from novelties introduced by false teachers. Thus *sola scriptura* did not rule out the subordinate religious authority of the church fathers, the ancient creeds, and the doctrinal decrees of the ecumenical councils but found itself buttressed by these factors. The councils were an authority above the individual but subservient to the scriptures.

Luther: A Bull Let Loose

While leading figures such as the humanist Erasmus and reformer Wolfgang Capito urged him to be self-controlled and moderate in his attack on the Church, Luther took an opposite stance, declaring that reformers must, no matter what, take firm stands on issues without wavering: "To take no pleasure in assertions is not the mark of a Christian heart; indeed, one must delight in assertions to be a Christian at all . . . by assertion I mean staunchly holding your ground, stating your position, confessing it, defending it and persevering in it unvanquished."[22] Eventually, he was to express contempt for Erasmus' lack of aggressiveness: "You desire to walk upon eggs without crushing them . . . and among glasses without breaking them."[23]

Luther was tough as fibrous leather. Indeed, a man softened to refined speech would have shrunk from so mortal a combat. It took a thick skin to fend off papal excommunications, imperial bans, and threats on

21. Melanchthon, *Selected Writings*, 74–6.

22. Luther, *The Bondage*, 66.

23. Quoted by d'Aubigné, *History Vol. III*, 274

his life; and he laughingly called himself "poor stinking maggot fodder." Admittedly, pride occasionally peeked through his humility—he was dogmatic against dogma, intemperate in zeal, granting no quarter to his opponents, denouncing intolerance while giving it a nod. Here was no paragon of consistency or perfecter of virtue, but a man as contrary as life and scorched with the powder of warfare. The former monk rocked the heavens with his Jacobic prayer-fests. He spoke to God—now imperiously, as one who had struggled mightily in the battles of the Lord, now meekly as a child lost in infinite space. Confident that God was on his side, he faced insuperable obstacles and won. He was what he had to be to do what he had to do.

Luther had been forced to take theological positions on a public stage with no time to hone and polish them. Now he began thinking through them more thoroughly and modifying them somewhat as he churned out his famous writings. In addition to *On the Freedom of a Christian Man*, it was during the summer of 1520 that Luther also delivered to the printers *The Sermon on Good Works*, *The Papacy at Rome*, *Address to the German Nobility*, and *The Babylonian Captivity of the Church*. These publications may very well be among his most exceptional writings.

While Luther stirred the masses with his preaching, his sermons were extended the most significant impact when they were produced in written form. In 1519 Johann Froben, Luther's publisher, informed him that his writings had reached France, Spain, Italy, England, and Brabant. Capito concurred that the writings were rampant throughout those regions. In November 1520, Swiss humanist, Glarean, reported from Paris that "no books are more eagerly bought up than those of Luther. . . . One bookshop alone has sold 1,400 copies. Everywhere people speak highly of him, but the chain holding the monks is long."[24] Luther admitted he could not supply the printing presses the demands they made of him.[25]

Luther and the Popular People's Priest Zwingli

As the chapter title indicates, Luther's participation in the Leipzig debate set northern Europe—especially Germany and Switzerland—abuzz. At this time, one of the prominent Swiss reformers, Ulrich Zwingli, was well aware of Luther's work and sought to disseminate the monk's writings

24. Quoted by Spitz, *The Protestant Reformation, 1517-1559*, 196–7.
25. Simon, *Luther Alive*, 207.

widely, even recommending them from his pulpit. However, he tempered his exuberance by exclaiming, "I began to preach the Gospel in the year of grace 1516, that is to say, at a time when Luther's name had never been heard in this country. It is not from Luther that I learned the doctrine of Christ, but from the Word of God. If Luther preaches Christ, he does what I am doing; and that is all."[26] Zwingli indicated that this period (1516) was the beginning of the Swiss Reformation.[27] Nonetheless, there was general enthusiasm in Zürich for Luther, of which Zwingli joined in. He knew that the public would be more ready to accept his teachings with a man of Luther's newfound prominence. Thus, Luther's works were sold from house to house—partly due to the influence of Zwingli.

Zwingli was undoubtedly irritated when the canons explained to him that his primary and most crucial function was collecting the revenues and squeezing tithes and dues from even the poorest of his great congregation. As months passed, Zwingli would begin shooting occasional potshots at the Roman See. He attacked monks for indolence and wealth, he rejected the veneration of saints, and he challenged the Church to clarify fact and fiction in the accounts. He cast doubts on hellfire, asserted that unbaptized children are not damned, questioned the right of excommunication, and even wondered if the Church could *demand* tithes from all citizens. Finally, Zwingli rejected his papal pension and began attacking the destructive mercenary system, declaring that it was only resulting in the death of many of Switzerland's finest young men simply to line the pockets of Swiss nobles.

In the spring of 1522, with Zwingli absent, the Smaller Council in Zürich laid complaints about him before the magistrates. If the magistrates had decided against him, it could have wholly crippled the Swiss Reformation movement. However, certain magistrates sympathetic to the preacher appealed to the Great Council (known as the Two Hundred)[28], and they finally agreed to admit the Reformation preachers to the hall and hear their case. First, the Catholic Coadjutor gave a long speech

26. Quoted by d'Aubigné, *History Vol. II*, 281.

27. d'Aubigné, *History Vol. II*, 307.

28. The canton of Zürich was governed by the Large Council of Two Hundred (in actually 212) and the Small Council of fifty. Members of the Large Council consisted members of thirteen guilds plus the Small Council. The Small Council exercised the greater power but was obligated to include the board of 162 in making far-reaching decisions related to alliances, certain taxes, war, ambassadors, and courts of appeal. For additional information on the Zürich councils see Gäbler, *Huldrych Zwingli*, 8–9.

stating in brief that the "new teachings" constituted heresy, and only through the Roman Church can salvation be granted. After the speech, the coadjutor and his colleagues headed speedily for the doors. Zwingli interrupted them and constrained them through the council to remain and hear his defense, which was brilliant. The council refused to vote out the reformers and determined that Zwingli should continue to preach the Gospel and "By the people's will, therefore: Zürich is to be Protestant."[29]

Conflict with Luther

After a few years of admiration for Luther, Zwingli rejected him, though V. H. H. Green suggests that Zwingli had greater respect for Luther than the German had for him.[30] Luther maintained that the Devil influenced Zwingli and his friend Oecolampadius and their teachings were no better than those of the Papists.[31] On Zwingli's part, when his critics accused him of being "tied to Luther's aprons-strings," he exclaimed, " I don't want the Papists to call me Lutheran."[32] Furthermore, and as noted earlier, he claimed his Reformation principles came to him in ways independent of Luther.

At first glance, one would assume the two reformers had much in common. While they were united in their opposition to many Catholic doctrines—such as papal authority, purgatory, devotion to Mary, transubstantiation, and the veneration of relics—they strongly disagreed over many issues, to the point of accusing each other as heretics.

> ▸ Luther rose up against the excesses of those who destroyed the images in the churches; Zwingli stood present as people destroyed idols in the churches. While Luther hoped to remain united to the Catholic Church, Zwingli wished to carry out a complete transformation of the Church.[33]

> ▸ Both reformers preached the doctrine of justification by faith. However, Luther's reform was directed more towards the Jewish influence—pharisaical notions of salvation by human works or

---

29. Farner, *Zwingli*, 51. See also, d'Aubigné, *History Vol. II,* 369–273

30. Green, *Luther*, 170.

31. Green, *Luther*, 170.

32. Quoted by Farner, *Zwingli*, 109.

33. d'Aubigné, *History Vol. 3*, 243.

self-righteousness; Zwingli's reform was directed more towards the misguided pagan worship of Rome and established the universal sovereignty of God.[34]

> The two reformers disagreed on the nature of Christ. Luther emphasized the deity of Christ, emphasizing His omnipotence. Zwingli emphasized the humanity of Christ, noting His presence at the right hand of God with His omnipresence fulfilled through the Holy Spirit. He kept the dual natures of Christ separate.

> Concerning the Lord's Supper, both rejected the Catholic doctrine of transubstantiation. However, Luther believed that when Christ said this is my "body," and this is my "blood," it should be taken literally, whereas it was Zwingli's notion that the body and blood simply represented Christ.

They attempted to resolve their differences at the disputation of Marburg, Germany, and were able to do so on many points but failed to agree on the nature of Christ and the Eucharist. At this point, an estrangement within the Protestant ranks was apparent.

Conclusion

Luther was no rebel—at least it was not in his mindset to become one. Perhaps the less incendiary term *dissident* better describes him. Initially, he was more concerned with God's wrath and his own salvation than with what went on in the Vatican or anywhere else. He stood firm in support of the Church until his distress concerning indulgences eventually brought him into Leipzig's disputations. The Leipzig debate was the beginning of the end of his affiliation with Rome. By now, there were others on the Reformation scene, including the Swiss priest Zwingli, emboldened by the efforts of Luther at Leipzig. While their goals were in many ways similar, eventually, they had a falling out over their incompatible distinctions regarding the dual nature of Christ and Lord's Supper. The next chapter addresses the renowned Diet at Worms and a crisis that emerged in Wittenberg, very nearly derailing the German Reformation.

34. d'Aubigné, *History Vol. 3*, 244.

5

Luther

Diet at Worms and the Wittenberg Crisis

"On the sixteenth of April, Luther entered Worms in a Saxon two-wheeled car with a few companions. The imperial herald preceded, wearing the eagle upon his cloak. Although it was the dinner hour, two thousand turned out to conduct Luther to his lodging. On the following day at four o'clock Luther was waited upon by the herald and the imperial marshal, who conducted him furtively, to avoid the crowds, to a meeting of the emperor, the electors, and a portion of the estates. The monk stood before the monarch, who exclaimed, 'That fellow will never make a heretic of me.'"[1]

—ROLAND BAINTON

"The Diet of Worms might well appear as the climacteric of Luther's career, and in a sense it was so, since as a result of his meeting with the Emperor Charles V the latter decided to implement the papal decision. As a result the principal secular and ecclesiastical authorities combined to stamp out the challenge to their order. The drama of the ensuing situation has so gripped the historians' imagination that the importance of the Diet itself has been sometimes obscured."[2]

—V. H. H. GREEN

1. Bainton, *Here I Stand*, 140–1.
2. Green, *Luther*, 101.

IN 1500, A SON was born to Philip the Handsome, King of Castille. He was named Charles, and could accurately be called a prodigy. He learned to speak German, Spanish, Italian, and French; he pretended to piety but carefully studied the art of war and intrigue; he read Phillippe de Commines and learned early on the tricks of diplomacy and the immoral affairs of state. At age fifteen, he assumed the governments of Flanders, Holland, Franche Comte, and Burgundy. At age sixteen, he became Charles, King of Spain, Sicily, Sardinia, Naples, and Spanish America. When only nineteen, he aspired to be emperor and spent 850,000 florins to gain the office. Now he was thrust into a no-win situation regarding an "errant monk." Having exhausted ecclesiastical means to bring Luther to his knees, the Church in Rome urged Charles V to summon the professor before a council of German leaders in Worms, Germany, in 1521. Plans for such were on-again, off-again for six months as the parties jockeyed for acceptable conditions. Then the Church did an about-face. The pope sent Jerome Aleander to convince Charles to cancel the Diet and send Luther in chains to Rome. As Aleander journeyed to meet Charles, he was amazed to find that "ninetenths of the Germans cried 'Luther,' and the other one-tenth, 'Death to the pope.'"[3] This was an embellishment, of course, but Aleander was sufficiently incensed. Negotiations were finally initiated, and a meeting of two men—Luther and Charles V—was set. No one could anticipate how this critical meeting would impact Western Europe's history as the Diet opened a new chapter of the Reformation. His appearance before the Diet was not the end for Martin Luther—rather, it sparked a new beginning. This chapter addresses the celebrated Diet at Worms, the exile of Luther to the castle at Wartburg, and the ensuing crisis of Wittenberg.

The Diet Seals Luther's Notoriety

Already declaring him to be a heretic, by February 1521, Charles V showed contempt for Luther by tearing up a personal letter from him and Aleander was desperate to have Luther delivered to the Church authorities. Aleander harangued the German representatives for three hours, promising a hundred crowns for the emperor's secretary, a benefice for the underage son of a member of the electoral courts, and other tempting

3. Quoted by Bainton, *Here I Stand*, 130.

advantages. In the end, the German leaders voted to give Luther his just day in court. An immature twenty-year-old Charles V was thrust unwillingly into one of the most potentially incendiary situations he would face in his reign. On March 6, the Emperor "invited" Luther to appear at the Edict of Worms. He gave Luther twenty-one days in which to arrive and promised him safe conduct. Though he was given safe conduct, several of his friends and colleagues warned him not to go—Luther rejected all pleas and alternative options. He proclaimed that he would go even if he were too sick to stand on his feet. "I will go," declared Luther, "though as many devils took aim at me as there are tiles on the roofs of the houses."[4]

His dogged determination was reflected in his letter of February 9, 1521, to Johann von Staupitz, his spiritual supervisor while at the monastery. Whereas he was not explicit on his insistence on attending Worms, he was brutally forthright in his resistance to recantation in any form, to the point of reproaching his dear friend for taking a middle path between Christ and the pope: "This is not the time to tremble but to cry aloud, while our Lord Jesus is being condemned, burned, and blasphemed. Wherefore as much as you exhort me to humility I exhort you to pride. You are too yielding, I am too stiff-necked. . . . I write this more confidently because I fear you will take a middle course between Christ and the Pope, who are now in bitter strife. . . . Truly your submission has saddened me not a little, and has shown me that you are different from that Staupitz who was the herald of grace and of the cross."[5]

George Spalatin, Frederick's court preacher and secretary, warned him not to go. However, to Spalatin, he wrote on March 19, 1521, "If I am summoned solely for the sake of recantation I shall not come, seeing that it is all the same as if I had gone thither and returned here. For I can recant just as well here if that is their only business. But if he wishes to summon me to my death, holding me an enemy of the Empire, I shall offer to go. . . . The Lord's will be done."[6] A short time later, and as he was nearing his destination, he wrote to Spalatin, announcing, "I shall enter Worms in the face of the gates of hell and the princes of the air."[7]

Catholic moderates, led by Jean Glapion, the Emperor's confessor, wished that the case against Luther could be resolved out of court.

---

4. Quoted by von Ranke, "The Beginning," 42.
5. Quoted by Smith and Backhouse, *The Life and Letters*, 109.
6. Quoted by Smith and Backhouse, *The Life and Letters*, 111.
7. Quoted by Smith and Backhouse, *The Life and Letters*, 112.

In an interview with Martin Bucer, Ulrich von Hutton, and Franz von Sickengen,[8] Glapion suggested that instead of a public appearance, Luther should meet in private with him at a nearby castle. Bucer raced on horseback to intercept Luther, overtaking him at Oppenheim, and beseeching him to come and argue his case at Sickingen's Ebernburg castle. Luther flatly rejected the idea, not wishing to jeopardize his safe-conduct, still valid for another three days. It is possible that Bucer then trailed Luther to Worms and was so captivated by Luther's defense, that he went on to make God's love his overarching theme more than did Luther himself.[9]

When he arrived in Worms on April 16, 1521, in the open wagon loaned to him by the council of Wittenberg, trumpeters announced him from the cathedral tower. The imperial herald led the procession, Saxon nobles accompanied him to his quarters, and throngs of people jostled in the streets to catch a glimpse of the ex-monk—all much to the chagrin of Aleander. The next day an unending list of callers—including nobility and Imperial knights—visited Luther in his quarters. Among them were princes Philip of Hesse, William of Henneberg, and William of Braunschweig.[10] Biographer Heintz Schilling recently likened Luther, in today's language, to "a best-selling author and media star."[11]

He was summoned before the Diet at about 4:00 P.M. on April 17, but was not admitted until nearly 6:00. At Worms, so many affluent individuals wished to observe the proceedings that authorities switched the meeting to the cavernous bishop's palace. In it waited the six German electors, nobles, territorial princes, Spanish troops, representatives from Rome, and, of course, the young emperor. The majority probably gazed at Luther for the first time. It is not certain what they expected, but the general description of him likely did not fit the image many had imagined: "He was of medium height, haggard and emaciated from much study, but retained the vigor of manhood. His voice was clear and distinct; he was

---

8. Hutton and Sickengen were leaders of the Holy Knights of the Holy Roman Empire and were sympathetic to Luther and the Reformation movement. However, unlike Luther and other reformers who sought change through Church reform, they endeavored to procure a reformation through a military crusade. They were defeated in 1523.

9. Bainton, *Here I Stand,* 140; von Ranke, "The Beginning," 41–2; Smith and Backhouse, *The Life and Letters,* 112.

10. Von Ranke, "The Beginning," 42 and Schilling, *Martin Luther,* 176–7.

11. Schilling, *Martin Luther,* 175.

not arrogant or gloomy—he came across as cultivated, affable, cheerful, and occasionally jocose. With the exception of his first meeting, where he appeared to have lost some of his self-assurance, he gave the impression of confidence."[12]

When Luther appeared before the Diet, his writings lay piled on a table, and after being warned not to speak unless questioned, he was asked whether he was willing to retract them. It is remarkable how prolific Luther had already become. Among the writings were pieces on the art of dying, Holy Communion, baptism, the Lord's Prayer (for both adults and children), and comments on the Psalms, Galatians, the Ten Commandments, penance, marriage, usury, the sufferings of Christ, confession, and comforts for the troubled and distressed. He then acknowledged that these writings were his but quietly asked for time to think before he either stood by them or retracted. He was no doubt in somewhat of a state. He had expected a chance to defend the writings and beliefs—a disputation—not a point-blank recantation. Some observers interpreted Luther's subdued answer as a reflection that his spirit was broken. However, the papal nuncio, Aleander, had tried desperately to deny Luther a chance to speak to the council. Pope Leo wanted the secular ruler to condemn and punish Luther as a heretic immediately. When Charles granted Luther a chance to defend himself the following day, it not only assisted the radical monk but also showed the pope that secular rulers were beginning to reject the idea of being church marionettes.

The next day's affairs delayed Luther's appearance until nightfall, so candles lighted the great hall. The place was so packed that the heat had risen, and Luther was visibly perspiring. His address took only about ten minutes in German, but he was magnificent. Luther first asked forgiveness if his behavior was not in keeping with the noble etiquette expected—he was only a lowly monk who did not know better. Humbly, he voiced submission to the assembled rulers as a loyal subject. He said that recanting was a complicated process: some of his writings were about simple, orthodox faith so clear that even his enemies were compelled to regard them as worthy of Christian reading. Other writings indicated how the Church was harming Germany through her evil characters and false papal teachings. Should he recant these, he would open the door to more tyranny and impiety, and it would be all the worse, appearing that he was doing so at the command of the Holy Roman Empire. Luther

---

12. Boehmer, *Road to Reformation,* 272.

admitted that still others of his writings did attack individuals. If his language was occasionally too caustic or harsh, he could not deny them until his error was proven. He claimed he was motivated for Germany's well-being, which was being oppressed by papal demands and felt it was his duty to bring the light of Scripture to bear upon such matters. If he had occasionally exceeded the bounds of propriety, he had only been impelled by an inner drive for the truth. When pressed for a clear answer of whether he would recant his writings or not, Luther did not hesitate: "Since then your Majesty and your lordships desire a simple reply, I will answer without horns and without teeth," Luther continued emotionally. "Unless I am convicted by Scripture and plain reason—I do not accept the authority popes and councils, for they have contradicted each other— my conscience is captive to the Word of God. I cannot and I will not recant anything, for to go against conscience is neither right nor safe. God help me. Amen."[13] Some of the earliest versions added the words, "Here I stand, God help me. I cannot do otherwise."[14]

Charles V gave a signal to the herald, and the meeting was over. It was, Thomas Carlyle would later claim, "The greatest moment in the Modern History of Men."[15] The boyish side of Luther emerged as he left the hall, smiling and waving his arm to supporters in a salute to victory as opponents shouted, "To the flames with him!" German nobles and delegates quickly formed a protective circle around him and escorted him back to his lodgings. As he reached his lodgings, he cried out, "I made it through!" It is ironic that this emperor, who seemed at the time so determined to defend the Roman Church, would, within years, send troops who would sack Rome and entrap the pope.[16]

The next day the young emperor called in the electors and princes and read to them a paper reflecting his opinion. He declared, "A single friar who goes counter to all Christianity for a thousand years must be wrong." He concluded by stating, "I regret that I have so long delayed in proceeding against him and his false teaching. I will have no more to do with him. He may return under his safe conduct, but without preaching

---

13. Quoted by Bainton, *Here I Stand*, 144.

14. Bainton, *Here I Stand*, 144.

15. Carlyle, *The Selected Works*, 184.

16. Friedenthal, *Luther*, 278–9; Green, *Luther*, 116.

or making any tumult. I will proceed against him as a notorious heretic, and ask you to declare yourselves as you promised me."[17]

A Kidnapping for Safekeeping

It is not entirely certain if Luther suspected that Frederick would do any-thing following Worms to protect his increasingly notorious professor. Frederick purposely kept himself out of the loop on this, possibly because he wanted to deny all knowledge of the details. Luther certainly seemed in no great hurry to return to Wittenberg. He departed Worms on April 26, 1521, and dismissed the safe-conduct guards on April 29.

Not far from Eisenach in the Thuringian forest horsemen suddenly burst through the trees. With drawn crossbows, they converged upon the small party. Caught by complete surprise, the monk's Imperial escort fled into the forest. With much cursing and a display of violence, they pulled Luther to the ground. They placed him upon a horse and led him for a whole day by a roundabout way through the forest until well after dusk at about eleven o'clock they arrived at the medieval fortress of Wartburg Castle high above Eisenach. Luther awoke in the castle the next morning after his kidnapping. His head was still throbbing from the tension and rough handling of the night before, and his legs and rump were aching from the hard riding. A message was sent to him, which stated that his identity had been changed.

Junker Jörg: Ten-Month Knight

To hide his identity, he was to pose as an itinerant knight named Junker Jörg, meaning Knight George. Several days afterward, the two servants who attended to him wakened him at dawn and led him down dim hall-ways until they reached a rather large courtyard. Several knights greeted him curtly and told him he must learn the skills of a knight, but he heard them muttering to one another that he would not exceed the level of a page.

His horsemanship was adequate for a typical commoner of that time, but of course, the knight's skill must be exceptional—especially when it came to controlling the over-sized and sturdy warhorses. They would never attempt to try Luther on such a mount. They started him

17. Quoted by Bainton, *Here I Stand*, 145.

out circling the courtyard on a tall but tame bay. After riding, they intro-duced him to the most elemental swordplay, using wooden swords and shields. They laughed at his clumsiness and grinned snidely when Luther became red-faced and winded after an hour or two of training. The monk was not portly at this time, but the life of a theologian did not include much physical exertion. They sent him back to his room, but he was to return most mornings save the Sabbath.

He was given a small room in which to write and study. From the lone window, he could peer down the sheer castle wall into deep chasms, over which stood magnificent ranges of silent forested mountains. To further disguise himself, Luther let his hair and beard grow wild. He was holed away deep in the castle in cramped quarters—a desperate insomni-ac—on his own Isle of Patmos. His two attendants brought him his meals and tried to comply with his requests, but the castle accommodations were sparse, and it was not equipped like a monastery. He lived for letters from Spalatin as there was little correspondence from anyone else. Luther seemed closer now to inner destruction than almost any other time of his life. He wrestled angels and demons, sometimes not sure, which was which. The black depression that would periodically plague him all his life threatened to wring any remaining bit of vitality from his soul. He wrote, "I can tell you in this idle solitude there are a thousand battles with Satan. It is much easier to fight against the incarnate Devil—that is, against men—than against spiritual wickedness in the heavenly places. Often I fall and am lifted again only by God's right hand."[18]

He agonized in prayer, questioning his faith and wondering whether the reformation fever that was now sweeping Germany and beyond was really of God. He then wrote to Spalatin, "Now is the time to pray with our might against Satan. He is plotting an attack on Germany, and I fear God will permit him because I am so indolent in prayer. I am might-ily displeasing to myself."[19] Isolated from the conflict, he wrote, "I had rather burn amid fiery coals than rot here" and "I wanted to be in the fray."[20] Months passed, and the theologian complained of many ailments, including constipation, hemorrhoids, depression, and insomnia. He fell into a spiritual stupor. To Spalatin, he wrote, "I sit here inactive and out

18. Quoted by Bainton, *Here I Stand,* 151.
19. Quoted by Bainton, *Here I Stand,* 151.
20. Quoted by Bainton, *Here I Stand,* 151.

of sorts the whole day long."[21] At one point, he confessed to his friend Melanchthon "For the last eight days I have written nothing. I neither pray nor study, partly on account of the trials of the flesh, partly because I am tormented with another malady."[22]

Finally, Luther went to work, turning out an enormous body of work in his edgy mood. To a friend he summarized his efforts: "I have brought out a reply to Catharinus and another to Latomus, and in German a work on confession, expositions of Psalms 67 and 36, a commentary on the Magnificat,[23] and a translation of Melanchthon's reply to the University of Paris. I have underway a volume of sermons on the lessons from the epistles and Gospels. I am attacking the Cardinal of Maintz and expounding the ten lepers."[24]

Between December 4 and 10, 1521, he made a secret visit to Wittenberg and stayed in Philip Melanchthon's home. Melanchthon urged him to take up the work of translating the Bible into German. Luther headed back to Wartburg and labored night and day to translate the New Testament into the German of the common citizen, completing the mammoth rough draft in eleven weeks. Luther's translation of the German Bible, called the September Bible, was likely his ultimate achievement.

Shortly before he visited Wittenberg, on May 26, 1521, the Emperor had already officially declared Luther a convicted heretic. He called him a pagan and a demon in monk's clothing. His followers were also condemned, and his books eradicated from the memory of humanity. His friends and colleagues despaired. Some of them thought that perhaps Luther had been carried off; others supposed him murdered. Erasmus, however, wrote, "The Lutheran drama is over. Would that it had never been brought to this stage. . . . Now that Luther has gone to ashes, the preaching friars and the divines congratulate each other, not, however, with much sincerity."[25] Erasmus confessed candidly that he did not think himself cut out for martyrdom and moved to Basel. Wolfgang Capito wrote in anguish to Erasmus, "Someday, far from now, the decree of Emperor Charles will be different. . . . Christ will undoubtedly make an end

21. Quoted by Green, *Luther*, 125.

22. Quoted by Green, *Luther*, 125.

23. The Magnificat was an ancient hymn of Mary based on The Gospel of Luke 1:46–55.

24. Quoted by Bainton, *Here I Stand,* 152.

25. Froude, *Life and Letters,* 292.

to these evils. Certainly no one can prohibit preaching and reading the gospels; nothing is accomplished by burning books."[26]

The Reformation Goes Awry as Luther Steams

With Luther in secluded exile, the Reformation took a violent turn. Throughout the countryside and towns, revolts began to break out. In Wittenberg, anarchy reigned, and while reports reached Luther in Wartburg, he did not take them seriously—at least initially. However, on December 4, 1521, as noted above, Luther, sufficiently disguised, decided to risk life and arrest by visiting Wittenberg. The day before his arrival, there had been a riot: "Students and townsfolk, with knives under their cloaks, invaded the parish church, snatched the mass books from the altar, and drove out the priests. Stones were thrown against those saying private devotions to the Virgin Mary. On the morrow the very day of Luther's arrival, the Franciscans were intimidated."[27] He did sense a revolutionary temper among the people, and more violence was to follow, but Luther, according to Lucien Febre, returned to Wartburg "with confidence and hope"[28] albeit with a warning to the people against any resorting to violence. Luther wrote a treatise in absentia: *A Sincere Admonition to all Christians to Guard against Insurrection and Rebellion,* but it did not do much to quell the growing unrest.

What had happened? Carlstadt and other reformers assured Luther that now everything was under control, and the riots were over, but this was clearly a cover-up. Luther had hoped that Melanchthon would continue to spread the reforms, and he chided him in letters: "I cannot believe what you write, that you are going astray without a shepherd. . . . As long as you, Amsdorf, and the others are there, you are not without a shepherd."[29] However, Melanchthon was more the brilliant writer than the gifted leader, and the rioting was likely due to a lack of strong leadership.

26. Quoted by Kittelson, *Wolfgang Capito,* 81.

27. Bainton, *Here I Stand,* 159.

28. Febvre, "The Crisis of 1521–1525," 47.

29. Luther, *Luther's Works Vol. 48,* 234.

Müntzer: The Wild Revelator Assumes Leadership

Several years earlier, Luther had seen promise in a German preacher named Thomas Müntzer. He mentored Müntzer and even recommended him as the priest in Zwickau. The young man now began to attract attention based partly on his oratorical skills. However, he began expressing increasingly radical ideas, claiming that he was a *bona fide* prophet, that direct revelations to him superseded the Word of God, and that the Kingdom of God would reign over all kingdoms, beginning with the ones ruled by German princes and nobles. This, of course, appealed to oppressed peasants but did not go over well with city councils.

Müntzer entered a pastorate at St. John's Church in Allstodt after being expelled from both Zwickau and Prague for his radical message and volatile nature. Regrettably, the rejections played into his developing theory that the Elect will naturally suffer persecution. At first, the princes of Saxony bent over backward to give him a fair hearing, and Müntzer preached his infamous Furstenpredigt sermon to them there. However, they found it difficult to stomach his accusations of, "all the eels and snakes coupling together immorally in one great heap. The priests and all the evil clerics are the snakes . . . and the secular lords and rulers are the eels."[30]

When Müntzer became unwelcome in Allstodt, on December 27, 1521, he collected his three fellow revelators (known as the Zwickau prophets)—Nicholas Storch, Mark Stübner, and Thomas Drechsel—and journeyed to Wittenberg.[31] Early on, Müntzer had written to Melanchthon in an effort to win him over. Now, surprisingly, Melanchthon seemed to be somewhat taken by teachings such as their "Spirit theology," and their so-called direct revelation of a looming apocalypse from which only the Elect could survive. Luther wrote Melanchthon a letter on January 13, 1522, from his place of hiding warning him to beware of those who testify of themselves but have not proven their wisdom and supposed divine revelations. The letter stated, "Thus far I hear of nothing said or done by them that Satan could not also do or imitate. . . . God has never sent anyone, not even the Son himself, unless he was called through men

---

30. Quoted by Scott, *Thomas Müntzer*, 73.

31. These so-called revelators claimed to be prophets of God and that they had received revelations directly from God.

or attested by signs."[32] Melanchthon gradually detected the falseness and danger of the teachings of Müntzer.

Müntzer's streak of vindictiveness aroused the hostility of Luther and in retaliation Müntzer began more boldly to denounce Luther's theological teachings directly. In turn, Luther refused to countenance Müntzer's claim of direct revelation even if "he had swallowed the Holy Ghost, feathers and all."[33] After fomenting uproar in Allstodt, Müntzer bungled his way into Muhlhausen, where a man named Heinrich Pfeiffer was already preaching doctrines somewhat like his own. Müntzer, however, was becoming more radical by the month. Soon he was denouncing established governments and advocating common Christian ownership of all. To the poor peasants, he declared, "Harvest-time is here, so God himself has hired me for his harvest. I have sharpened my scythe, for my thoughts are most strongly fixed on the truth, and my lips, hands, skin, hair, soul, body, and life curse the unbelievers."[34] He went on to incite them to, "Drive Christ's enemies out from among the Elect, for you are the instruments for that purpose. Dearly beloved brethren, don't put up any shallow pretense that God might do it without your laying on with the sword. . . . Christ is your master, so don't let them live any longer, the evildoers who turn us away from God. For a godless man has no right to live if he hinders the godly."[35]

His words appealed to the oppressed poor, and the powder keg of peasant unrest, which had for years been smoldering, began moving inexorably toward flashpoint. Luther saw the danger of revolt brought on by revolutionaries such as Müntzer and Pfeiffer from his damp rooms in Wartburg Castle and he warned the Elector Frederick in March of 1522, "there will be a real rebellion in the German territories, by which God will punish the German nation. For we see that this gospel is excellently received by the common people; but they receive it in a fleshly sense; that is, they know that it is true but do not want to use it correctly. Those who should calm such a rebellion only aid it. They attempt to put out the light by force, not realizing that they are only embittering the hearts of men by

32. Luther, *Luther's Works Vol. 48*, 366.

33. Quoted by Bainton, *Here I Stand*, 203.

34. Quoted by Cohn, *The Pursuit*, 237.

35. Quoted by Cohn, *The Pursuit*, 239.

this and stimulating them to revolt."[36] Luther's prediction came to pass in 1525–1526, instigated and supported in part by Müntzer himself.

Luther Again Takes the Reins

Luther was under heavy pressure from both outside and inside Wittenberg. A new pope, Adrian VI, took the throne and demanded enforcement of the Edict of Worms against Luther and his followers. Matters were spiraling out of control, and the Wittenberg congregation was urgently begging and pleading for him to return to the city and restore order. Luther himself wrote to Frederick giving three reasons for him to return to Wittenberg one of which was that, "Satan has intruded into my fold at Wittenberg. . . . Satan has injured some [sheep] which I cannot heal with my writing. I have to deal with them personally via mouth and ear. My conscience will no longer allow me to yield or procrastinate."[37]

Luther was finally convinced to come out of hiding and re-take the reins of the movement, his first concern being the restoration of order and confidence in his leadership. Despite Frederick's cautions, he rushed to Wittenberg and preached eight sermons between March 9 and 16, 1522, known as the *Invocavit*. Before touching on doctrinal principles, he declared, as summarized by Preserved Smith, that "mob violence is not the way to reform the Church—that sedition, even when provoked is always wrong, and that the people, in presuming to regulate spiritual matters, usurp an office which does not belong to them."[38] The violence that included demolishing altars, smashing images, and dragging priests by the hair was to Luther a greater miscarriage of justice than anything dealt him by Rome. He pleaded desperately:

> Do not suppose that abuses are eliminated by destroying the object which is abused. Men can go wrong with wine and women; shall we then prohibit wine and abolish women? The sun, the moon, the stars, have been worshiped. Shall we then pluck them out of the sky? Such haste and violence betray a lack of confidence in God. See how much has been able to accomplish through me, though I did no more than pray and preach. The Word did it all. Had I wished I might have started conflagration

36. Luther, *Luther's Works Vol. 48*, 396.

37. Luther, *Luther's Works Vol. 48*, 396.

38. Smith, *The Life and Letters*, 148.

at Worms. But while I sat and drank beer with Philip and Amsdorf, God dealt the papacy a mighty blow.[39]

Capito appeared covertly in Wittenberg and heard Luther preach one of these rallying sermons. When he was identified, Capito used the opportunity to have some private talks with the reformer. He came away full of admiration for Luther's pacifying influence on the revolutionaries and thoroughly convinced of the true Gospel and of Luther's mission to re-establish it. He wrote, "And now the authorities everywhere may come to know what a light and easy thing Christianity is and how completely a patient Christian differs from a seditious revolutionary."[40]

Andreas Carlstadt: Disgruntled "Purist"

Andreas Carlstadt, at one point, was a prominent member of the faculty at the University of Wittenberg. His advocacy of Luther's teachings, however, "prompted him to indulge in such blasts against critics that Luther himself was prone at times to wince."[41] Eventually he was escorted to the Elector and instructed to either stop preaching novelties or leave the city. He wrote an extreme treatise defending his tough line on icons. He then set aside his doctor's robe when lecturing and began addressing the young students as "dearest colleagues." In 1523, he accepted a post as vicar of Orlamünde, and soon he began spending more time on his farm outside town than fulfilling his academic obligations. He encouraged visitors to call him "neighbor Carlstadt." He avoided old friends and associates and found some solace in correspondence with Müntzer, the proverbial loose cannon—unfortunate because, as Bainton puts it, "neither was balanced and stable."[42]

Melodramatically, Carlstadt cast aside his senior academic's gown and began dressing as a peasant, asking that people call him Brother Andreas. His most severe extremism occurred after he settled in the parish of Orlamünde. In addition to his previous attacks on images and church music, he now denied the presence of Christ in the sacrament, a critical component of Luther 's theology. He likewise rejected infant baptism, another essential tenet of Luther's doctrine. Luther was encouraged to take

39. Quoted by Bainton, *Here I Stand*, 165–6.

40. Quoted by Kittelson, *Wolfgang Capito,* 85.

41. Bainton, *Here I Stand,* 81.

42. Bainton, *Here I Stand,* 200.

a preaching tour of Carlstadt's area with the intent of returning them to orthodoxy, but his message fell on deaf ears. As Carlstadt's ideas spread, Bucer wrote urgently to both Luther and Zwingli, asking for their stand on fundamental issues, which the professor was expounding with such abandon.

Undoubtedly feeling betrayed, Carlstadt called Luther a papist twice over, then forsook Wittenberg and was warmly received by Zwingli in Zürich. He published three pamphlets in which he supported Zwingli's view of the Lord's Supper, that there was no actual presence of Christ in the elements. The resultant link between Carlstadt and Zwingli irked Luther sorely, and it was unfortunate that the first encounter later between Zwingli and Luther was framed in Zwingli's geniality toward Carlstadt and the Zwickau ranters.

Luther's Support Network During the Crisis of 1521–1525

During Luther's absence, Johannes Bugenhagen arrived in Wittenberg and took the pastorate at St. Mary's. Early on, he had studied the arts at the University of Greifswald and had excelled. Though Bugenhagen was largely untrained in theology, he was ordained a priest in 1509. He began perusing Luther's writings. He vehemently disagreed with Luther and angrily threw *The Babylonian Captivity of the Church* on the floor. However, the more he read, the more he was drawn to the logic and power of the writings and joined Luther's cause in 1520. He concluded, "The entire world is blind, for this man is the only one who sees the truth."[43] He became a colleague of Luther on the faculty of Wittenberg and shared preaching duties with him at the Castle Church. He became Luther's confessor (or partner in confession). When Luther would suffer a breakdown or temptation, it was Bugenhagen who would "give him a good scolding, asking him what he meant by saying he was a victim of God's wrath."[44] He would speak for God: "What am I to do with this man? I have bestowed so many excellent gifts on him, and yet he insists on despairing of My grace."[45] This, admits Luther, had been a great comfort to him. With Melanchthon, Bugenhagen assisted in translating the Bible and became a chief reformer who was "loaned" to various territories, even to the king

43. Quoted by Kittelson, *Luther,* 186.

44. Friedenthall, *Luther,* 330.

45. Quoted by Friedenthall, *Luther,* 330.

of Denmark. Even through the most challenging times, Bugenhagen remained a faithful friend and supporter of Luther.

Among Luther's other close friends was Spalatin. They had studied law together at Erfurt and crossed paths again when Spalatin was secretary to Fredrick the Wise. In that capacity, he no doubt came to Luther's aid on more than one occasion. Other friends included Nicholas Amsdorf, lawyer Justus Jonas, and artist Lucas Cranach. Jonas was a fellow pastor at Wittenberg, shared Luther's passion for hymn writing, spent many hours at the family table of Luther, and preached Luther's funeral sermon. However, Melanchthon, among all of his colleagues and friends, stands out as the most notable, as described by Stephen Nichols: "They enjoyed a lifetime friendship, although they were quite different personalities. Luther once remarked that Melanchthon stabbed with pins and needles, while he himself stabbed with a heavy spear. Melanchthon was much quieter and more gentle, a chemistry that sometimes proved efficient and at other times proved quite frustrating to Luther."[46] When he made a secret visit to Wittenberg, he stayed in Melanchthon's home. Furthermore, it was Melanchthon who urged him to take up the work of translating the Bible into German.

Conclusion

Within a few short years of the notorious Diet of Worms, Luther had instigated a colossal religious and societal revolution. The prodigious output of the gifted Luther as reformer, preacher, author, counselor, and letter writer began to emerge in Wittenberg in a truly astounding fashion. He was a staunch believer in persistence, thoroughness, and tenacity, full concentration upon the task of the moment as a God-ordained mission. Now, as Friedenthal puts it, the world came to Wittenberg, and "Luther was overwhelmed with inquiries, requests and demands for his opinion."[47] This chapter addressed the period that launched Martin Luther into the center of the Reformation. We will revisit Luther in subsequent chapters, but in the next chapter, we transfer our attention to Philip Melanchthon, Luther's colleague and cherished friend.

46. Nichols, *Martin Luther*, 59.
47. Friedenthall, *Luther*, 329.

6

Philip Melanchthon

Luther's Brilliant Shrimp

"Melanchthon was . . . a prodigy of learning, enjoying already a European reputation. In appearance he was not prepossessing, as he had an impediment of speech and a hitch in the shoulder when he walked. Luther once, when asked how he envisioned the appearance of the apostle Paul, answered with an affectionate guffaw, "I think he was a scrawny shrimp like Melanchthon." But when the stripling opened his mouth, he was like the boy Jesus in the temple. He came as professor of Greek, not of theology, and without any commitment to Luther; but soon he succumbed to his spell. His conversion stemmed from no travail of spirit but from agreement with Luther's interpretation of the apostle Paul."[1]

—ROLAND H. BAINTON

MARTIN LUTHER'S EVENTUAL IMPACT on the event that not only transformed the Church but Western society as well came, to coin a modern phrase, with a strong supporting cast. In addition to the patronage of Prince Fredrick, Luther gained the support of distinguished scholars such as Andreas Carlstadt, George Spalatin, and John von Staupitz. However, the man who became Luther's dearest friend and closest colleague was Philip Melanchthon whose appearance was underwhelming: "He was young, below middle size, diffident, hesitating, of frail

1. Bainton, *Here I Stand,* 81–2.

body and stammering tongue, and carried one shoulder higher than the other."[2] However, upon the completion of his first oration, Luther proclaimed, "We have quickly abandoned the opinion we formed from his small stature and homeliness, and now rejoice and wonder at his real worth."[3] On his part Melanchthon, "filled with admiration at Luther's knowledge of the Scriptures, set him far above the fathers of the Church."[4]

The Bright Star Rising[5]

Philipp Schwarzerd (changed to Philip Melanchthon), Luther's eventual theological partner and friend, originated in the town of Bretten in the Electoral Palatinate, a town of not more than three hundred families. Bretten was primarily a farming community, though the trades of weaving and tanning brought a healthy income to a minority. Resting on a beautiful site, the buildings and fortifications reflected skilled and careful workmanship.

Melanchthon's father George was the Elector's armorer and had also served the emperor Maximilian. Given his almost constant travel, he had no time for courting, so when he was thirty-five years old, the Elector matched him with Barbara, the sixteen-year-old daughter of the Bretten mayor. Philip was born on February 16, 1497, followed later by a brother, George, and three sisters. When Philip was only eleven years old, he lost his father to a lengthy illness triggered by a drink from a polluted well. His mother then sent the boy to stay with relatives in Speyer. Philip always expressed tender sentiments toward his mother, though he saw her seldom after this.

The boy was brilliant, grave, with deep feelings and a sharp temper. As he matured, he so mastered the temper that stubbornness, harshness, and vindictiveness flashed through only rarely, when one of his crucial goals was attacked or belittled. Philip's first formal learning took place in a private school led by John Unger. Unger was a strict and skillful educator who must have had a fatherly side because none of Philip's future

---

2. Richard, *Philip Melanchthon*, 36.

3. Quoted by Smith, *The Life and Letters*, 70.

4. d'Aubigné, *History Vol. III*, 6–7.

5. Unless otherwise noted, content in this section is summarized from Steinmetz, *Reformers*, Stuperich, *Melanchthon*, and Richard, *Philip Melanchthon*.

teachers were recalled with such warm words as Unger. In addition to praising him as an illustrious scholar and teacher, he had this to say about his relationship with him: "He was a good man. He loved me as a son, and I him as a father. In a short time we shall meet, I hope, in eternal life. I loved him notwithstanding that he used such severity; though it was not severity, but parental correction which urged me to diligence."[6] Next, he spent one year in a Latin school in Pforzheim in which he was introduced to Greek, a language for which he showed an extraordinary affinity. It was here that he first came under the influence of his great-uncle Johann Reuchlin who observed the excellent talents in the twelve-year-old boy. During this time, Reuchlin determined that such a clever young man should not go by the unattractive name of Schwartzerd (meaning black earth) and that he be called by the Greek equivalent Melanchthon.

On October 14, 1509, Melanchthon matriculated at Heidelberg and, within two years, had completed the requirements for a Bachelor of Liberal Arts. However, when he applied to receive the master's degree, he was refused, being only fourteen years of age. Thus, he transferred to Tubingen in 1512, and there made many friends, including the eventual reformer, Oecolampadius. The young man loved learning in every field and pursued mathematics, juristics, and even medical studies. As mentioned earlier, Melanchthon was the grandnephew of the great Hebrew scholar, Reuchlin, and became like a son to him. Reuchlin gifted him with a Latin Bible, and he became so engrossed with it he even read it covertly during Mass. In January of 1514 he received the degree of Master of Liberal Arts.

As a Master, Melanchthon also received his license to teach and began delivering lectures on classical authors such as Virgil and Cicero. The newly published *Dialectics* by Agricola stimulated him profoundly in the method of establishing basic concepts, deducing from them essential viewpoints, and from the context, developing conclusions. By the age of twenty, he had written a Greek grammar. Thus, a shimmering star edged over the horizon, a young man who was to become, not only a colleague but also one of Luther's most cherished friends.

As early as 1515, Desiderius Erasmus lavished high praise on Melanchthon: "Eternal God, what expectation does not Philip Melanchthon raise, who though a youth, yea, rather, scarcely more than a boy, deserves equal esteem for his knowledge of both languages! What sagacity in

6. Quoted by Richard, *Philip Melanchthon*, 7.

argument, what purity of style, what comprehension of learned subjects, what varied reading, what delicacy and almost royal elegance of mind."[7]

The Reformers Become Great Friends

Elector Frederick the Wise inquired whether Reuchlin knew of a capable and suitable Greek instructor for his newly established University of Wittenberg. Without a moment's hesitation, he recommended his grand-nephew, and Melanchthon was hired as an instructor over the scholar, Peter Mosellanus. He arrived in Wittenberg on August 25, 1518, and his inaugural address, delivered on August 29 under the title *On Improving the Studies of Youth,* caused a great stir. Among the audience was Luther, who described him as slight, homely, and spoke with a lisp. However, Luther and others very quickly disregarded his appearance "and saw in him only the David who was destined to go forth against the Goliath of Scholasticism."[8] To Spalatin, a few days after Melanchthon's inaugural address, Luther wrote: "We have quickly abandoned the opinion we formed from his small stature and homeliness, and now rejoice and wonder at his real worth, and thank our most illustrious Elector and your good offices too, for giving him to us."[9] Luther was even more grandiose to Staupitz in his praise for Melanchthon: "If Christ please, Melanchthon will make many Luthers and a most powerful enemy of the devil and of scholasticism, for he knows both the trumpery of the world and the rock of Christ, therefore shall he be mighty."[10] Publicly, Luther described him as scrawny shrimp, like the apostle Paul, but declared that when he speaks, "he was like the boy Jesus in the temple." [11] Though he taught with a stammer and his voice was harsh and shrill, four hundred students flocked to Melanchthon's first classes, and by 1520 sometimes as many as six hundred people crowded into his classrooms. Word spread far and wide about the prodigy.

Reuchlin moved to Ingolstadt, where he lived in the same house as Catholic professor John Eck and pleaded with Melanchthon to come to him. The young man wrote back, "I love my homeland but I must also

7. Richard, *Philip Melanchthon,* 28.

8. Stupperich, *Melanchthon,* 32.

9. Quoted by Smith, *The Life and Letters,* 70.

10. Smith, *The Life and Letters,* 71

11. Bainton, *Here I Stand,* 82.

heed whither Christ calls me, not whither my own pleasure may draw me."[12] He asserted to his uncle how close he had already become with Luther and confessed, "I will die rather than allow myself to be torn from Luther."[13] Reuchlin, concerned that he would now be associated with hints of heresy already drifting out of Wittenberg, told Melanchthon that he could no longer correspond with him.[14]

Choosing to remain at Wittenberg proved to be a praiseworthy decision. Melanchthon had the remarkable opportunity to continue cultivating his relationship with Luther and eventually playing a notable role in the Reformation. While there was mutual respect and admiration for each other, their friendship was not without its struggles. Despite his timidity and gentle qualities, Melanchthon had a terrible temper and consequently, Luther felt that Melanchthon was sometimes too harsh with his students. On the other hand, Luther sensed that he, for the sake of maintaining harmony with his foes, was too ready to make concessions.[15]

The two scholars also differed on theological issues. For example, regarding the law, Luther believed that as a justified person, there is no need for the law, whereas Melanchthon taught that there was no place for lawlessness in the Christian life. Concerning Scripture, Luther believed that not all parts were to be considered of having equal authority, whereas Melanchthon appeared to view all of Scripture as carrying the same weight. In regards to philosophy, Luther insisted on a theology of the cross that disregarded all philosophical theology while Melanchthon took "up the tools of philosophy to ground, clarify, and order the biblical theology of Luther."[16] Furthermore, he believed that the Christian needed philosophy to make sure of what he or she believed.

Expert Educator and Productive Writer

Melanchthon was a skillful teacher at all levels of education. He set up a private school in his own home to give pupils a better preparation for university than what the typical Latin school provided. Not only did he teach the ancient languages, he instructed his students in mathematics,

12. Quoted by Stupperich, *Melanchthon,* 35.

13. Stupperich, *Melanchthon,* 35.

14. Stupperich, *Melanchthon,* 35.

15. Stupperich, *Melanchthon,* 35.

16. Stupperich, *Melanchthon,* 74.

Aristotelian physics, and ethics. He eventually composed a small spiritual handbook for his pupils, that included the Decalogue, the Lord's Prayer, the Creed, an alphabet, sayings of the seven sages, and numerous prayers that emphasized praise for God and His creation. This handbook was then used with some modifications for children in the churches.

At the University of Wittenberg his classroom popularity grew. From all over Germany and foreign countries, students flocked to Wittenberg to hear his lectures. In the fall of 1520, there were 600 students at one of his lectures. So successful was his teaching that Luther declared, "Whoever does not recognize Philip as his instructor, is a stolid, stupid donkey carried away with his own vanity and self-deceit. Whatever we know in the arts and true philosophy Philip has taught us. He has only the title of Master, but he excels all Doctors. There is no one living adorned with such gifts."[17] Melanchthon also became known as an experienced organizer and administrator of schools at all levels. He helped rebuild the Latin schools in Eisleben, Nuremberg, and Magdeburg. He assisted in founding new universities such as Marburg and Konigsberg and helped reorganize the schools in Tubingen, Leipzig, and Heidelberg. His expertise in education and his role in improving schooling in Germany earned him the esteemed title of *praeceptor Germaniae* (Germany's Principle Teacher).

Melanchthon was a productive writer, authoring textbooks on Latin and Greek grammar, dialectic (reasoned argumentation), rhetoric (persuasion through speech), history, and religion, to name a few. But Melanchthon was also very much drawn to theology and biblical studies. He penned commentaries on Daniel, the Psalms, Proverbs, the Gospel of John, Romans, and Colossians. In the years 1520 and 1521, he drafted a system of basic concepts that he anticipated would bring Christ closer to readers, strengthen their conscience, and establish their souls against Satan's power; he titled the small book *Loci Communes*.[18] Finished in April of 1521, it was published sometime later that year. Melanchthon was dissatisfied with the book—he thought it too elementary—and tried to suppress its publication. Nonetheless it appeared in December of that year and was read to such an extent that, within four years, eighteen editions had been to press. The publication, notes James Richard, became

---

17. Quoted by Richard, *Philip Melanchthon*, 44.

18. The title in English is *Common Places in Theology* or *Fundamental Doctrinal Themes*. *Loci Communes* are common places where an individual may place and organize things—whether it be in the mind or in a book—and recovered as necessary.

Melanchthon's most significant theological work: "It systemizes what he and Luther had taught and lays the foundation for the *Evangelical Dogmatic*. For the time being it was the Wittenberg Confession of Faith and was the forerunner of the Confession of Augsburg."[19] It addresses fundamental doctrines such as sin, free will, grace, justification, and faith. Luther was so impressed with the *Loci*, he called it "an invincible book, worthy not only of immortality, but of being placed in the Canon."[20]

Communion and the Wittenberg Concord

Melanchthon had gradually become the chief Protestant negotiator with Catholic leaders as well as divergent evangelicals. Though he continued teaching off and on in Wittenberg, his life became more and more a series of theological colloquies and diets he felt obligated to attend—sometimes against his wishes. He would not entirely give up on the hope that Catholic and Protestant parties could agree on significant matters of theological doctrine.

Regarding Luther's belief that Christ's body and blood are truly present in the Supper—and after discussions with Calvin—Melanchthon omitted that statement in a later edition of the Augsburg Confession. He merely affirmed at some length that with the bread and wine, the body and blood were offered. Luther did not attack his friend directly upon this development but remarked sharply, "everything is too long and nothing but eyewash . . . a great babbling; I surely smell that chatterbox Bucer in it."[21] There was undeniable tension between Luther and Melanchthon late in their relationship, but during his final year, Luther would still write that Philip was "a divine instrument which has achieved the very best in the department of theology to the great rage of the devil and his scabby tribe."[22]

There was not only the seemingly impossible schism between the Roman Church and evangelicals but also schisms between evangelical groups. Still desirous of a Protestant union after the Marburg Colloquy's partial failure, Melanchthon contacted Martin Bucer in Strassburg. "I desire nothing more," he wrote, "than that the monstrous scandal of this

19. Richard, *Philip Melanchthon*, 95.
20. Quoted by Richard, *Philip Melanchthon*, 102.
21. Quoted by Stupperich, *Melanchthon*, 99.
22. Kirn, "Melanchthon, Philipp," 282.

schism, which so manifestly hinders the course of the gospel, may be eliminated."[23]

Along with Bucer, Wolfgang Capito had spent a great deal of time and energy trying to reconcile the evangelical views of the Lord's Supper. Together they set forth their understanding of the matter in a letter to Ulrich Zwingli: "The bread and the cup are external things (whatever they may be), and by themselves they accomplish nothing for salvation; but the memory of the Lord's death is both beneficial and necessary. Therefore, we admonish our [parishioners] to eat the Lord's bread and to drink the cup for this purpose while passing over other things."[24] Clearly, they had been attempting to appease both Luther and Zwingli by tossing each a bone.

The controversy on the Lord's Supper alone could be easily expanded into a book. Suffice it to say that there was never a complete unity established between the evangelicals on this doctrine. However, there was a moment in 1536 when it appeared that primary parties had mellowed enough to possibly come to a final negotiation. At the landgrave's invitation, Melanchthon and Bucer met for new negotiations in Kassel. Bucer was able to unite the Swiss theologians in a confession that differed from Melanchthon's formula so little that an agreement seemed imminent. The final meeting was to take place on May 14, 1536, and though the turnout was sparse, preliminary cohesion was evident. Luther was ill, so Bucer and Melanchthon went to Luther's home for final discussions.

On May 29, the sides came to an agreement. Capito, Bucer, and other German theologians finally reached an agreement on the Lord's Supper at what came to be called the Wittenberg Concord. While alienating Zwinglians, who held to a symbolical understanding of the sacrament, the settlement brought agreement between the Lutherans of the north and other evangelicals in the southern German cities.[25] In addition to Capito and Bucer, South German signees were Matthaus Alber, Martin Frecht, Jakob Otter, and Wolfgang Musculus. Lutheran signatories included Luther, Melanchthon, Johannes Bugenhagen, Justus Jonas, Caspar Cruciger, and George Spalatin. Later, Bucer disavowed his agreement due to Swiss differences with the Lutherans over what Scripture means by "unworthy participants" of the Eucharist. Still, the agreement held

23. Quoted by Stupperich, *Melanchthon*, 105.
24. Quoted by Kittelson, *Luther*, 198.
25. Spitz, *The Rise*, 118.

symbolic importance. The statement was approved by Wittenberg theologians Amsdorf, Spalatin, and Agricola. However, when the Diet of Schmalkald met, Melanchthon entreated delegates to save themselves some trouble and rest their case on the already-established Augsburg Confession, so Luther's articles were signed by leaders, but never discussed, and the Catholic legate was rejected.

In February 1539, Melanchthon had to accompany his elector to a conference in Frankfurt. Here he met John Calvin for the first time, and through theological discussions between them and others, many a misunderstanding was absolved. Melanchthon began calling Calvin "the theologian." In the end, the Protestants and Romanists acquiesced to a fifteen-month armed truce, but no theological agreements occurred. Melanchthon was obliged to attend another conference in Worms at the end of October 1540, and he had decided he would not bow to doctrinal pressures from the electors. He wrote to Camerarius, "With God's help, I shall work to explain clearly without subterfuge and with all earnestness the important doctrines for which we contend. I can do so all the more eagerly, since I have ceased to worry over the will of the princes, and thus I am more at ease than formerly."[26]

At first, the Worms discussions seemed rather pointless, as had other colloquies with the Romanists. However, the Catholic, Johann Gropper, met secretly with Bucer, and they wrote up a theological agreement known thereafter as the *Regensburg Book*, which still contained doctrines to which neither Catholics nor Protestants would agree. Melanchthon was thoroughly frustrated. He responded, "It is not arms and violence that I fear but deceitful speeches and sophistry."[27]

Calvin was again present with his Strassburgers as Melanchthon took the battlefield against Eck. Evangelicals could not agree on the doctrine of justification as expressed in the book, so they left the book and discussed it in free dialogue. After many efforts by Melanchthon, Eck, Cardinal Contrarini, and Gropper, a common formula was found upon which all parties agreed. A tenuous measure of unity on this subject was reached on May 2, 1541. He advised the Elector of Brandenburg about the cautious introduction of reform measures, which would not enrage Rome. Through his friend, Bucer, he kept open the dialogue with Swiss and Strassburg reformers. He corresponded with Cardinal Albrecht of

26. Quoted by Stupperich, *Melanchthon*, 113.
27. Quoted by Richard, *Philip Melanchthon*, 290.

Mainz, calling on him to act as a mediator, along with the Archbishop of Cologne.

In 1541 and 1542, Melanchthon contended with two Catholic leaders, Cardinal Contrarini and Gian Pietro Carafa. Contrarini was an Italian who, with brutal frankness, let the pope know what sweeping moral and administrative reforms the Roman Church desperately needed. Carafa, a founding member of the Theatines, a brotherhood committed to pious works among the poor, had the opposite reaction. He declaimed the reformers as incorrigible and only worthy of death. So bloodthirsty was he that he claimed he would pile sticks around his own father if he were to embrace such heretical ideas. Luther and his elector withheld final judgment regarding Melanchthon's many negotiations, but he asked the princes not to treat his friend too harshly lest he "die of grief."

Calvin, however, was ecstatic. He wrote to Guillaume (William) Farel, "You will marvel when you see what has been obtained from the adversaries. Our side has upheld the summary of the true doctrine. There is nothing in the formula which is not found in our writings."[28] The legate, Contrarini, may have given the statement his approval, but Rome was of another opinion and repudiated the article on justification, thus nullifying the significant breakthrough.

Like a mastiff, Charles V continued to cling to the hope that Protestants would finally bow to the Romanists, so the pope called another council in Trent in 1542. However, war between the emperor and Francis I of France made this impossible. Another diet was scheduled in Speyer for 1544, and it, too, was postponed. In 1545 a diet was called for Worms, but to gain time, the Protestants asked that it be put off for a later meeting in Regensburg.

The Council of Trent and The Saxon Confession

On May 1, 1551, Pope Julius III reconvened the Council of Trent.[29] The Emperor had covertly prepared a book in which the Romanists laid out the points to which evangelical Protestants had to capitulate:

---

28. Stupperich, *Melanchthon*, 117.

29. The Council of Trent was held between 1545 and 1563 in Trent, Northern Italy, as a council of the Catholic church. It was effected by the Protestant Reformation and denounced what the Catholic church considered to be heresies of the Protestant reformers.

> justification was presented from the Catholic perspective;

> the Mass was interpreted as a commemorative sacrifice;

> the Lord's Supper was allowed under both forms;

> the marriage of the clergy was referred to the council for judgment;

> transubstantiation and church practices were not compromised.

The Emperor promised Protestants safe conduct to the council for a hearing. Melanchthon was called upon to attend but did not go. However, he was commissioned to further refine the Augsburg Confession, which was printed as the *Repetition of the Augsburg Confession*, later named the *Saxon Confession*. It was an elaborate restatement of all the Christian doctrines according to the Lutherans and was meant to be presented to the Council of Trent, but this never happened. It was later printed without his knowledge.[30] Meanwhile, Charles V attempted to force the German princes to return to Catholicism, but the 1552 Treaty of Passau[31] recognized the right of Lutherans to practice religious liberty. The treaty laid the basis for the religious Peace of Augsburg (1555), which gave each German prince the freedom to choose a religion for his state.

Conclusion

Melanchthon's influence on Luther and the impact he had on the Reformation of the church are profound, three of which are highlighted here. First, in 1521 Melanchthon published what was to become his most significant work, the *Loci Communes* (literally "common places" or less literal "basic concepts"), a systematic manual or discourse on the fundamental teachings of Luther. Second, while both Luther and Melanchthon were committed to the education of the masses, Melanchthon was the true reformer of education in Germany and is credited with establishing the school and university systems. As early as 1520, he established a private school in his home with the purpose of giving students better preparation for university. His expertise in education earned him the honored title of *praeceptor Germaniae*. Third, and perhaps his most significant contribution to the Reformation was his role as the primary architect of

---

30. Richard, *Philip Melanchthon*, 353–5.

31. The Treaty of Passau was agreed upon in 1552 between the Emperor of the Holy Roman Empire, Charles V, and Protestant princes led by elector Maurice de Saxe.

the Augsburg Confession, a summation of the Lutheran faith presented to Emperor Charles V at the Diet of Augsburg on June 25, 1530. Church historians today recognize Melanchthon as one of the foremost reformers and stands alongside Luther as one of the founders of the Lutheran church. In chapter seven we shift our focus to the Swiss Reformation and its leader Ulrich Zwingli.

7

Ulrich Zwingli

Leader of the Swiss Reformation

"Thirteen small composed a simple and brave nation. Who would have looked in those sequestered valleys for the men whom God would choose to be the liberators of the church conjointly with the children of the Germans? Who would have republics, placed with their allies in the center of Europe, among mountains which seemed to form its citadel, thought that small unknown cities—scarcely raised above barbarism, hidden behind inaccessible mountains, on the shores of lakes that had found no name in history—would surpass, as regards Christianity, even Jerusalem, Antioch, Ephesus, Corinth, and Rome? Nevertheless, such was the will of Him who 'causeth it to rain upon one piece of land, and the piece of land whereupon it raineth not, withereth.'" (Amos 4:7).[1]

—MERLE D'AUBIGNÉ

THE WINDS OF REFORMATION change quickly made its way from Germany into Switzerland. Known at the time as the Swiss Federation, the country consisted of thirteen independent states or cantons. Ulrich Zwingli was the leader of the Protestant Reformation in German-speaking Switzerland, and along with Martin Luther and John Calvin was one of the three "Fathers of the Reformation." Though he did not get quite the credit Luther and Calvin did for the Protestant Reformation

1. d'Aubigné, *For God and His People*, xxiii.

(some would say undeservedly so), he fought for ecclesiastical change before Luther did. He rejected Catholic doctrine and practices such as the sale of indulgences, clerical celibacy, purgatory, the Mass, and priestly mediation. Zwingli also vehemently opposed the use of Swiss mercenaries to serve in Catholic wars. Calvin would later surpass him as a theologian and Swiss reformer but would stand squarely on the broad shoulders of Zwingli.

Zwingli's Early Years

Less than two months after Luther's birth, Zwingli was born on New Year's Day, 1484, in Wildhaus (the Wild-house), in the Toggenburg valley of the Lower Alps of Switzerland. He was the third of what would become nine siblings, and like Luther, his parents noticed intellectual promise in him as a boy. Though a farmer, Ulrich's father was a leading magistrate of the town and made sure that his son received an excellent education beginning with years of tutoring by his uncle.

At ten years of age, Ulrich was sent to St. Theodore's in Basel for three years to learn Latin. He boarded with the humanist Henry Wolfflin and learned from Lupulus, who included Homer, Democritus, Plutarch, Cicero, Caesar, Seneca, Pliny the Younger, and Tacitus in his repertoire of significant works. It was there that the Dominicans tried to persuade him to join their order, and he may have been received temporarily as a novitiate. Meanwhile, he enrolled in the University of Vienna in the winter semester of 1498 but was apparently expelled. Whatever problem precipitated it must have been resolved because he re-enrolled in 1500 and continued studies there until 1502 when he transferred to the University of Basel, where he received a Master of Arts degree. He taught for a time in St. Martin's school and thus was able to earn his way for the first time. It was here also that he met Wolfgang Capito, who was to become one of his closest friends.

In November 1505, a professor by the name of Thomas Wittembach arrived to teach at Basel, and many young men, including Zwingli, flocked to him to learn the Scriptures. Ahead of his times, he predicted, "The hour is not far distant in which the scholastic theology will be set aside and the old doctrines of the church revived. For Christ's death is the only ransom for our souls."[2] Wittembach attacked indulgences, clerical celibacy, and the Mass, doctrinal motifs Zwingli would later tackle.

Though his degree was not in theology, Zwingli became a Catholic priest, and at twenty-two took his first ecclesiastical post as pastor in the town of Glaris, Switzerland, in September of 1506. He labored there for ten years until 1516. In addition to performing his pastoral duties, which included preaching and teaching, he methodically studied both Greek and Hebrew. He read the Greek and Roman philosophers, as well as the works of the humanist Erasmus. He reverently read Erasmus, with whom he would eventually have correspondence, every night as a prelude to sleep.

There was a tradition of Swiss armies hiring out as mercenaries in the wars of other nations. Zwingli agreed to be the chaplain for several of these armed forces, and for this was offered an annual pension of fifty guldens by the Roman Church. Then in the dreadful battle of Marignano, ten thousand young Swiss were slaughtered by French artillery. By 1513, Zwingli had become thoroughly disillusioned by this practice, believed it was immoral, and alleged that it disturbed Swiss unity. This conviction would become an increasingly troublesome one for him in the years to follow.

Budding Evangelical

In February 1513, Zwingli wrote to his friend Joachim Vadian: "In order to be able to draw from the fountainhead of truth the doctrines of Jesus Christ, I am determined to apply myself to Greek and no one shall be able to turn me aside from it. I do it not for glory, but for the love of sacred learning." Noting Zwingli's progressive leanings toward evangelical ideas, one priest told him, "Master Ulrich, I am informed that you are falling into this new error: that you are a Lutheran." Zwingli answered, "I am not Lutheran, for I learned Greek before I had ever heard the name of Luther." Zwingli was rapidly developing a great reverence for the Scriptures. He stated, "They have a very mean idea of the gospel who consider as frivolous, vain, and unjust all that they imagine does not accord with their own reason. Men are not permitted to wrest the gospel at pleasure that it may square with their private sentiments and interpretation."[3]

2. Quoted by d'Aubigné, *For God and His People*, 6.
3. Quoted by d'Aubigné, *For God and His People*, 12.

In 1514, Desiderius Erasmus arrived in Basel. By this time, Zwingli had made friends with three men who would figure powerfully in the Swiss Reformation: Capito, Oswald Myconius, and John Hausschein (Oecolampadius in Greek). Myconius was the rector of the school of Basel, and Oecolampadius had been appointed preacher in Basel through the influence of Capito. All of these men exulted in the presence of Erasmus.

As usual, Erasmus was complimentary in the presence of his admiring readers. He told Myconius, "I look upon you schoolmasters as the peers of kings."[4] To Oecolampadius, he dedicated the commencement of his Gospel of St. John with the exhortation: "There is but one thing that we should look for in Holy Scripture and that is Jesus Christ."[5] To Zwingli, he wrote, "I congratulate the Helvetians that you are laboring to polish and civilize them by your studies and your morals, which are alike of the highest order."[6] It is no wonder that initially, these emerging reformers thought of Erasmus almost reverently. In response to Erasmus' praise, Myconius said, "I do but crawl upon the earth. From my childhood, there has been something humble and mean about me."[7] Oecolampadius kept the old master's book dedication suspended to his crucifix that "I might always remember Erasmus in my prayers."[8] And after their meeting, Zwingli wrote to him: "I should be unable to sleep if I had not held some conversation with you. There is nothing I am prouder of than of having seen Erasmus."[9] Zwingli's admiration was to grow to the point that in 1522 he would invite Erasmus to come to Zürich to live.

Zwingli at Einsiedeln

Zwingli's sexual indiscretions were well known, and in 1516 he fell prey to carnal weakness and did so again a year and a half later. He repented with humiliation and claimed to doubt that he would remain in the grasp of this evil habit. He resolved, though not without struggle, to lead a righteous life and when accused did not deny his guilt. He would eventually

4. Quoted by d'Aubigné, *For God and His People*, 16.
5. Quoted by d'Aubigné, *For God and His People*, 17.
6. Quoted by d'Aubigné, *For God and His People*, 15.
7. Quoted by d'Aubigné, *For God and His People*, 16.
8. Quoted by d'Aubigné, *For God and His People*, 17.
9. Quoted by d'Aubigné, *For God and His People*, 17.

confess: "Having no one to walk with me in the resolutions I had formed many even of those about me being offended at them, alas! I fell, and like the dog of which St. Peter speaks (2 Pet 2:22), I turned again to my vomit. The Lord knows with what shame and anguish I have dragged these faults from the bottom of my heart, and laid them before that great Being to whom, however, I confess my wretchedness far more willingly than to man."[10]

Nonetheless, in that same year and despite his sexual transgressions, "after a hard contest with the temptations of the flesh, and after a hard but prayerful striving after truth,"[11] he was accepted into the positions of priest and preacher in Einsiedeln, a celebrated place of religious pilgrimage from southern Germany and Switzerland. It is here that Zwingli commenced his work as a reformer, preaching against particular beliefs of the Roman Church, such as justification by works.

In May of 1517, Zwingli began transcribing the epistles of St. Paul by hand. He learned these epistles by heart and later added other New Testament books as well as a portion of the Old. His gradual movement toward Reformation convictions is evident in this quote from the pulpit during this period: "Do not imagine that God is in this temple more than in any other part of creation. Whatever the country in which you dwell, God is around you. . . . Can unprofitable works, long pilgrimages, offerings, images, the invocation of the Virgin or of the saints, secure for you the grace of God? What avails the multitude of words with which we embody our prayers? What efficacy has a glossy cowl, a smooth-shorn head, a long and flowing robe, or gold-embroidered slippers. . . . God looks at the heart and our hearts are far from him!"[12]

It was also here where Zwingli first came into conflict with Bernhard Samson, a Franciscan monk from Italy who was Switzerland's answer to Johann Tetzel. In 1518 Samson came barefooted through the St. Gotthard pass boldly offering indulgences to the people of Einsiedeln. He declared that he could "forgive and absolve all sins; heaven and hell stand under my dominion; and I sell the merits of Jesus Christ to each and everyone who is willing to pay in ready money for an absolution."[13] To this, Zwingli responded by proclaiming, among other things, "Jesus Christ is

10. Quoted by d'Aubigné, *For God and His People*, 32–3.

11. Quoted by Christoffel, *Zwingli*, 13.

12. Quoted by d'Aubigné, *For God and His People*, 24.

13. Quoted by Christoffel, *Zwingli*, 31.

the only sacrifice, the only gift, the only way."[14] This occurrence would not be the last time the two combatants would encounter one another.

Zwingli Transfers to Zürich

The hour had come when Zwingli would leave Einsiedeln and embark on a new sphere of ministry. When the position of preaching priest in Zürich became vacant, Zwingli's good friend Myconius immediately recommended him to the post. Though there were some dissenters, a vote of affirmation was taken on December 11, 1518. He arrived on December 27, and on New Year's Day of 1519, he appeared in his pulpit and announced to his congregation that he intended to preach through the Gospel of Matthew beginning to end, paying no notice to the commentaries of men. "No one suspected yet that with this new man," notes biographer Oskar Farner, "they had handed themselves over to a Reformer."[15]

Zwingli's criticisms of the church continued. His contempt grew for Catholic Church officials as described by Ulrich Gäbler: "Bad preachers of the gospel, as well as 'speculative' scholastic theologians and ecclesiastical lawyers, were denounced. He turned against one group of people in particular: monks. He accused them of indolence and high living. He said that in the confessional in Einsiedeln he had heard plenty of examples of their immoral lifestyle."[16] He also rejected the veneration of saints, the damnation of unbaptized children, as well as the practice of forced tithing that amounted to nothing more than revenue-raising. For these causes and his strident personal attacks from the pulpit, opposition was materializing, though opponents remained in the minority. An anonymous note was sent him: "Snares surround you on every side. . . . A deadly poison has been prepared to take away your life. Never eat food but in your own house and only what has been prepared by your own cook. The walls of Zürich contain men who are plotting your destruction. . . . I am your friend; you shall know me hereafter."[17]

At the same time, Zürichers visiting Lucerne were forced to watch the reformer's effigy dragged to a scaffold and hanged. In Wildhaus, it was with confusion and alarm that Zwingli's brothers heard that their

14. Quoted by Christoffel, *Zwingli*, 32.
15. Farner, *Zwingli*, 30.
16. Gäbler, *Huldrych Zwingli*, 49.
17. Quoted by d'Aubigné, *For God and his People*, 81.

brother was preaching heresy and condemning the church, and they pictured him dragged before a bishop, burned at the stake. They wrote to him, describing their offense and fears. Zwingli sent them a response:

> So long as God shall permit me, I will execute the task which he has confided to me without fearing the world and its haughty tyrants. I know everything that can befall me. There is no danger, no misfortune that I have not carefully weighed long ago. My own strength is nothingness itself and I know the power of my enemies. But I know that I can do everything in Christ who strengthens me. Banish all anxiety, my dear brothers. If I have any fear, it is lest I have been milder and gentler than suits our times. All my labors have no other aim than to proclaim to men the treasures of happiness that Christ hath purchased for us, that all might take refuge in the Father through the death of His Son.[18]

Though there was significant skepticism, the townspeople flocked to hear the salty-tongued preacher. He was bold and energetic in the pulpit, affable to all he met in the streets or public places, often seen in company halls or peasant stalls conversing casually or explaining the essential features of the Christian doctrine. He spoke to peasants and nobles with the same geniality and often invited country people to dine with him.

Samson—Preacher of Indulgences

In February of 1519, Samson, the Franciscan preacher of indulgences, once again emerged on the scene, now headed toward Zürich. He arrogantly boasted that although he knew Zwingli would speak against him, he would stop his mouth. However, as Samson moved toward Zürich, Zwingli began preaching with vigor and power against indulgences. "No man," he declared from his pulpit, "can remit sins: Christ, who is very God and very man, alone has this power. Go! Buy indulgences . . . but be assured that you are not absolved. Those who sell remission of sins for money are the companions of Simon the magician, the friends of Balaam, and the ambassadors of Satan."[19]

Word began to spread that Samson was a cheat and seducer, and the council of state resolved to oppose the monk's entry into Zürich. He

18. Quoted by d'Aubigné, *For God and his People*, 97.
19. Quoted by d'Aubigné, *For God and his People*, 46.

was allowed to address the council but was quickly dismissed, at which point he left the hall in a fit of anger. Soon after, the pope recalled him to Italy. The pope sometime later sent a papal brief to Zwingli through a legate, which still addressed him as a beloved son and assured him of his special favor, to the point of inviting him to "labour in the affairs of us and the apostolic chair, whereby you will have reason to rejoice in our very peculiar favour and regard."[20] Myconius asked what the pope had commissioned to offer to Zwingli, and the answer was: "All but the papal chair."[21]

Zwingli Proves his Mettle

When the dreaded plague struck the city in August of 1519, 2,500 inhabitants fell victim to it. Instead of fleeing, Zwingli stayed and tenderly ministered to the sick and dying. One in four citizens perished; the disease struck Zwingli as well, and those still healthy in the city began praying day and night for his survival. Word came of Zwingli's death, and when those in Basel heard, the whole city went into deep mourning. His friend, Kaspar Hedio, exclaimed, "The preserver of our country, the trumpet of the gospel, the magnanimous herald of truth, is cut down in the flower and springtide of his life."[22]

Then Zürich sent out a second message: *Zwingli is clinging to life— weak as a baby—but still alive.* Even Johannes Faber, who was later to become Zwingli's bitterest antagonist, wrote to him: "I heartily rejoice," he exclaimed, "that you have been delivered out of the jaws of the murderous plague, for I entertain towards you so lively a friendship that nothing in this world would pain me more than the intelligence that any calamity had befallen you, which God in his mercy avert."[23] Faber's loyalty to his countrymen helped convince them of his compassion and sincerity. It may be that this also proved a time of spiritual consecration for Zwingli, as reflected in the final stanza of a poem written during his illness:

> Yet on I go with gladness,
> Since 'tis Thy holy will,
> With joy yet mixed with sadness,

20. Quoted by Christoffel, *Zwingli,* 209.
21. Quoted by Christoffel, *Zwingli,* 210.
22. Quoted by d'Aubigné, *For God and his People,* 52.
23. Quoted by Christoffel, *Zwingli,* 81.

My journey to fulfil;
To wage 'gainst sin the strife,
And when life's toils are ended,
There will at length b'extended
To me the crown of life. [24]

His spiritual zeal became increasingly fearless, his life more holy, his preaching more free and powerful.

The Beginning of the Zürich Reformation

The Zürich Reformation began "officially" on Sunday, March 9, 1522, with citizens of the city gleefully eating sausages in Zwingli's presence, a provocative violation of Catholic compulsory fasting regulations. He declared that no general rule against particular foods could be validly located in the New Testament, so to transgress such a command of the Roman Church was not a sin. The "ostentatious eating of sausages" as a planned incitement, occurred at the home of the printer and bookseller Christoph Froschauer. Though Zwingli himself abstained from the eating of sausage, a dozen participants, including another Swiss Reformer by the name of Leo Jud, deliberately disobeyed the fasting rule "in order to proclaim Christian liberty."[25] Other fasting violations followed, and an enthusiastic mood pervaded the city of Zürich.

On January 29, 1523, the Great Council of Zürich convened a conference to address the disturbances that had been taking place; a great crowd of 600 participants attended. For his part, Zwingli came prepared with *Sixty-seven Conclusions* or theses. Sometimes compared to Luther's *Ninety-five Theses*, these conclusions demonstrated how "thoroughly he had already thought out the Reformation to its consummation."[26] Zwingli debated these theses with priests before the Zürich city council. The first fifteen statements expressed positive matters of faith whereby he determined that "The sum and substance of the gospel is that our Lord Jesus Christ, the true Son of God, has made known to us the will of his heavenly Father, and has with his innocence released us from death and reconciled God.[27] In his sixteenth thesis, Zwingli commenced an unyielding repu-

24. Taken from Christoffel, *Zwingli*, 82.
25. Gäbler, *Huldrych Zwingli*, 52.
26. Farner, *Zwingli*, 48.
27. Quoted by Aland, *Ulrich Zwingli*, 86.

diation of the Church of Rome. He renounced practices such as the Mass, intercession of the saints, good works, compulsory fasting, pilgrimages, indulgences, purgatory, celibacy of priests, and iconic images.

The Catholic bishop frostily sent word that such a judgment was beyond the power of a city council. He refused to attend and sent his aide Faber. After reading the theses, Faber was very reluctant to argue them but was eventually drawn into the debate. Halfway into the second day, it was evident that Zwingli was winning points. Faber protested that he had not been given enough time to prepare. The council deliberated and resolved that until Zwingli was scripturally refuted, he could proceed with his reforms: "Master Zwingli shall continue to proclaim the Holy Gospel, as hitherto, according to the Spirit of God, until such a time as he be instructed by a better authority; and, likewise shall all the other pastors preach in their parishes only that which they can uphold by genuine divine Scripture. By the people's will, therefore Zürich is to be Protestant."[28] Thus the Zürich Reformation had begun.

The Kappel Wars and Zwingli's Fateful Transformation

In the late 1520s, Zwingli regressed from a discerning pacifist to a political radical. From the beginning, Zwingli had limited his religious reforms to those gradually permitted by the Zürich city council. However, as the Reformation progressed, he had increasing involvement with the government. Zwingli began considering military means of securing the survival and spread of the Reformation in other parts of Switzerland. When matters grew tense between Zürich and Berne, he drew up very detailed plans of military defense. In 1528, he wrote a noteworthy paper regarding strategies, weaponry, and deployment if evangelicals were to face the Holy Roman Empire, France, other European states, and even fellow Swiss cantons in battle.

As Swiss citizens in surrounding cantons began to show some interest in Reformation ideas, the Catholic cantons appealed to Austria for military assistance. They threatened that France or the Holy Roman Empire might come to their aid. Zürich responded with outrage, but Niklaus Manuel, a leader from Berne, appeared and urged a peaceful approach, stating that one cannot really "bring faith by means of spears and halberds. Let us not be so hasty. . . . The Word of God enjoins peace. It is

28. Quoted by Farner, *Zwingli*, 51.

not with pikes and lances that faith is made to enter the heart. For this reason, in the name of our Lord's sufferings, we entreat you to moderate your anger."[29]

If Zwingli had only taken these words to heart, it might have saved a great deal of bloodshed. However, the Swiss account becomes a reckless march toward violent ends. On May 29, 1529, Jacques Keyser, an evangelical pastor in the Gaster district, was burned alive for his faith. In June, many believers fled in fear to Zürich. As the military posturing increased, Zwingli's ire was up as was that of the Zürich council. Protestant cantons led by Zwingli declared a state of war against the Catholic cantons who had allied with Ferdinand of Austria on June 8, 1529.

The two forces met near Kappel, but war was averted due to the intervention of Hans Aebli, a Zwingli friend, who pleaded for an armistice. He proclaimed, "The five Catholic cantons are prepared but I have prevailed upon them to halt if you will do the same. For this reason I entreat my lords and the people of Zürich, for the love of God and the safety of the Confederation, to suspend their march at the present moment. In a few hours . . . I hope, with God's grace, to obtain an honorable peace and prevent our cottages from being filled with widows and orphans."[30]

Zwingli did not fully trust Aebli and stated that the man might be creating a ruse so that the Catholics could catch Zürich unawares; Aebli claimed no ulterior motive. Berne again claimed that they would use all means to keep the peace. Zwingli warned that in a month or so, when they had laid down their arms, the Catholics may come and crush them. However, warriors from both sides were quite genial, even sharing food and necessities. On June 15, the parties signed a treaty that did not grant free preaching of the Word of God but did stipulate freedom of conscience. The Catholic alliance with Austria was retracted, and the family of the martyred Pastor Keyser was given financial compensation. However, even the signing of the First Kappel Peace Treaty on June 26, 1529, did not pacify Zwingli. While the accord secured a legal basis for the establishment of the Reformation in sizable areas of north and east Switzerland, he felt his strategies for Confederation reform were stymied.[31] At this point, notes d'Aubigné, Zwingli "advanced more and more along the fatal path into which he was led by his character, his patriotism,

29. Potter, *Zwingli,* 364.

30. Quoted by d'Aubigné, *For God and His People,* 191.

31. Gäbler, *Huldrych Zwingli,* 119–22; d'Aubigné, *For God and His People,* 189–97.

and his early habits. . . . From this period, the reformer almost entirely disappears, and we see in his place the politician, the great citizen, who, beholding a formidable coalition preparing its chains for every nation, stands up energetically against it."[32]

The emperor, Charles V, had recently formed a closer alliance with the pope, and this also threatened Zwingli. Again, justifying physical violence, he preached: "A single individual must not take it into his head to dethrone a tyrant. This would be a revolt and the kingdom of God commands peace, righteousness, and joy. But if a whole people with common accord, or if the majority at least, rejects him without committing any excess, it is God Himself who acts."[33] Abuse of evangelicals by the Roman Catholic Five Cantons continued—some individuals were arrested, fined, physically tormented, or expelled from their cantons.

While the first Kappel encounter was settled without the sides going to battle, many of the tensions were not resolved, leading to Kappel's second war. Accusations and incitements on behalf of both Catholics and Protestants continued culminating in a food blockade by Zürich and Berne against the Five Cantons in May 1531. The cities' intent of the blockade was to cut the five states off from necessary imports and provoke the umbrage of the commoners, in turn forcing the Catholic states to go to war or surrender. The Five Cantons responded by declaring war on Zürich on October 9, 1531. Rough estimates pit seven thousand Catholics against thirty-five hundred poorly deployed Zürichers led by Zwingli—the other Protestant cantons were very slow to respond. [34]

On October 11, 1531, the Second Battle of Kappel was at its height. Zwingli, dressed in a dark green mantle under armor, continued to fight as a common soldier. He advanced with the disorganized Protestant troops, but the Catholic force was much larger. The two forces crashed together in brutal hand to hand combat and gun volleys. The bloody outcome was determined within an hour, with five hundred Zürichers losing their lives compared to approximately one hundred Catholics.[35]

Though he was no trained soldier, Zwingli found himself amid the battle. Early in the confrontation, the military leaders requested Zwingli to speak to the people and encourage them: "Warriors!" he implored,

32. d'Aubigné, *For God and His People,* 200–1.

33. Quoted by d'Aubigné, *For God and His People,* 201.

34. Gäbler, *Huldrych Zwingli,* 150.

35. Gäbler, *Huldrych Zwingli,* 150–1.

"fear nothing. If we are this day to be defeated, still our cause is good. Commend yourselves to God."[36] Very shortly, as he bent over to comfort a dying soldier, he was struck on the head by a stone hurled at him. Twice more, he was hurled to the ground by the advancing forces, incurring severe injuries—one in the thigh—but in each case, he rose again. On the fourth occasion, the spear of a soldier from the Unterwald Canton pierced him beneath his chin. As he fell to his knees, he is said to have murmured, "What matters this misfortune? They may indeed kill the body, but they cannot kill the soul."[37] Enemies propped the bloody corpse against a tree and tried and condemned him as a heretic. They then quartered the body and burnt the pieces atop a pile of dried excrement, spreading pig's entrails over the charred chunks. Zwingli was forty-seven when he died, and "a great light had been extinguished in the church of God."[38] "Unfortunately," presumes d'Aubigné, "Zwingli had wielded an arm that God had forbidden. His body was no more than a handful of dust in the palm of a soldier."[39]

Heinrich Bullinger—Successor to Zwingli

After Zwingli's death, Zürich church leaders knew they needed a firm hand to steer them back to theological stability and growth. They selected Heinrich Bullinger, a young man whom some might have considered an unlikely individual to take the reins of such a significant and influential movement. However, Philip Schaff describes him as a man of "firm faith, courage, moderation, patience, and endurance" who was "providentially equipped" to preserve and consolidate the Swiss Reformation in such difficult times.[40] Bullinger was born at Bremgarten on July 18, 1504, and was educated in the school of the Brethren of the Common Life and University of Cologne.

At the tender age of twenty-seven, he was appointed religious leader in Zürich to sort out the debacle at Kappel and preserve the legacy and life efforts of Zwingli. Schaff notes that "Bullinger faithfully maintained the doctrine and discipline of the Reformed Church against the Roman

36. Quoted by d'Aubigné, *For God and His People,* 241.

37. Quoted by d'Aubigné, *For God and His People,* 246.

38. d'Aubigné, *For God and His People,* 250.

39. d'Aubigné, *For God and His People,* 250.

40. Schaff, *History Vol. VIII,* 205.

Catholics and Lutherans with dignity."[41] While exhibiting loyalty to Zwingli, he tactfully and tacitly modified aspects of that legacy, which might prove troublesome. For example, "His theory of the sacrament was higher than that of Zwingli. He laid more stress on the objective value of the institution" and wrote that "the bread is not common bread, but venerable, sacred, sacramental bread, the pledge of the spiritual real presence of Christ to those who believe."[42] Unlike Zwingli, he decided to avoid public involvement in political issues. He also reached far beyond Switzerland in an effort to breach the theological divide created at Marburg and bring unity to the fractured Protestant factions. He spent over fifty years writing letters that crisscrossed the Continent in a veritable spider's web. Indeed, twelve thousand of his letters survive.[43]

He was compelling both theologically and administratively, was a prolific writer, tireless preacher, devoted pastor, and compassionate counselor. While opposing some aspects of Anabaptist doctrine, he sought more peaceful methods of co-existing with them and seeking to convert them to Reformed doctrine. Though Luther's writings had originally won Bullinger to evangelicalism, the disagreements between Luther and Zwingli carried over into Luther's relationship with Bullinger. His actions and impact went far beyond the frontiers of Zürich. He embraced and reached out to Christians in all their differences and distinctions to the point of receiving Protestant fugitives from all over Europe. Bullinger died on September 17, 1575, remembered as one of the foremost, second-generation Reformers.

Conclusion

Luther and Calvin each had about three decades to shape their theological ideas and achieve their Reformation accomplishments. Zwingli, on the other hand, had twelve years. Nonetheless, he is considered one of the three Reformation fathers. Though Zwingli's name is not widely recognized, his legacy lives on in the doctrines of Reformed churches today. In Zwingli's final years, a change took place as political affairs consumed a more substantial portion of his efforts. Unfortunately, Zwingli's name is attached to one of the great blights of the Reformation—the persecution

41. Schaff, *History Vol. VIII*, 209.

42. Schaff, *History Vol. VIII*, 209–10.

43. MacCulloch, *The Reformation*, 172.

of the Anabaptists. Chapter eight addresses his clash with this group led by Conrad Grebel, a one-time ardent supporter of Zwingli.

8

The Swiss Anabaptist Movement

"The cause of the gospel is in a very bad way here. It all started to go this way at the assembly . . . when the Word of God was thrown down and trampled on by the ones who should have been its proclaimers, learned as they are. . . . Instead of obeying the divine teaching against saying the mass they have shrewdly come up with a compromise, but it's a devilish one. It means the mass is going to have to be said. . . . Whoever thinks or believes or says that Zwingli acts like a true Christian pastor thinks and believes and speaks wickedly."[1]

—CONRAD GREBEL

WHEN ULRICH ZWINGLI AND his followers stood before the town council in October of 1523, the reformer seemed to convince some listeners that the mass as such should be terminated. However, the council moved on to deal with the issue of purgatory without making a ruling. Zwingli accepted their delay at this point because he felt that reform would take place more placidly and more universally if he made certain that supporters and city leaders were ready for each new step. Conrad Grebel stood and referred back to the subject of the mass, requesting, again, further discussion of abuses in the mass and a policy whereby the saying of the mass should be outlawed. "It is not enough to have disputed about the Mass," he spoke, "We must put an end to its abuses." Zwingli replied, "The council will draw up an edict on the subject."

1. Quoted by Ruth, *Conrad Grebel*, 83.

Agreeing with Grebel, Simon Stumpf, another of Zwingli's disciples rose and cried out, "The Spirit of God has already decided. Why refer to the decision of the council?"[2] What the dissenters clearly meant was that the governing council cannot make a law regarding the mass, since this is already against the Word of God and must cease immediately. However, Zwingli acknowledged the "government's right to find the way it deems appropriate to draw consequences from the debate."[3]

Grebel was beginning to view Zwingli in a slightly different light. They still interacted much, but there was now a tension that existed between them. Zwingli had said that the divine Word is as unstoppable as the Rhine, yet he was handling the city council with kid gloves in the mind of Grebel and his religious allies such as Stumpf and Felix Manz. "Be rid of the State," they said, "and let us have a Free Church."[4] On his part, Zwingli supported government and insisted that a Christian government is the best assurance of the wellbeing of the people.[5] Thus a chasm began to develop in the Zürich Reformation between the reformers led by Zwingli and the dissenters, eventually to be known as the Anabaptists, led by Grebel, Stumpf, Manz, Balthasar Hubmaier, and Wilhelm Reublin.

A Rift Among Zürich Reformers

As things progressed sluggishly in Zürich through much discussion and Scripture searching, Grebel and other young men came also to believe that government-collected church tithes gave politicians unfair power over the church. They began to press Zwingli to support church rejection of forced political tithes, even offering to pay Zwingli's salary themselves. They presented a program in which church discipline would be handled by church leaders, pastors would be supported by voluntary tithes and offerings of church members, believers would share with those who had little, and worldly and nominal members would be admonished. But the reformer considered their ideas confusing and unrealistic. As weeks turned into months, Zwingli began painting these young radicals as divisive, self-righteous, pharisaical, and arrogant. He was concerned that this

---

2. Quoted by d'Aubigné, *For God and His People,* 110–1.

3. Gäbler, *Huldrych Zwingli,* 78.

4. Quoted by Farner, *Zwingli,* 59.

5. Gäbler, *Huldrych Zwingli,* 88.

radicalism could only lead to sectarianism and the undermining of both government and ecclesiastical authority.[6]

The Zürich governmental authorities appeared stalled regarding the banning of the Catholic mass. An impatient and impulsive Grebel now found himself turning against his mentor. Where was the Zwingli, he wondered, who had thundered that, if the city council did not follow the Word, it would be brushed aside by the irresistible tide of truth? In December 1523, Grebel rashly wrote a friend, "The cause of the gospel is in a very bad way here. . . . Whoever thinks, believes or says that Zwingli acts like a true Christian pastor thinks and believes and speaks wickedly. I'll stand by that."[7]

It had been wonderful to see the first stages of the Reformation in Zürich. Zwingli's sermons had skillfully exposed the pagan and abused rites and beliefs lurking beneath the surface of Christianity in Switzerland. But now it seemed he was backing down and allowing the secular authority to dictate when and how church reformation would occur— certainly in the minds of the dissenters. As Grebel and about a dozen others continued engaging in their own Bible study, they began asking harder questions of Zwingli: "When will you release the Christian church from its captivity to the public tax system? How can you be an employee of the city of Zürich and a free prophet of Christ? Who will break the news to the people that Christ calls on His followers to lay aside violence, even the common sword of self-defense? How long will you wait for the Council to let you abolish the repetitive sacrifice of the mass? What keeps you from giving up the baptizing of infants who can't possibly repent and believe in the gospel? When will the rule of Christ become the rule of the church, whether or not the world is ready for it?"[8]

By the summer of 1524, many Zürich pastors were calling Grebel and his group the *rebaptizers*, a pejorative term not originally embraced by the radicals. Across Switzerland, cantons began taking sides for or against Zwingli and there were hostilities. Grebel wrote a couple of missives to Andreas Carlstadt setting forth his case. Carlstadt responded by traveling to Zürich and meeting with the young men in October of 1524, but despite some similarities, no alliance between the two occurred and, within a few days, Carlstadt quietly departed. Grebel also wrote Luther

---

6. Farner, *Zwingli*, 59.

7. Quoted by Ruth, *Conrad Grebel*, 83.

8. Quoted by Ruth, *Conrad Grebel*, 89.

expressing his beliefs and grievances regarding Zwingli. Luther could think of no appropriate reply but sent word through a friend of sympathetic interest in the Bible-searching brothers in Switzerland.

Meanwhile, Grebel heard that Thomas Müntzer and his associates were beginning to stir up peasants with their radical brand of the kingdom message. In a comprehensive ten-page letter, using Scripture to undergird everything, Grebel wrote to Müntzer that September, agreeing with him on some issues and politely disagreeing on others. But before he could mail the letter, he heard that Müntzer had been preaching that where leaders did not yield to biblical reformation, Christians may violently overthrow them. In an anxious postscript, he condemned this extreme view and advocated pacifism. Müntzer did not receive the letter because he had already gone into hiding and it was eventually returned to Grebel.

From this point, the controversy regarding infant baptism grew until it seemed the primary bone of contention. Grebel and company believed that according to the Word of God infants should not be baptized but should wait until they came of age and were able to testify to their own faith. The Anabaptists claimed that they had concluded this from Scripture as well as outside sources, including Zwingli's statements. Early on, Melanchthon also taught that baptism was merely an external symbol and was not necessary for salvation. Interestingly, though Zwingli rigidly held to infant baptism, he rejected infant baptism as a means of grace and agreed with the Anabaptists that it simply announced that, "the baptized belong to God" and "stands at the beginning of a path."[9] For the Anabaptists, however, this was not good enough, as they believed baptism symbolized a change that already had occurred (conversion) and was a commitment to a new way of life in Christian community.[10] They felt that Zwingli had not completely broken with the Roman church.

The Birth of Anabaptism

The public break between the Zwinglians and the radicals came about as a result of a disputation that took place on January 17, 1525, whereby the opponents of infant baptism were to present their position. The Zürich city council determined that the defense was unsuccessful and their

9. Gäbler, *Huldrych Zwingli*, 128.
10. Gäbler, *Huldrych Zwingli*, 128.

position was declared heretical. Furthermore, they issued a ruling that all families were to have their infants baptized; a refusal would result in complete banishment from the canton of Zürich. Grebel and Manz were warned to refrain from private meetings and public debates.[11]

Grebel's wife bore her second child, a daughter they named Rachel. Seeking to make a statement, Grebel refused to have her baptized. Manz and George Blaurock, another of the radical leaders, did the same regarding their newborns. The deciding moment came on January 21, 1525, when Grebel's party met covertly in the home of Manz. They felt they must make a decisive step. Blaurock, a converted priest, turned to Grebel and begged him, for God's sake, to give him a true Christian baptism. Manz, the illegitimate son of a Roman Catholic priest, was in full agreement. In a momentous act, Grebel reached for the water and poured it over the man's bowed head. Blaurock then baptized Manz and the other brethren. In this act, they declared that infant baptism in no way provided salvation for an individual; rather, baptism should follow a conscious act of repentance and faith in Jesus Christ.[12] Anabaptism had been birthed and as expressed by John Ruth, those fiery dissenters could not know "that in this act is inaugurated a fellowship that shall spread beyond Europe to every continent."[13]

The following day Grebel celebrated the Lord's Supper in the neighboring village of Zollikon and in the subsequent week other baptisms were administered. The now-organized Anabaptist groups took their missionary activity to nearby cantons of Schaffhausen and St. Gallen. Meanwhile, the Zürich Council warned the Schaffhausen Council of the debates with Grebel's group and their expulsion from Zürich. Lacking success in Schaffhausen, Grebel himself ventured to St. Gallen. During his two weeks there, hundreds of people thronged to the hall of the weaver guild to hear him, and many demanded to be baptized. On April 9, 1525, great crowds—perhaps five hundred—streamed to the banks of the River Sitter to be baptized by him. This was surely one of the most rewarding days of Grebel's life. When he left St. Gallen, he turned the ministry over to Bolt Eberli. However, the city council asked him to depart or be

---

11. Gäbler, *Huldrych Zwingli*, 126.

12. Gäbler, *Huldrych Zwingli*, 10–11.

13. Ruth, *Conrad Grebel*, 106.

banished in three days. Eberli soon became the first martyr of the Swiss Brethren when he was burned at the stake in the canton of Schwyz.[14]

Both Zwingli and Grebel tried desperately to win Vadian, Grebel's former best friend, to their side. In the end, Vadian chose for Zwingli, perhaps for the reason of his own gain and self-protection. In May 1525, Grebel wrote again to Vadian, stating that he and the Brethren were ready to testify to their faith by death, a death that he believed was already being prepared for them by Zwingli. Between June and October, Grebel spread his message door to door throughout Grüningen, his boyhood home. He encountered phenomenal success as many were persuaded that his teachings carried the ring of truth. Periodically he stole back home for a day or two to see his wife and children.

Zwingli and his followers had popularized the term Anabaptists or rebaptizers in reference to Grebel and his party. Grebel challenged Zwingli to publicly debate the question of baptism using only the Scripture as a reference. If Zwingli proved him wrong, Grebel agreed to be burned as a heretic. If he proved Zwingli wrong, he would demand no such punishment for him. But the challenge fell on deaf ears. Tense months wore on. Then in October of 1525, Grebel and Blaurock were arrested as they preached at an open-air gospel meeting. Manz escaped but was captured three weeks later. It is interesting to note that, though Grebel's movement had been tagged a seditious rebellion, the crowd of deeply committed followers reacted peacefully, though with much grief, at the arrests.

Anabaptist Leaders Suffer Arrests and Deaths

Grebel finally got his wish. Zwingli debated with Grebel, Manz, and Blaurock for three full days in November. The debate finally broke down, with each side trying to outshout the other. Following the debate, predictably, the city council declared Anabaptist teachings heretical and the prisoners were immediately subjected to a trial and found guilty on November 18, 1525. They had been convicted on weak testimony and charges were based on perverse accounts of what the Anabaptists believed. They denied they held to the notion that "community of goods" should be the hallmark of Christian living but affirmed the notion that Christians ought to share with the needy. Furthermore, they continued to denounce

14. Ruth, *Conrad Grebel*, 114.

infant baptism and confirmed that adult or believer's baptism was the true sign of membership in the church.[15]

Junker Jacob Grebel, Conrad's father, was a member of the city council. Understandably, he urged leniency while Zwingli fumed. In a second briefer trial on March 5-6, 1526, after two days of deliberation, the council sentenced Grebel and eight others to be permitted no visitors, be bedded in straw, and fed only bread and water until death. Death by drowning was now announced as a penalty for anyone caught rebaptizing. About two weeks later, a prisoner noticed that a window shutter in their dungeon cell was open. Breaking through the heavy shutters, the party hoisted each other up and out of the cell. At first Grebel, Manz, and Blaurock resisted the opportunity to escape but were finally persuaded to do so and they slid down the tower wall with a rope and ratchet. Each of the prisoners fled separately; Grebel went north and began preaching in distant townships.[16]

Conrad Grebel Succumbs to the Plague

Still a fugitive, Grebel appeared in the summer of 1526 in the Maienfeld area in the Canton of Grisons where his oldest sister lived. Within weeks, his fragile body capitulated to the plague at twenty-eight years of age. Though Eberli was counted the first Anabaptist martyr Grebel's death may have done the most to fire the determination of Anabaptists to remain steadfast in spite of all. Only twenty months or less comprise the complete ministry of Grebel, a crucial figure in the Anabaptist movement that continues to this day.[17]

Jacob Grebel is Beheaded

Zwingli's city council then pieced together a case against Jacob Grebel. The senior Grebel was accused of having accepted foreign pensions contrary to the laws of the canton. When he claimed innocence, they tortured him on the rack in an effort to force a confession. On October 30, 1526, he was judged guilty and immediately taken to the Zürich fish

---

15. Estep, *The Anabaptist Story*, 29.

16. Estep, *The Anabaptist Story*, 29–30; Ruth, *Conrad Grebel,* 137.

17. Estep, *The Anabaptist Story*, 30.

market where he was beheaded. While dismay spread throughout the city of Zürich, Zwingli was gratified over the death sentence.

Felix Manz is Drowned

With the death of Grebel, Manz was no doubt the most influential leader of the Brethren and a danger to the Swiss Reformation. He was arrested again and released, allegedly on the promise to leave Zürich and not continue re-baptizing. But he and Blaurock were apprehended in Grüningen. On January 5, 1527, one of the most sinister moments of the Protestant Reformation occurred—a blight on the movement. The mandate demanding the death of anyone rebaptizing was pronounced in March of 1526 and Manz would be the first victim on January 5, 1527, at three o'clock in the afternoon. Estep summarizes the tragic event as follows:

> Manz, according to the sentence, was taken bound from the Wellenberg prison past the fish market to the boat. All along the way, he witnessed to the members of the dismal procession and those standing on the banks of the Limmat River, praising God that even though a sinner he would die for the truth. Further, he declared that believer's baptism was the true baptism according to the Word of God and the teachings of Christ. His mother's voice could be heard above the subdued throng and the ripple of the swift-flowing stream, entreating him to remain true to Christ in the hour of temptation. After the sentence was pronounced, he was placed into a boat just below the Rathaus, which moved downstream to a fish hut that was anchored in the middle of the Limmat. As his hands and legs were being bound, he sang out with a loud voice, "*In manus tuas, Domine, commendo spiritum meum*" (Into Thy hands O Lord, I commend my spirit). A few moments later the cold waters closed in over the head of Felix Manz.[18]

George Blaurock is Burned at the Stake

Blaurock, considered the Hercules of the Anabaptists, was stripped to the waist and beaten with rods the day that Manz was drowned. He was then expelled from Zürich never to return. From Zürich he went to Bern, then Biel, and finally to the canton of the Grisons and town of Appenzell.

18. Quoted by Estep, *The Anabaptist Story*, 32.

His final and most fruitful ministry was in the Adige Valley of Austria where he pastored an Anabaptist church and preached to great crowds throughout the area. Finally, on August 14, 1529, Blaurock was taken into custody by Innsbruck authorities along with Hans Langegger. On September 6 they were both burned at the stake by Roman Catholics of Tyrol. Blaurock's ministry surpassed his Swiss Brethren Manz and Grebel in both scope and efficacy as God, in His sovereignty, allowed him to successfully spread the message of Anabaptism for two and a half years before his tragic martyrdom.[19]

Conclusion

The Reformation in Zürich progressed under the guidance of Zwingli and attracted a following of like-minded protestors. However, by 1523 it was evident that there was a growing dissatisfaction amongst some of his most dedicated disciples led by Grebel and Manz. The dissenters felt that Zwingli was moving too slow, disputed his stand on the Mass, and especially differed with him on the view of infant baptism. The public break with the Zürich reformers occurred on January 21, 1525, when a number of the dissenters were baptized. Anabaptism was born and in the words of Estep, was "clearly the most revolutionary act of the Reformation."[20] However, in the mind of the Zürich Council led by Zwingli, there could be no greater opposition to the Gospel than rebaptism.[21] Thus, dark days were to follow before Anabaptism prospered. Grebel succumbed to the plague at the young age of twenty-eight and Manz and Blaurock were tragically put to death. While the movement all but vanished in Zürich, persecution forced the Brethren to spread and consequently Anabaptism spread to other parts of Europe and the movement flourished—the theme of the next chapter.

19. Estep, *The Anabaptist Story*, 33–7; Ruth, *Conrad Grebel*, 143.
20. Estep, *The Anabaptist Story*, 11.
21. Ruth, *Conrad Grebel*, 117.

9

Anabaptism Grows Amidst Persecution

"In the decade between the end of the sanguinary Great Peasants' War in Germany in 1525 and the collapse of the polygamous Biblical commonwealth of misguided peasants, artisans, and burghers in Münster in 1555, the gravest danger to an orderly and comprehensive reformation of Christendom was Anabaptism, which because of a profound disappointment with Martin Luther, Ulrich Zwingli, their clerical associates, and their magisterial supporters, withdrew into separatist conventicles. Anabaptists were regarded as seditious and heretical."[1]

—GEORGE HUSTON WILLIAMS

"From the beginning, the Anabaptist trek across Europe was a 'martyr's pilgrimage' yet it was something more; it was a march—a march to Zion. Joining step with the condemned were numbered those of every tongue and nation of Europe."[2]

—WILLIAM R. ESTEP

RELIGIOUS PERSECUTION OF MINORITIES for their beliefs or practices rarely, if ever, brings about the desired or intended outcomes of the oppressors. More often than not, the opposite rings true—rather than eradicating a sect or religious movement, it often prompts one of two things or both. First, it elicits a zeal or intensity of the persecuted that

---

1. Williams, *The Radical*, xxiii.
2. Estep, *The Anabaptist Story*, 73.

may be otherwise restrained. Second, it forces the persecuted to flee the region of existence and spread to other regions, bringing their religious beliefs with them. Anabaptists were severely persecuted in the 16th and 17th centuries by both Protestants and Catholics. However, the oppression only served to stoke the passion of the Swiss Brethren, causing the radical Reformation movement to spread like wildfire throughout Europe. A zeal for the extremist evangelical message transformed them into missionaries of the Anabaptist movement. Michael Sattler labored in Württemberg, Wilhelm Reublin and Balthasar Hubmaier made their way to Waldshut where they baptized hundreds, Hans Denck went on a missionary journey down the Rhine Valley, and Hans Hut evangelized throughout Austria and Moravia. Menno Simons founded the Mennonite movement in the Netherlands and Germany while Jacob Hutter reorganized the Anabaptist brethren in Moravia.

Swiss Brethren Leaders Persevere

In 1531 Sebastian Franck, the sixteenth-century chronicler of certain European countries penned the following words concerning the Swiss Brethren:

> The Anabaptists spread so rapidly that their teaching soon gained a large following and baptized many thousands, drawing to themselves many sincere souls who had a zeal for God. For they taught nothing but love, faith, and the cross. . . . They increased so rapidly that the world feared an uprising by them, though I have learned that this fear had no justification whatsoever. They were persecuted with great tyranny, being imprisoned, branded, tortured, and executed by fire, water, and sword. In a few years, very many were put to death. Some have estimated the number of those who were killed to be far above two thousand.[3] They died as martyrs, patiently, and humbly endured all persecution.[4]

3. Wenger indicates that this number was recorded before the movement in the Netherlands was established. In this country, another twenty-five hundred followers were put to death for their Anabaptist beliefs.

4. Quoted by Wenger, *Even Unto Death*, 103.

Michael Sattler

One of the most notable leaders of the Anabaptist movement, especially after the deaths of Conrad Grebel and Felix Manz, was Michael Sattler. Born in the South German town of Staufen in the Breisgau around 1490, he entered the Benedictine monastery at Freiburg. Along the way, he learned Greek and Hebrew and studied the Pauline epistles for himself. Believing Catholic doctrine to be in error, he left the Church and united with the Swiss Brethren in Zürich. Banished from Zürich on November 18, 1525, he moved to Württemberg and became a dynamic evangelist in that region, specifically in the towns of Horb and Rottenburg. On February 24, 1527, he presided over a conference of the Brethren at Schleitheim where he presented a confession of faith consisting of seven articles of faith that were enthusiastically accepted by the Swiss Brethren. Sattler was captured by Roman Catholic authorities in Horb, tried on May 17, then tortured and burned at the stake on May 21, 1527.[5] Pieces of flesh were ripped from his body with red-hot tongs, and his tongue was torn. He was still able to whisper, "Almighty, eternal God, thou art the way and the truth; because I have not been shown to be in error, I will with thy help to this day testify to the truth and seal it with my blood."[6] His wife was drowned in the Neckar a few days later.

Wilhelm Reublin

One of the leading figures of the Swiss Anabaptist movement was Wilhelm Reublin, born in 1484 in Rottenburg. Reublin was a pastor in Basel where he advocated church reform. After being expelled from Basel for his Reformation views, he eventually joined Grebel and Manz and the Swiss Brethren in Zürich. During Easter of 1525, Reublin baptized about sixty men and women who had been driven out of Zürich and fled to Waldshut, a German town right on the Swiss border. Among those who were baptized was Balthasar Hubmaier, to whom Reublin had explicated the principles of Anabaptism. He later baptized Sattler in Rottenburg. He spent some time in Strassburg, where he was arrested and eventually made his way to Moravia, where he had a ministry of mixed results with the Hutterites. Expelled from the colony in Auspitz, he returned to

5. Wenger, *Even Unto Death*, 24–8
6. Quoted by Estep, *The Anabaptist Story*, 47.

southern Germany, where he gathered about three hundred Anabaptists together. Not much is known of his latter days, except that he eventually ceased to be a leader in the Anabaptist movement.[7]

Balthasar Hubmaier

Balthasar Hubmaier was born around 1481 in the Austrian town of Freiburg. One of the most influential and respected Anabaptist theologians of the Reformation, he received his doctorate in theology in 1512 under John Eck, one of the most revered instructors of the time. Ordained to the priesthood, he rose quickly in the ranks to become vice-rector of the University of Ingolstadt then chief preacher at a new cathedral in Regensburg. In 1522, he journeyed to Basel, where he met Desiderius Erasmus and Heinrich Glarean, Grebel's former teacher. These encounters spurred him into an in-depth study of the New Testament, and he subsequently adopted evangelical views. He married and began preaching Reformation doctrine. Hubmaier challenged his old instructor to debate twenty-six evangelical articles of faith he had drawn up, but there is no indication Eck paid any attention to it.[8] While Grebel's party was solidifying their convictions in Zürich, Hubmaier was moving in a similar direction and showing himself to be in accord with the radical movement. As noted above, Hubmaier was baptized by Reublin in an Easter service, and on Easter day, he baptized over three hundred men, and on Monday and Tuesday after Easter baptized seventy to eighty others. In July of 1525, Hubmaier disputed Zwingli on the subject of baptism in a document titled *The Christian Baptism of Believers*.[9] In December of 1525, Hubmaier was imprisoned in Zürich and, while stretched on the rack, he finally uttered the required recantation. Deeply penitent for his revocation, he silently slipped out of the city. The Moravians in Nikolsburg welcomed him, and in one short year, he baptized over six thousand believers. He was executed by burning on March 10, 1528, in Vienna. As his tormentors rubbed sulfur and gunpowder into his long beard, he said, "Oh, salt me well, salt me well." Then, raising his head, he cried out, "O

7. Estep, *The Anabaptist Story*, 82–3; Vedder, *Balthasar Hübmaier*, 111–2.

8. Vedder, *Balthasar Hübmaier*, 89–91.

9. Vedder, *Balthasar Hübmaier*, 112–3.

dear brothers, pray God he will give me patience in this my suffering."[10] His wife was drowned three days later in the Danube.

Hans Denck and Hans Hut

Along the way, Hubmaier met Hans Denck, a distinguished graduate of the University of Ingolstadt with recognized proficiency in Latin, Greek, and Hebrew. Denck became convinced that Hubmaier's convictions were biblical, and he converted to Anabaptism. One of Denck's first converts was the erratic Hans Hut, once a follower of Thomas Müntzer. While Denck went on an extended missionary journey down the Rhine Valley, Hut evangelized through Franconia, Austria, and Moravia. Denck labored for a time in Nurnberg and later in Ulm. He received permission from Oecolampadius, an old friend, to enter Basel, where he died a victim of the plague. Hut was imprisoned in Augsburg and tortured mercilessly for four months. Very soon after Denck passed, Hut died in prison of asphyxiation from a fire some say he lit himself. His deceased body was taken to court, tried in absentia, and burned at the stake.

Pilgram Marpeck

In 1528, an Anabaptist named Pilgram Marpeck appeared in Strassburg after being compelled to leave Rattenberg, Austria, for his beliefs and refusal to co-operate with officials in apprehending Anabaptists. Originally interested in Lutheranism he embraced Anabaptism and upon his arrival in Strassburg made contact with Anabaptists who met in private homes. Marpeck was forthright in expressing his theological views such as believer's baptism and separation of church and state. While Martin Bucer admitted Marpeck and his wife were of unblameable character, he accused him "of being an obstinate, stiff-necked heretic, lacking in love and overconfident in his own supposed knowledge."[11] Bucer debated publicly with him on several occasions, and on January 18, 1532, Marpeck was banished from the city. At one time the undisputed leader of the Anabaptist movement in Strassburg, he wandered as an evangelist for the next twelve years and finally settled in Augsburg, where his engineering expertise was much esteemed. While he experienced brief imprisonment,

10. Vedder, *Balthasar Hübmaier*, 243.
11. Williams, *The Radical Reformation*, 274.

Marpeck was one of the few early Anabaptist leaders who did not die a martyr.

The Fringe Element—Militant Dissenters

One of the unfortunate features of Anabaptism is that virtually any evangelical group that remained outside the circle of established state churches was branded as Anabaptist. That meant that extreme dissenters whose practices and theologies were not necessarily in line with the more moderate Anabaptists were considered part of the movement. Some extremists believed in the violent overthrow of established government, some considered themselves prophets bleating forth God's judgments, some were violent apocalyptic doomsayers, some were communal, a few were polygamists.

While Anabaptism is considered to have originated in Switzerland, similar movements sprang up simultaneously in southern Germany, Austria, Moravia, and the Netherlands. Movements emerged so quickly and spread so unevenly that even true Anabaptists would reach out to a group only to discover that certain core beliefs were hopelessly irreconcilable with their own. Furthermore, it was convenient for both Roman Catholics and Protestants to paint with the same brush, every group that did not pay homage to them in theology or practice. Anabaptism became a catchall term—usually negative—tacked onto a wide range of nontraditional approaches to Christian teaching and practice. At times, both Protestants and Roman Catholics misunderstood and misinterpreted Anabaptism.

One such example of religious extremism occurred in Münster, Germany. In early 1534, free elections were held in the city, which resulted in a militant Anabaptist majority—in reality, a contradiction in terms. They began enacting legislation that reflected their aggressive religious convictions. Many citizens, including councilors, departed the city and complained to both Catholics and Protestants of what they called Anabaptist excesses. This evacuation resulted in even more radical individuals entering Münster. Though Bernt Knipperdolling was the mayor, Jan Matthijs and Jan Bockelson arrived and rose to prominence—Matthijs assuring military victory against all opposition and Bockelson promising a New Jerusalem. Some began practicing polygamy, claiming Old

Testament legitimacy, and a few even indulged in public nudity, claiming a return to Eden.

Incidental skirmishes with cities in the proximity ratcheted up the intensity. Bishop Franz von Waldeck, as well as other Protestant and Catholic civic leaders, placed the city under siege, and when Matthijs made a wild sortie outside the city, he and his party were killed. His severed head was placed on a pole for all citizens to see, and his genitals nailed to the city gate. Under Bockelson, the city held out for about two years, but, in the end, citizens considered even rats and vermin delicacies. A few escapees betrayed weak spots in the defenses, and on June 25, 1535, the walls were stormed, and the city was re-captured. The assailants tortured Bockelson and Knipperdolling and put them to death in January of 1536. As a gruesome memoriam, they placed the bodies of the leaders in an iron cage suspended from the church steeple, executing all initiators of the debacle.[12]

Strassburg and the Anabaptists

Dissenters against Catholicism of various stripes began fleeing to Strassburg, viewing it as religiously tolerant. At the height of the movement, some two thousand people lived in the city; it appeared that almost anyone who was persecuted made way to the city. A couple who faithfully reached out to Protestant refugees—including Anabaptists—were Matthew and Katharina Zell. Matthew was an influential pastor in the city and Katharina was one of the first women to marry an ex-priest—even before the marriage of Katharina von Bora to Martin Luther. While Matthew used his influential pulpit in the Strassburg cathedral to proclaim the evangelical message, motivate widespread enthusiasm, and draw more and more leading clergymen to his side, his wife, Katharina, was at least as active in her own right.

Though she was a gifted hymn writer and pamphleteer, her primary ministry involved hospitality and service to Protestant refugees, some of whom were well-known reformers of the day. Many of those who were exiled, however, were ordinary people who simply needed temporary shelter while fleeing persecution. Katharina always cared deeply for the destitute. At one point, when relief for the poor was being mismanaged,

---

12. See Bax, *Rise and Fall,* 195–331 (chapters VII to IX) for an expanded account of the Münster movement.

she stepped in boldly, pleading that the government restore all such services to the disadvantaged. There was an investigation and significant reform took place. Katharina was not shy in attacking the religious bigotry against the Anabaptists. In defense of one leader, she exclaimed, "Why do you rail on him? You talk as if you would have him burned like the poor Servetus at Geneva. . . . You behave as if you had been brought up by savages in a jungle. The Anabaptists are pursued as by a hunter with dogs chasing wild boars. Yet the Anabaptists accept Christ in all the essentials as we do."[13]

With the support of the Zells, Wolfgang Capito, a leading minister of the Reformed Church in Strassburg, was for years most responsible for the city's relatively tolerant attitude toward religious dissenters. In 1527 he wrote, "I frankly confess that in most [Anabaptists] there is in evidence piety and consecration and indeed a zeal which is beyond any suspicion of insincerity. For what earthly advantage could they hope to win by enduring exile, torture, and unspeakable punishment of the flesh. I testify before God that I cannot say that on account of the lack of wisdom they are somewhat indifferent toward earthly things, but rather from divine motives."[14] Initially, Bucer also held the same sentiments. He took the Anabaptists seriously theologically and through many conversations with them realized that he shared some beliefs in common with the less radical groups, including matters such as the central role of the Holy Spirit in the life of the believer, God's election of the faithful, the meaning of the sacraments, and the importance of church discipline. However, he was troubled by those Anabaptists who seemed to be attaching more importance to Christ as an ethical model than as a crucified Savior.

Bucer and Capito's first debate with an Anabaptist occurred with Sattler. The primary point of contention seemed to be the Strassburgers' emphasis on political responsibility for the common good as opposed to Sattler's emphasis on strict adherence to the Sermon on the Mount. However, Bucer and Capito came away with great respect for Sattler's Christian qualities and were much grieved at his brutal execution by Austrian authorities only a few weeks later. In *A Faithful Warning*, a July 1527 publication, the two reformers penned these words: "Thus we do not doubt that Michael Sattler, who was burned at Rottenburg, was a dear friend of God, even though he was a leader in the baptism order;

13. Bainton, *Women of the Reformation*, 73.
14. Quoted by Estep, *The Anabaptist Story*, 72.

yet much more qualified and honorable than some others. He also spoke concerning baptism, in such a way that you can see that he only rejected that infant baptism, through which one thinks he can be saved. For, as a printed booklet concerning him reports, he proved his point by arguing that faith alone can save. Furthermore, he pled for instruction from biblical Scripture and offered to accept the same. Therefore we do not doubt that he is a martyr of Christ."[15]

Capito did take a public stand against those so-called Anabaptists who were fractious, such as Denck. Of him, he wrote to Zwingli: "He has disturbed our church exceedingly. His apparent sacrificial life, brilliance, and decent habits have wonderfully captivated the people. . . . He left yesterday. His going left some disturbances behind; but the remaining problems can be easily settled with diligence and caution."[16] For a time, Capito harbored an Anabaptist named Martin Cellarius in his home. Bucer was greatly troubled by it, and he begged Zwingli and Oecolampadius to convince Capito to rid himself of the man. Bucer seemed to be over-reacting because Cellarius was by no means one of the more extreme individuals that had been placed under the umbrella of Anabaptism. In any case, Capito finally sent Cellarius on his way, but the Anabaptists benefited much from the sympathy shown them by such a highly respected churchman.

Just the same, on April 13, 1534, a decree was published in Strassburg that if Anabaptists did not sign a statement providing for the baptism of all infants, they must leave the city within eight days. This sanction was apparently not enforced for long because, within a year or two, their numbers again began increasing. Other Anabaptists gravitated to Philip of Hesse's territory because it did not uphold capital punishment. In 1538, not knowing how to handle the Anabaptist phenomenon, Philip asked the Strassburg city council to send Bucer to him. Bucer met with Anabaptist leaders that fall and was able to make significant progress. Peter Hesch, a highly respected Anabaptist leader, even declared that he and his followers were willing to return to the Protestant fold if it would exercise true church discipline and if the Anabaptists were given ample time to readjust to its pastors and congregations. Bucer guaranteed both conditions. After he left Philip's territory, his vision of the Church

---

15. Quoted by Sattler and Yoder, *The Legacy*, 19.
16. Quoted by Estep, *The Anabaptist Story*, 76.

left a true impact, but the church ordinances he espoused through the civil servants failed.

Between 1525 to 1529, in Strassburg, Zell, Bucer, and Capito fought for morality in the city and stood against the practice of Mass. Much disorder in the city resulted from the controversy, and in April 1525, a raucous mob broke into Capito's home. This activity moved the pastors to action, and the battle raged on for several years. Capito wrote to Zwingli, "We are again directing every trick against the Mass."[17] Public morals did gradually improve, and there was also a momentous victory regarding the Mass. Capito wrote to his friend Ambrosius Blaurer on February 21, 1529, "Grace and peace, dearest brother. Yesterday the Mass was abolished among us. . . . Thanks be to the Lord who has given us at last to defy the vain threats of the tyrants."[18] The reformers had finally gained a victory. In decades to follow, though, the persecution only grew worse for Anabaptists throughout Europe.

Menno Simons and the Dutch Mennonite Movement

Menno Simons is to Mennonites what John Calvin is to the Reformed movement, and Luther is to Lutheranism. There is no more significant name among sixteenth-century Mennonites—indeed all Anabaptists—than his. Simons, born around 1496, entered the priesthood in 1524. Though trained and consecrated as a priest, he admitted that he had never read the Bible for fear it would mislead him. Eventually, he would be forced to study the Scriptures to find answers to his doubts. John Wenger identifies three incidents that would drive the heretofore-convinced Catholic to turn to an evangelical Anabaptist faith.[19] First, during the celebration of the Mass, he suddenly doubted the veracity of the doctrine of transubstantiation. This uncertainty drove him to the New Testament Scriptures, where he found nothing supporting the Roman Catholic view of the sacrament. Second, he heard of the beheading of a man by the name of Sicke Snijder for being rebaptized. It seemed strange to him to hear of a second baptism. Once again, he went to the Scriptures and found nothing in support of infant baptism. Third, the death of his brother at the hands of the authorities for his baptism caused

17. Quoted by Kittelson, *Capito,* 134.

18. Quoted by Kittelson, *Capito,* 139.

19. Wenger, *Even Unto Death,* 43–4.

Simons to yield to Christ fully: "My heart trembled within me. I prayed to God with sighs and tears that He would give to me, a sorrowing sinner, the gift of His grace, create within me a clean heart, and graciously through the merits of the crimson blood of Christ forgive my unclean walk and frivolous easy life and bestow upon me wisdom, Spirit, courage, and a manly spirit so that I might preach His exalted and adorable name and holy Word in purity."[20]

Simons remained in his appointment in the Catholic parish for under a year, but on January 30, 1536, he renounced his Catholic faith as well as his post. He was later baptized and ordained as an elder in the Anabaptist fellowship by Obbe Philips. A prolific writer, he authored twenty-five books, his most significant publication the *Foundation of Christian Doctrine*, a forthright presentation of Anabaptist faith and practice. In his writings, Simons emphasized—among other teachings— obedience to God's Word, the supremacy of Christ, justification by faith, baptism of the true believer, God's grace, and holy living. Initially, Simons labored in his home country, where his leadership position became solidified shortly after the Bockholt congress of 1536. In 1543 he moved to North Germany, where due to his rising influence, the German and Dutch Anabaptists became known as Mennonites.

While the Mennonite leader never suffered as severe persecution as some Anabaptists, he did grumble against the harsh life which he compared to the relative ease of the priests of the state church: "I with my poor, weak wife and children have for eighteen years endured excessive anxiety oppression, affliction, misery, and persecution. . . . Yes, when the preachers repose on easy beds and soft pillows, we generally have to hide ourselves in out-of-the-way corners. . . . We have to be on our guard when a dog barks for fear the arresting officer has arrived."[21] Simons passed away on January 31, 1561, after a brief illness.

Jacob Hutter and the Moravian Hutterite Movement

In the Tyrol of Moravia, an unlikely leader by the name of Jacob Hutter emerged to save the fragmented Anabaptist movement in this region. Unlike virtually all of the other reformers, whether Anabaptist, Reformed, or Lutheran, Hutter did not come out of the Roman Catholic clergy. A

20. Quoted by Estep, *The Anabaptist Story*, 118.
21. Quoted by Estep, *The Anabaptist Story*, 121.

hat maker by trade, Hutter came into contact with Anabaptists in the Carinthia area and became an Anabaptist preacher in 1529. He quickly emerged as a leader among the Anabaptists in the Tyrol. As persecution mounted in the region, Hutter left for Moravia, arriving in Auspitz in 1533. He assumed authority of the church from the elders and rescued the movement by introducing communal living and organization—the sharing of goods in production as well as consumption. Hutter's leadership amongst the Moravian Brethren though profound, was short-lived. He was arrested, taken to Innsbruck, and burned at the stake on February 25, 1536. Originally known as the Moravian Brethren, these Anabaptists took on the name of Hutterites after the death of their leader. They maintain their clearly defined communistic style of living in *Bruderhof* (house of brothers) colonies to the present day.[22]

Conclusion

Though Anabaptism would spread in pockets throughout Europe in the decades to follow, Grebel was not there to witness it. The young man with only a skeletal knowledge of the Bible had been one of many leaders of a movement that reverberates to this very day, including Mennonites, Amish, and Hutterites. As a whole, true Anabaptists were not seditious social visionaries or revolutionaries. Rather, they were a people who desired to create a believers' Church modeled on Apostolic Christianity. They objected to infant baptism because they believed baptism was a ceremony for believing saints. They also believed that sincere, regenerated Christians should have no carnal dealings with the pagan world and were against swearing total loyalty to earthly authority, engaging in wars, and placing the Church under secular governments' dominance. In the next chapter we return to the Reformation movement in Germany, more specifically the peasants' revolt of 1524–1525.

22. Estep, *The Anabaptist Story*, 92–97; Bax, *Rise and Fall*, 86–7;

10

The German Peasants' War

"Peasant risings were not uncommon in Europe for more than a millennium. . . . The fifteenth and early sixteenth centuries saw many local revolts. To the old standing grievances of the lords' tyranny, the heavy taxes and tithes, the game laws, the forced labour and serfdom, common cause of all these risings alike, new motives were added to make this last the most terrible, among them the prevalent intellectual unrest and the powerful leaven of the new religious teaching."[1]

—PRESERVED SMITH

THE REFORMATION WAS PRIMARILY a religious movement, but it was not without social tensions and insurgencies. In fact, historians consider the revolt to be a socio-religious conflict. The German Peasants' War of 1524–1525 was a series of insurrections among the German-speaking peasants and farmers of central Europe against the princes and rulers of the cities and provinces. Martin Luther preached and taught in favor of civil obedience and opposed insurrection, though he anticipated an insurgency. Many of his contemporaries, however, believed that his writings and teachings were responsible for the uprisings. For example, the Catholic controversialist Johann Cochlaeus concluded that "There are (unfortunately) still many Anabaptists, assailants of the Sacrament, and other mob-spirits awakened by Luther to rebellion and error. . . . I'd lay you odds, however, that among all the peasants, fanatics, and

---

1. Smith and Backhouse, *The Life and Letters,* 138.

mob-spirits not one could be found who has written more obscenely, more disdainfully, and more rebelliously than Luther has."[2] Two noticeable Protestant preachers who supported the peasants in their uprisings were Andreas Carlstadt and Thomas Müntzer.

Peasant insurgencies in Europe were not unusual in the Middle Ages, usually related to the prosperity gap between the wealthy and the poor classes, related income issues, and oppression. Such was the peasant revolt in Flanders (1323–1328), the Jacquerie revolt in France (1356–1358), and the Great Rising (labor strike) of England (1381). In Germany, the miserable plight of the peasants was highlighted by the feudal system's weighty demands and reinforced by reformation principles. Luther's teachings on Christian freedom and the priesthood of the believer, as well as the notion of equality among man, fueled the movement, especially when radicalized by the extremists such as Müntzer. The conflict began in the fall of 1524 in southwestern Germany and quickly swept north. The demands of the insurrectionaries were incorporated in the Twelve Articles, drawn up in early 1525 and implicitly accepted by most of the insurgents. The statement demanded the princes grant reforms related to matters such as tithing, serfdom, foresting, oppressive fish and game laws, feudal dues, and death taxes.

Müntzer Incites the Peasants—Luther Preaches Restraint

There would be no Peasants' War, suggests Roland Bainton, without Müntzer.[3] Whether his assessment is accurate or not, clearly Müntzer, along with Carlstadt, was a chief inciter of the insurgency. Müntzer took his message to the people, declaring to the German peasants that it was God's will to erect His kingdom by the destruction of the godless rulers: "Now is the time. If you be only three wholly committed to God, you need not fear one hundred thousand. On! On! On! Spare not. Pity not the godless when they cry. Remember the command of God to Moses to destroy utterly and show no mercy. The whole countryside is in commotion. Strike! Clang! Clang! On! On!"[4] The emboldened masses embraced the radicalized message and began gathering throughout the countryside. Luther had spoken clearly to the nobles much earlier, decrying the

2. Quoted by Edwards, *Printing, Propaganda*, 149.

3. Bainton, *Here I Stand*, 215.

4. Quoted by Bainton, *Here I Stand*, 216.

abuse of peasants and warning them that their behavior could result in a bloody explosion, which would shake Germany: "The people neither can nor will endure your tyranny any longer; God will not endure it; the world is not what it once was when you drove and hunted men like wild beasts."[5] That time had come.

Luther, however, believed God gave the sword to the magistrate, not to the minister, let alone the saints. In April of 1525, he wrote *An Admonition to Peace on the Twelve Articles of the Peasantry in Swabia*. There was a manifest attempt at being fair-minded and evenhanded. To the lords and clergy, he spoke words of admonishment: "We need thank no one on earth for this foolish rebellion but you, my lords, and especially you blind bishops, parsons and monks, for you, even yet hardened cease to rage against the holy gospel although you know that our cause is right and you cannot controvert it. Besides this, in civil government you do nothing but oppress and tax to maintain your pomp and pride until the poor common man neither can nor will bear it any longer."[6] To the peasants, he declared that violence was never an option for the Christian. He condemned the false prophets most severely and preached against insurrection: "If the government is bad and intolerable, that is no excuse for riot and insurrection, for to punish evil belongs not to everyone, but to the civil authority which bears the sword."[7] Müntzer despised Luther's warnings. He exclaimed,

> Luther says that the poor people have enough in their faith. Doesn't he see that usury and taxes impede the reception of the faith? He claims that the Word of God is sufficient. Doesn't he realize that men whose every moment is consumed in the making of a living have no time to learn to read the Word of God? The princes bleed the people with usury and count as their own the fish in the stream, the bird of the air, and the grass of the field. And Dr. Liar says, "Amen!" What courage has he, Dr. Pussyfoot, the new pope of Wittenberg, Dr. Easychair, the basking sycophant? He says there should be no rebellion because the sword has been committed by God to the ruler; but the power of the sword belongs to the whole community.[8]

5. Quoted by Smith and Backhouse, *The Life and Letters*, 138.

6. Quoted by Smith and Backhouse, *The Life and Letters*, 140.

7. Quoted by Smith and Backhouse, *The Life and Letters*, 140.

8. Quoted by Bainton, *Here I Stand*, 215.

Richard Friedenthal contrasts the moderate Luther with the radical Müntzer:

> In Thomas Müntzer Luther saw the spirit of evil, Satan, which had led humankind astray; Müntzer returned the accusation, or rather charged Luther first and foremost with corruption, with having flattered the princes and delivered the Gospel's cause into their hands. In Müntzer's teaching, the people, the peasants, were the "elect;" to what extent his followers in Thuringia, a few thousand in all, understood his apocalyptic utterances is unlikely ever to be known. It also seems to us unnecessary to go into his faults his short-sightedness, his failure at decisive moments or his utter unsuitability to play the part of military leader. He was no more a popular leader in action than Luther was a politician; he was a visionary, a prophet, an agitator, a man who sounded the alarm.[9]

Müntzer Drives the Peasant Hordes over the Edge

As already mentioned, the fanatical preaching of *Müntzer* and other radicals was the spark that transformed social unrest and discontent into an insurgency. In early 1524 he traveled throughout south and southwestern Germany preaching the emancipation of Israel and the institution of God's Kingdom on earth. "Strike hard on the anvil of Nimrod [the princes]" he exclaimed, "cast his tower to the ground because the day is yours."[10] His message moved the peasants to violence on August 24, 1524, when a group led by Hans Müller of Stühlinger calling themselves the evangelical brotherhood, marched on the town of Waldshut. The violent results were predictable, and the demands and grievances of the peasants were expressed in March of 1525 in the Twelve Articles briefly summarized as follows:[11]

1. The right to choose and remove their own pastors.

2. Pastors be paid from the great tithe and they be exempted from the small tithe (of grain).

---

9. Friedenthal, *Luther,* 417.

10. Quoted by Richard, *Philip Melanchthon,* 145.

11. Summarized from Richard, *Philip Melanchthon,* 145–6 and von Ranke, *History of the Reformation in Germany,* 341–2.

3. Relief from serfdom since everyone has been redeemed by Christ's blood.

4. The right to hunt and fish.

5. The forests be returned to all for domestic use.

6. An alleviation of feudal services.

7. Payment for any labor in addition to contractual agreements.

8. Just rents.

9. Be dealt fairly according to the old written law rather than constantly changing edicts.

10. Return of the meadows to the community.

11. The abolishment of heriot (sort of inheritance tax).

12. All of the articles must be submitted to the test of Scripture.

Revolts sprung up in various areas, the peasants often incited by the reading of the *Twelve Articles*. The insurrection reached the central states of Thuringia, a breeding ground of social unrest, and Saxony sometime in April 1525. On March 7, a pamphlet from the peasants begged Luther, along with Philip Melanchthon, Johannes Bugenhagen, and Elector Frederick the Wise to act as arbitrators between them and the lords. However, the Elector lay close to death at his castle in Lochau. On April 19–20, Luther wrote an *Exhortation to Peace on the Twelve Articles of the Swabian Peasants* in which he addressed both parties. In the first part he admonished the lords by saying, among other things, "We need thank no one on earth for this foolish rebellion but you" and to the peasantry in a second section, he exclaimed, "If the government is bad and intolerable, that is no excuse for riot and insurrection."[12] In a third section, he closed by charging each side to strive for peace and that which is right. He hoped this treatise would help bring both sides together for negotiation. However, his exhortations came too late, as the peasants were already burning and pillaging monasteries, castles, and towns.

Luther was unenlightened of the severity of the situation and the extent of the peasantry's unrest until he journeyed to Thuringia with Melanchthon. It was then he observed firsthand the excessive actions of the violent hordes. In May of 1525, Luther responded with another publication entitled *Against the Murderous and Thieving Hordes of Peasants*. In

---

12. Smith and Backhouse, *The Life and Letters*, 140.

this tract he harshly condemned the peasants: "If the peasant is in open rebellion, then he is outside the law of God, for rebellion is not simply murder, but it is like a great fire which attacks and lays waste a whole land. . . . Therefore, let everyone who can, smite, slay, and stab, secretly and openly, remembering that nothing can be more poisonous, hurtful, or devilish than a rebel. Just as when one must kill a mad dog, for if you do not strike him, he will strike you and the whole land with you."[13]

On May 5, 1525, Elector Frederick died, and on the 15th a mob of eight thousand armed peasants gathered near Frankenhausen. In hopes of coming to a peaceful agreement, Philip of Hesse met with peasants who seemed ready to negotiate. However, on May 12, Müntzer arrived with a force from Muhlhausen and roused the peasants back to a fanatic frenzy. The combined armies of Philip and several other princes met the peasants with a vengeance. When the troops attacked the horde on May 15, over 5,000 peasants were killed and 600 more taken prisoner. *Müntzer* fled to an attic and was eventually found cowering under a bed. Captured by knights of Philip, he was tortured and two days later executed by beheading. In what was known as the Battle of Frankenhausen, the soldiers now far exceeded the peasants in acts of violence, and the brutal conflict did not end until an excess of 100,000 peasants lay butchered.

Nonetheless, there was wanton destruction on both sides. In Thuringia, seventy cloisters were demolished, and in Franconia, the peasantry destroyed fifty-two cloisters and two hundred and seventy castles. Other insurrections fared no better, and despite all the carnage and butchery committed by both sides, the peasants gained virtually nothing.[14]

Sobered Luther Backpedals and Desperately Recants

With the peasants viciously crushed, Luther came under the denigration of his enemies. The Catholic princes held him responsible for the revolt, and the peasants accused him of betraying them—indeed seen as a traitor to their cause. Luther tried to counteract the effect of his condemning pamphlet (*Against the Murderous and Thieving Hordes*) by penning two tracts entitled *A Dreadful Story and a Judgment of God Concerning*

---

13. Quoted by Bainton, *Here I Stand*, 216–7.

14. Bainton, *Here I Stand*, 217, 220; Manschrek, *Melanchthon*, 127; Smith and Backhouse, *The Life and Letters*, 145–6.

Thomas Müntzer and *An Open Letter On the Harsh Pamphlet Against the Peasants* apologizing for the strong and harsh language against the peasants. He also urged mercy to captives. To Albert, Elector of Mainz, he wrote, "I humbly pray your Grace to consider that this insurrection has been put down not by the hand of man but by the grace of God who pities us all, and especially those in authority, and that you treat the poor people graciously, and that accordingly you treat these poor people graciously and mercifully as becomes a spiritual lord even more than a temporal one. . . . It is right to show sternness when the commonality are seditious and stubborn, but now that they are beaten down they are a different people, worthy that mercy be shown them . . . putting too much in a bag bursts it—moderation is good in all things." [15]

The state of affairs sobered Luther. To one friend, he wrote, "All is forgotten that God has done for the world through me. Now lords, priests, and peasants are all against me and threaten my death."[16] Perhaps he had misjudged his influence. Perhaps he could have somehow forced the raging parties together and hammered out some solution. In *An Open Letter on the Harsh Pamphlet Against the Peasants* he tried to explain why he had reacted against the rebellion. Melanchthon added his own popular *History of Thomas Müntzer*, in an effort to contrast the man's violent, fanatical approach with that of Luther and his followers. However, it was too little, too late. "As it was," writes Derek Wilson, "his movement lost and never regained the mass support of the common man. Lutheranism would develop as a state religion closely allied with the ruling class."[17] Moreover, Smith concludes, "It would have been more becoming of Luther, the peasant and the hero of the peasants, had he shown greater sympathy with their cause and more mercy. Had he done so, his name would have escaped the charge of cruelty with which it is now stained."[18]

It was during this general period that Luther also learned of two young Augustinians burned at the stake for proclaiming the gospel. Weeping, he expressed regret that he had not been chosen in place of the two "young boys" as early martyrs for the Reformation. It appears that these tragedies not only grieved Luther deeply but also terrified him. He became afraid, not so much of God, nor of the Devil, nor of himself, but

---

15. Quoted by Smith and Backhouse, *The Life and Letters*, 148–9.

16. Quoted by Smith and Backhouse, *The Life and Letters*, 147.

17. Wilson, *Out of the Storm*, 229.

18. Smith and Backhouse, *The Life and Letters*, 150.

of chaos and loose cannons. At times, this fear was to make him hard and un-discriminating, ready to call down judgment on anyone he imagined clones of Müntzer. For the most part, Luther relied upon rumors about Anabaptist behavior, and so did not investigate what the Swiss Brethren and their disciples actually taught. Thus, he never realized that most Anabaptists were pacifists committed to suffering persecution without violence in imitation of first-century Christians toward the Roman government. He made no distinction between militant and peaceful groups and labeled all factions Anabaptists if they held to dissenting views of baptism and communion.[19] Perhaps had Luther chanced on Zwingli's ideas and the Anabaptists minus Müntzer and Carlstadt, he might not have been so devoid of understanding of the peasant's plight and so implacable towards them.

It seemed to Luther that all men now presumed to criticize the Gospel—that "almost every old doting fool or prating sophist must, forsooth, be a doctor of divinity."[20] However, Luther never encouraged violence against those professing Christians who disagreed with him. He wrote, "Let not your graces interfere with freedom of speech; do not fear to let them preach to their heart's content, how and against whom they please. Sects there must be; and God's word must take the field and conquer."[21] At most, he advocated banishment, not physical arrest, torture, or murder.

Beginning with the radical Zwickau prophets, Luther would face apocalyptic mystics and extremists throughout his ministry. As noted earlier, some peasants and Catholic princes held Luther responsible for both the religious unrest and the peasant fiasco. However, there was an apparent heavy undercurrent of peasant unrest long before even Müntzer appeared on the scene, and it had nothing to do with religion. In contrast, Luther engaged in no overt conflict with the true Anabaptist movement or movements like theirs. Though he generally opposed them, he wrote: "It is not right, and I am deeply troubled that the poor people are so pitifully put to death, burned, and cruelly slain. Let everyone believe what he likes. If he is wrong, he will have punishment enough in hellfire. Unless there is sedition, one should oppose them with Scripture and God's Word. With fire you won't get anywhere."[22]

19. Bainton, *Here I Stand,* 207; Friedenthall, *Luther,* 484.

20. Luther, *The Table Talk,* 27.

21. Stork, *The Life of Martin Luther,* 262

22. Quoted by Bainton, *Here I Stand,* 294.

The reformer was learning both the positive and devastating results of his broad influence and power. Throughout his life, he would battle impulsive anger that sometimes resulted in rash words and actions. He also faced depression at times. In a letter to a friend in 1536, Luther wrote, "Don't mind my ways, for you know that I am so hard and cross, gross, gray, and green, so overladen, overcrowded and overstocked with business that once in a while, for the sake of my poor carcass, I have to break out to a friend."[23] However, most of the time, Luther exhorted those in his circle to be cheerful. His advice to a friend in 1530, was "Whenever this temptation [depression] comes to you beware not to dispute with the Devil nor allow yourself to dwell on these lethal thoughts, for so doing is nothing less than giving place to the Devil. . . . Be strong and cheerful and cast out those monstrous thoughts."[24]

Contrasting Impact on Carlstadt and Melanchthon

It is worthy to note the lasting effects of the Peasants' Revolt on two other reformers—Carlstadt and Melanchthon. History was much kinder to one than the other. After the wars, Carlstadt was threatened with prosecution for alleged involvement with the Peasant Revolt; his name, unfortunately, was linked to Müntzer. For a time, up to early 1525, he wandered about Germany with his wife and child. He eventually fled back to Luther, begging for protection. He pleaded with Luther to intercede with the Elector to grant him access again to Orlamünde, the parish from which he was exiled. Luther attempted to do so but to no avail. The reformer provided his one-time opponent and his family hospitable lodgings in Wittenberg for eight weeks. During this time, Carlstadt wrote a short book in which he retracted most of the charges he had leveled against Luther.[25]

Carlstadt spent his last few years in Switzerland, where he was accepted in 1534 as an instructor at the University of Basel and minister of the university church. Unlike Melanchthon, his name vanished into theological obscurity. On December 24, 1541, he perished, due to an outbreak of the plague in Basel. David Steinmetz concludes that while his writings influenced the early Anabaptist movement, "the dominant impression which he has left on history is that of a man who like Lear

23. Quoted by Smith and Backhouse, *The Life and Letters,* 234.

24. Quoted by Smith and Backhouse, *The Life and Letters,* 231.

25. Kittelson, *Luther,* 200–1.

'hath known himself but slenderly' and who therefore found it difficult to guard against those rash and impetuous acts which, ironically enough, thwarted his own ambitions and made his aspirations for reform even more difficult to attain."[26]

History was much kinder to Melanchthon. His refutation of the peasants was both sympathetic and severe, and his moderate stance to the revolt undoubtedly contributed to a more forgiving posture on behalf of the German people. In his *Confutation of the Articles of the Peasants*, he expressed an understanding of their concerns while believing that it was the princes' responsibility to establish peace and order. Furthermore, the educational accomplishments of Melanchthon beginning in 1524 tempered the backlash towards him and helped preserve the impact of the Reformation. His influence upon the secondary and higher education in Germany is above all estimations, and he goes down in history, as noted elsewhere, as the preceptor of Germany. He authored the famous Augsburg Confession and stands alongside Luther as a founder of Lutheranism.

Conclusion

The Peasants' War was by far the most devastating consequence of the reforming church. In an age of anger, social injustices, and wealth gaps between the rich and poor, insurgencies were not uncommon. In Germany, the Protestant Reformation helped fuel the insurrection. When the peasant Christians began to read the Scriptures for themselves, their notions of justice began to change. What right did feudal overlords and princes have to enslave them and rule unjustly? Reformers took sides with the two parties—the peasants and the nobility. Two Protestant preachers who buttressed the peasants in their uprisings were Carlstadt and Müntzer—the most radical and influential being Müntzer. Luther spoke out against both the peasants and the princes though he drew the ire of the peasants by urging the princes to strike hard against the insurgents. Melanchthon held a moderate and sympathetic view towards the peasants, though condemned their actions. The revolt eventually failed—in fact, failed devastatingly and few, if any, of the demands were realized by the suffering masses. Approximately 100,000 of the poorly armed farmers and peasants were slaughtered. The social disorders may have decelerated

26. Steinmetz, *Reformers*, 185.

the spread of the Reformation, but the evangelical movement eventually regained momentum. The next chapter focuses on Luther's most productive years, beginning with his marriage to Katharina von Bora.

11

Luther's Finest Years

"I am richer than all the papal theologians in the whole world, for I am contented with what I have. I have three children born in honorable wedlock, which no papal theologian has. Again, I am richer than all the nobles in the land, although I rob my gracious prince in order that I may give to others."[1]

— MARTIN LUTHER

THE PEASANTS' WAR BEHIND him, Martin Luther turned his thoughts in an unexpected direction. To the surprise of his peers and colleagues—even to himself—Luther became betrothed to the former nun Katharina von Bora. Katie, accounts one of his biographers, "had been in their midst for two years and not one of them had the slightest idea that Luther was attracted to her."[2] Luther himself expressed wonder at the sudden events: "God knows that I had no thought of going so far in this matter as I have gone. I thought only to attack indulgences. If anyone had told me, when I was at the Diet of Worms: 'In six years you will have a wife and be sitting at home.' I should not have believed it."[3] The marriage proved to be successful in virtually every way. Katie was masterful in caring for the extensive household, and devotedly cared for her husband in health and sickness. Consequently, they were industrious

1. Luther, *Table Talk*, 57–8.
2. Kittelson *Luther*, 201.
3. Luther, *Table Talk*, 41.

and prolific years for Luther. Despite chronic illnesses, he was able to continue to be highly productive. He was able to teach, preach, write, and equip men to be pastors in the Lutheran churches. "The essential difference between the early years and these later ones," notes James Kittelson, "was that external circumstances and the requirements of the Evangelical movement ushered in a new and somewhat different phase of life. He was still creative as he was in prior years, but in a far more official way. He became less the professional and academic theologian and more the churchman, pastor, bishop, and even defender of the faith."[4]

Adventurous Nuns of the Nimbschen Cistercian Convent

On April 4, 1523, twelve nuns convinced of the evangelical teachings of the reformers were smuggled out of the Nimbschen Cistercian convent near Grimma in herring barrels by a Torgau burgher named Leonhard Coppe and his nephew. None other than Luther himself orchestrated the clandestine escape. Three of the sisters went home to their families, and the remaining nine went to Wittenberg, where they all eventually married. One of the nuns, Katharina von Bora, who had spent twenty-one of her twenty-six years in the convent, was the last to marry. She was intelligent and robust, unwilling to marry the first man who grudgingly accepted her, perhaps as a glorified slave. Instead, she worked for two years as a servant in the home of the rich and honorable Reichenbach, where she learned housekeeping and where Luther visited periodically. She met some noblemen such as Lucas Cranach the artist, King Christian II of Denmark, and Luther's friend Philip Melanchthon. She approved of a suitor named Jerome Baumgartner, but his family talked him out of the marriage. Luther thought she should marry Caspar Glatz, a theologian and pastor. She complained about this to Luther's friend, Nicholas von Amsdorf, who, in turn, scolded Luther for his matchmaking efforts: "What in the devil are you up to that you try to persuade good Kate and force that old skinflint, Glatz, on her? She doesn't go for him and has neither love nor affection for him."[5]

Katharina was also invited from time to time to the dwelling of Lucas Cranach, the famous artist. Luther often appeared at the home when she was there, and he could not hide his enjoyment of the break from

4. Kittelson *Luther*, 213.
5. Bornkamm, *Luther*, 404.

the stress of attackers and his heavy workload. Boldly, von Bora said she would marry Luther himself if he would but ask, but Luther was as stubborn as she and refused. He had told George Spalatin in a letter that his refusal was not because he did not have the sexual desires of a man, for he was neither wood nor stone, but he expected the possibility of a sentence of death before long.[6] He did not take her suggestion seriously until he visited his parents. What he took as a joke his father apparently took seriously with the possibility of a son to pass on the name. Luther finally admitted to the possibility of marriage. In May of 1525, he wrote, "I believe in marriage, and I intend to get married before I die, even though it should be only a betrothal like Joseph's."[7]

A Welcome Surprise—Marriage and Family

On June 13, 1526, Luther unexpectedly married the nun, though for reasons other than romantic love. He confessed that "I married to gratify my father, who asked me to marry and leave him descendants. . . . I was not carried away by passion, for I do not love my wife in that way, but esteem her as a friend."[8] At forty-two years of age, Luther now awoke in the morning to find a pair of pigtails on the pillow next to him. That was only one of the many adjustments he had to make. Luther admitted, "Before I was married the bed was not made up for a whole year and became foul with sweat. But I worked all day and was so tired at night that I fell into bed without noticing that anything was amiss"[9] Though Luther stated at the time of his marriage that he did not love von Bora romantically, his feelings changed with time, and the marriage did indeed turn out to be a happy one. He came to respect her for more than her wifely and motherly skills. He said, "Katie understands the Bible better than any papists did twenty years ago."[10] He called her his "rib" and once remarked at the dinner table, "I would not change my Katie for France and Venice, because God has given her to me, and other women have much worse faults, and she is true to me and a good mother to my children. If a husband always kept such things in mind he would easily conquer the temptation to

6. Smith and Backhouse, *The Life and Letters*, 156.

7. Bainton, *Here I Stand*, 224–5.

8. Quoted by Smith and Backhouse, *The Life and Letters*, 160.

9. Quoted by Smith and Backhouse, *The Life and Letters*, 151.

10. Quoted by Smith and Backhouse, *The Life and Letters*, 163–4.

discord which Satan sows between married people."[11] Luther expressed his enjoyment "with the woman who has been joined to me by God I may jest, have fun, and converse more pleasantly."[12] Perhaps it is surprising that the "old monk" and his "nun" provided a worthy example of marriage to many in that age who sorely needed a positive role model.

The marriage turned out to be a good one, and his Katie was indeed a godsend for Luther. One particular provision Katie provided for him was health care. Through the years, Luther was often sick, suffering at various times from ringing in the ears, headaches, gout, insomnia, catarrh (runny nose), hemorrhoids, constipation, and dizziness. He described the ringing in his ears "like all the bells together of Halle, Leipzig, Erfurt, and Wittenberg."[13] He periodically suffered from kidney stones and while attending the Schmalkald League in 1537 almost died from inability to urinate. He left for home in a carriage and the elongated excursion over a rough road apparently dislodged his stones and saved his life: "After I requested that I be taken away from Smalcald in order that I might not die and be buried there in the presence of that monster [the papal legate Vorstius], I arrived in Tambach, where I drank a little red wine in the inn. Soon afterward by God's grace my bladder was opened."[14] His wife was a master of herbs, poultices, and massage, and no doubt was responsible for adding some years to his life with her expertise in medicine and health care.

The Luthers were to bear six children of their own—two of which died at young ages—and adopt four orphans whose parents had been victims of the plague. Besides rearing these children, Katie was also responsible for the many guests and boarders that moved in and out of the Black Cloister, as the dwelling was known, and she did so as cheerfully as possible. When money was tight, Luther attempted to provide income through gardening and woodworking but failed miserably in both projects. Katie, on the other hand, bred pigs, brewed beer, grew vegetables, and took care of bookkeeping duties. She typically rose at four in the morning to begin her duties. Luther rose at dawn and devoted the morning to lecturing and preaching. Between his writing, preaching, and personal appointments, Luther stayed exceedingly active.

11. Quoted by Smith and Backhouse, *The Life and Letters,* 164.

12. Quoted by Brecht, *Martin Luther,* 235

13. Bainton, *Here I Stand,* 228.

14. Quoted by Gritsch, *The Wit,* 95.

The main meal of the day came at ten in the morning, after which the entire afternoon was occupied with writing and additional matters. Supper was served at five. Though others conversed, the primary focus of attention at the daily event was invariably Luther himself. The most knowledgeable at the table, he posed questions of all kinds to others and commented boldly, no matter what the subject matter. Multiple reporters recorded the conversations, and Luther's private secretary Johannes Aurifaber became the first editor of what became famously known as *Table Talk*. Luther was aware of this practice, of course, but still spoke with unusual candor, sometimes engaging in timely humorous entertainment. After dinner, he devoted the evening to visits from outsiders, reading, or other work until about nine, which was bedtime.

Despite his heavy work schedule, Luther was undoubtedly no wet blanket or killjoy. He thoroughly enjoyed his home life, loved children, relished his beer and wine, approved of all innocent forms of entertainment, played a good game of chess, believed cards to be a harmless diversion of children, liked outdoor sports, enjoyed the theater, and even approved of dancing if it was done decently and with honorable chaperones. He also had a keen sense of humor and wit and used it to denigrate his adversaries and occasionally poke fun at his wife. His wit came in the form of satire, clever word plays, self-deprecation, vulgarity, and subtlety. Eric Gritsch suggests Luther acquired a well-developed sense of humor "to balance his bouts of depression and melancholy"[15]

Along with boarding students, the home was a respite for needy relatives, infirmed sufferers, penniless priests, and at times distinguished visitors. In 1542 a guest by the name of George Held described the house as "inhabited by a miscellaneous and promiscuous crowd of youths, students, girls, widows, old maids, and children, and was very unrestful."[16] Of course, this man's perspective cannot erase the enormous spirit of hospitality that must have motivated the Luthers to receive so many guests and care for them with such warmth.

Prolific Author, Preacher, and Teacher

With the horrors and distresses of the Peasants' War behind him, Luther settled into a mollifying family life and was able to promote the

15. Gritsch, *Martin*, 198
16. Quoted by Atkinson, *Martin Luther*, 323.

Reformation through writing, teaching, and speaking. Between 1520 and 1546, fully one-third of all literature published in the vernacular in Germany came from Luther's pen.[17] However, he chose to refuse any payment from the publishers: "God has given me all things without price. The printers offered me four hundred gulden per annum for my manuscripts but I declined them, not wishing to sell God's free gifts. . . . I have enough, and thank God who has given me a wife and children, that fair blessing; and the elector who voluntarily gives me three hundred gulden per annum. . . . I have never sold a manuscript nor lectured for money my whole life long."[18]

Luther the Pamphleteer

One of the popular ways of spreading religious messages during the Reformation was through the publication and dissemination of pamphlets—brief (usually less than twenty pages) unbound publications written by preachers and theologians. Known as pamphleteers, these writers found this strategy an inexpensive and efficient way to reach the masses with their messages. Among the pamphleteers were well-known reformers such as Zwingli and Luther as well as lesser-known authors such as Heinrich von Kettenbach and Eberlin von Gunzburg. The pamphlets were intended to be read aloud in the public square as well as by private readers.

> The Reformation perfected the use of the small booklet or pamphlet as a tool of propaganda and agitation. Frequently in quarto format—that is, made up of sheets folded twice to make four leaves or eight pages—and without a hard cover, these pamphlets were handy, relatively cheap, readily concealed and transported, and accordingly well suited for delivering their message to a broad audience. They could be easily transported by itinerant peddlers, hawked on street corners and in taverns, advertised with jingles and intriguing title pages, and swiftly hidden in a pack or under clothing when the authorities made

17. Luther's works are published in English by Fortress Press and Concordia Publishing House with fifty-five volumes. The Weimar edition of his works is a complete edition of all of his writings and verbal statements. They were begun in 1883 and finished in 2009 with 121 volumes.

18. Luther, *Table Talk: Conversations*, 52.

an appearance. They were ideal for circulating a subversive message right under the noses of the opponents of reform.[19]

The pamphleteers were surprisingly innovative with their powerful metaphors, vivid contrasts between Christ's ministry and the popes, caricatures of Romanists, and role-playing conversations between those with differing spiritual convictions. Clearly, Luther was the most prolific of pamphleteers both before and after his marriage. He out published the other evangelicals in the vernacular during the period between 1518 and 1525, producing in excess of eleven times as many printings of works as the next nearest publisher Carlstadt. As noted above, he continued to be productive after his marriage as "He churned out controversial pamphlets attacking the Pope and the curia with almost hysterical passion."[20]

Luther the Equipping Professor

Despite all his other responsibilities, Luther continued to teach at the University of Wittenberg. His foremost influence or contribution to the new and emerging church lay in his role as university professor, where he would help equip a generation of pastors who would provide ecclesiastical leadership.[21] Moreover, as Luther's fame grew, so did the university. From an enrollment of 162 in 1516, it expanded to 552 in 1520. Enrollment plunged in 1526 to below one hundred and then gradually expanded to over eight hundred in 1554 (immediately after the peasant's revolt). Between 1520 and 1560, approximately sixteen thousand students from all over Europe matriculated from this bastion of the Reformation.[22]

Initially much Reformation preaching was sub-par and in time the monastic orders and the mendicants began supplying the vast vacuum of empty evangelical pulpits. Recognizing the indispensable nature of the spoken word, Luther declared, "The Church is a mouth-house, not a penhouse."[23] However, ecclesiastical reform in Germany was not taking place in an organized fashion, and Luther became aware that most pastors were woefully ignorant of the Scriptures and were not equipped to teach or preach effectively. In January 1526, a church visitation program revealed

19. Edwards, *Printing, Propaganda,* 15.

20. Green, *Luther,* 175.

21. Kittelson, *Luther,* 247.

22. Spitz, *The Rise of Modern Europe,* 94.

23. Quoted by Spitz, *The Rise of Modern Europe,* 93.

that only ten of some thirty-five ministers had an acceptable grasp of the Word, and one of the ten was given to alcohol. Over a decade later, Justus Jonas reported that many preachers were still Catholic at heart and preached evangelically only to draw their salary. Luther claimed that even though the gospel was being preached with clarity, people's morals did not advance. Everywhere he turned, he saw rioting and carousing, vices of every sort, ignorance, and signs of ingratitude toward God.[24]

In 1524 Johann Frederick, Elector of Saxony, suggested that some form of church government be established, and in 1527 a plan was implemented. Luther and Melanchthon, as well as other capable leaders, were sent around to the various parishes to assess the pastors' capabilities and found many of the priests were clinging to old church ways and were ignorant of Bible content, and in some cases were immoral. Subsequently, Luther and Melanchthon set up a detailed plan for supervisors to instruct the priests in various doctrinal themes. Based on the parish needs they found, the eventual handbook Melanchthon and Luther authored was entitled *Instructions for the Visitors of Parish Pastors in Electoral Saxony*, appearing in 1528. In it were matters related to doctrine, the sacraments, the organizing of the worship service, and school and curriculum issues.

In his observations of the clergymen, Luther came across many priests and clerics who preached the identical few sermons over and over due to a lack of biblical and hermeneutical understandings. Consequently, he compiled his own sermons and published them for preachers to use in the pulpit. Luther had distinct ideas about how Lutheran preachers should be trained: "A good preacher should have the following qualifications: 1. Ability to teach. 2. A good mind. 3. Eloquence. 4. A good voice. 5. A good memory. 6. Power to leave off. 7. Diligence. 8. Wholesouled devotion to his calling. 9. Willingness to be bothered by everyone. 10. Patience to bear all things."[25] He also taught that a preacher should, "be diligent with the catechism and serve out only milk, leaving the strong wine of high thoughts for private discussions with the wise. . . . It would be a foolish gardener who would attend to one flower to the neglect of the great majority."[26]

Luther also explained how to write a sermon: "When he [a pastor] is about to treat a subject, he should first set it forth, then define it; third,

24. Spitz, *The Rise of Modern Europe*, 113.

25. Luther, *Table Talk: Conversations*, 189.

26. Quoted by Smith and Backhouse, *The Life and Letters*, 236.

adduce passages of Scripture in support of it; fourth, illustrate it with examples from the Bible and elsewhere, fifth, adorn it with parables; sixth, administer reproof to the wicked, the disobedient, the slothful, and others."[27] Simplicity from the pulpit was emphasized rather than sheer eloquence. Luther taught, "It is best not to preach long sermons, and to speak simply and like a child, for one must preach to little Hans, and little Martin, and the young. Preaching is meant for the children. . . . Christ had an extremely simple way of talking, and still he was eloquence itself."[28] The reformer also cared more about the content being communicated in churches than the formalities. For example, Lutheran pastor George Buchholzer complained to Martin that his elector required him to wear Roman vestments and lead processions with the Eucharistic elements. Luther replied by poking fun at the demands of the Elector:

> Why don't you, for heaven's sake, march around wearing a silver or gold cross, as well as a skullcap and a chasuble made of velvet, silk, or cotton? If your superior, the Elector, thinks that one cap or one chasuble is not enough, then put on two or three. . . . If your Electoral Excellency thinks one procession is not enough, marching around with singing and with bells, then do it seven times, just as Joshua did in Jericho. . . . Perhaps your Electoral Excellency might even jump around and dance in front of all the people with harps, drums, cymbals, and bells, just as David did before the ark of the covenant. . . . I completely approve of such things, as long as they are not viewed as necessary for salvation or binding to the conscience.[29]

Luther as Pastor

More than anything else, Luther was pastor to the parishioners of Wittenberg, defined primarily by teaching and preaching. This meant, "that he baptized, celebrated the Lord's Supper, heard confessions, preached at marriages and funerals, visited the sick, comforted the grieving, and even held the dying in his arms."[30] Moreover, as a pastor, he implemented innovations and changes in liturgy that "arose not merely out of speculation about what constituted 'correct evangelical worship' but out of care

27. Luther, *Table Talk: Conversations*, 187.
28. Luther, *Table Talk: Conversations*, 195.
29. Quoted by Gritsch, *The Wit*, 59–60.
30. Wengert, "Introducing," 12.

to see that the gospel was preached and celebrated in Wittenberg and among his dear Germans."[31]

Undoubtedly, one of the most pastoral of all his works emerged as an outcome of the disheartening visitations to the parishes. This was the publication of two catechisms in 1529. He was appalled by the ignorance of the common people towards the Gospel and the proper lifestyle of the Christian that he had discovered in his visitations. In the preface to the *Small Catechism*, he wrote: "Good God, what wretchedness I beheld! The common people, especially those who live in the country, have no knowledge whatsoever of Christian teaching, and unfortunately many pastors are quite incompetent and unfitted for teaching. Although the people are supposed to be Christian, are baptized, and receive the holy sacrament, they do not know the Lord's prayer, the Creed, and the Ten Commandments, they live as if they were pigs and irrational beasts, and now that the gospel has been restored they have mastered the fine art of abusing liberty."[32]

The *Large Catechism* was written for adults, particularly clergymen and heads of households, divided into five parts: the ten commandments, the Apostles Creed, the Lord's prayer, baptism, and the Eucharist. The *Small Catechism* was a book of doctrine written primarily for children's training and to be used in church and the home. It addressed subjects similar to those found in the *Large Catechism*, such as the Lord's prayer and the ten commandments, much of which was in question and answer format. It also included instructions on how to do various blessings or prayers. For example, for the evening blessing, he recommended the following: "I give you thanks, heavenly Father, that you have protected me this day through your dear son, Jesus Christ. I ask you to forgive all my sin and the wrong that I have done. Graciously protect me during the coming night. Into your hands I commend my body and soul and all that is mine. Let your holy angels have charge of me, that the wicked one may have no power over me. Amen."[33]

Luther was also concerned with revising worship—liturgy and music in particular. Regarding changes in the liturgy:

1. He desired to keep as much as the service or Mass as possible.

2. He wanted to exclude all pretensions to human merit as possible.

31. Wengert, "Introducing," 12.
32. Quoted by *Kittelson*, Luther, 216–7.
33. Quoted by *Kittelson*, Luther, 218,

3. He opposed the sacrificial aspect of the Mass.

4. He believed sermon should be the focal point of the service.

Luther determined that for the peasants to understand the Mass it must be in German. Thus in 1526, he wrote the German Mass, retaining the evangelical essentials included in his earlier revision of the Latin mass.

Improving church music was very high on Luther's agenda as well, and he wrote some lyrics himself. Bainton suggests that the most far-reaching adjustments to the liturgy lie in the realm of music.[34] He often played and enjoyed music with whoever expressed an interest in it. In a letter of October 1530, Luther expressed his enthusiasm for music:

> Music is a fair and lovely gift of God which has often wakened and moved me to the joy of preaching. . . . I have no use for cranks who despise music, because it is a gift of God. Music drives away the devil and makes people gay; they forget thereby all wrath, unchastity, arrogance, and the like. Next after theology I give to music the highest place and the greatest honor. I would not exchange what little I know of music for something great. Experience proves that next to the Word of God only music deserves to be extolled as the mistress and governess of the feelings of the human heart. We know that to the devils' music is distasteful and insufferable. My heart bubbles up and overflows in response to music, which has so often refreshed me and delivered me from dire plagues.[35]

Among Luther's many hymnodies is his best-known, *A Mighty Fortress Is Our God*, written sometime between 1527 and 1529.

Conclusion

This chapter has highlighted Luther's years beginning with his marriage to Katharina von Bora in 1525 to his death in 1546, which we have titled "Luther's Finest Years." One could argue that his most significant accomplishments came before his marriage, including the publication of his *Ninety-five Theses*, his courageous stand against Rome at the Diet of Worms, and completion of the New Testament into German. While this is true, he also had to endure excommunication, exile to the Wartburg

---

34. Bainton, *Here I Stand*, 266.

35. Quoted by Bainton, *Here I Stand*, 266–7.

Castle, and the Peasants' War. We propose that overall, and despite his health issues, he experienced some of his best and most productive years post marriage. His marriage to Katharina was a good one, and his domestic life was an oasis in a world that was still unstable. His settled lifestyle enabled him to be industrious, engaging in preaching, lecturing, writing, and pastoring. He expressed his satisfaction with his life with some of the words with which we began the chapter: "I am richer than all the papal theologians in the whole world, for I am contented with what I have. I have three children born in honorable wedlock, which no papal theologian has. Again, I am richer than all the nobles in the land."[36] The next chapter addresses some of the conflicts that threatened to disrupt the unity within the Reformation movement.

36. Luther, *Table Talk*, 57–8.

12

Protestants Break Ranks

The Marburg Colloquy

THE REFORMATION WAS BELEAGUERED with conflict—reformers against princes and electors, peasants against the aristocracy, Protestants against Catholics, and reformers against fellow reformers. After 1525 in Germany and Switzerland, the Reformation took on political ramifications as princes and electors of the Holy Roman Empire[1] adopted opposing stances based on theological perspectives, in particular the Sacramentarian Controversy. The theological debate over the meaning of four simple words, "This is my body" emerged in controversy between Martin Luther and Ulrich Zwingli. Luther and his supporters held that Christ's body was present (real) in the Lord's supper (consubstantiation) while Zwingli and his followers believed that Christ's presence in the communion elements was spiritual only, not material. Philip, Landgrave of Hesse, wished to unite the Protestant factions, which in turn he anticipated would help create a political alliance against Catholic rulers, so he took the initiative of inviting the conflicting reformers to settle the divisive doctrinal article through debate and discussion. The key attenders were Luther, Philip Melanchthon, John Oecolampadius,

---

1. The Holy Roman Empire was a loosely knit conglomeration of primarily Germanic lands in Western and Central Europe during the Middle Ages between A.D. 962 and 1806. The Holy Roman emperor during much of the early Reformation was Charles V, ruling between 1519 and 1556.

Martin Bucer, and Zwingli. With some hesitation, Luther accepted the invitation to assemble with the German and Swiss theologians in Philip's picturesque castle on a hill overlooking the towers of Marburg and the river, Lahn. The prominent group of theologians assembled, and all participants appeared to desire unity. Ultimately the reformers were able to agree on fourteen of fifteen articles[2] presented but could not come to terms on the last—the doctrine of the Lord's supper.

Egos and Convictions Collide in Marburg

The debate between Zwingli and Luther did not surface at Marburg as the two reformers had disputed at least two years prior. In February 1526, Zwingli published a pamphlet titled *A Clear Explanation of Christ's Supper*, where he presented his position that the elements were simply bread and wine. Luther replied with his own publication in March 1527 titled *That the Words of Christ, "This is My Body," Still Stand Against the Ranting Spirits*. The two continued their controversy through subsequent publications. Zwingli had significant respect for Luther, but he wanted to be considered an equal colleague in the Reformation cause instead of a subdued follower. In April 1527, Zwingli wrote a letter to Luther explaining his position on the Lord's Supper. Preserved Smith suggests the letter was pastoral in tone and pedagogical in nature and probably intended to be inoffensive and conciliatory.[3] On the other hand, the often-polemic Luther was irritated by Zwingli's letter and replied, "You have produced nothing on this subject worthy either of yourself or of the Christian religion, and yet your ferocity daily increases."[4] The accusations and barbs went back and forth until Philip of Hesse was able to engage the two factions in a public discussion at Marburg. Luther possibly viewed Zwingli as indirectly disputing his position as the primary reformer and first re-discoverer of the gospel. Luther was put off by Zwingli's public demonstration of his humanistic knowledge and sometime after Marburg, he spoke his mind regarding this display:

---

2. Known as the "Schwabach Articles," they were prepared by Luther and Melanchthon in July 1529 prior to the Marburg Colloquy. After the colloquy, the articles also became known as the "Marburg Articles."

   3. Smith and Backhouse, *The Life and Letters*, 188.

   4. Quoted by Smith and Backhouse, *The Life and Letters*, 188-9.

> People always want to seem more learned than they are. When we were at Marburg, Zwingli wanted to speak Greek. Once, when he was absent, I said "Why isn't he ashamed to speak Greek in the presence of so many classicists—Oecolampadius, Melanchthon, Osiander, and Brent? *They* know Greek." These words were carried to him, wherefore the next day he excused himself in the presence of the Landgrave by saying: "Illustrious Lord, I speak Greek because I have read the New Testament for thirteen years." No, indeed! It is more than reading the New Testament, it is vainglory that blinds people. When Zwingli spoke German he wanted everyone to adopt the Swiss dialect. Oh, how I hate people who use so many languages as did Zwingli: at Marburg he spoke Greek and Hebrew from the pulpit.[5]

Landgrave Philip recognized the crucial importance of a united Protestant front to stand against the power of the Holy Roman emperor and See. However, he experienced fierce resistance to a meeting of the minds. Theoretically, Luther and Zwingli, the two primary antagonists summoned to Marburg, should not have been at odds. "Influenced by Paul, Augustine, and Erasmus, both were biblical scholars, ordained priests who became married pastors, leaders of evangelical movements, on the outs with Rome, and especially critical of the Mass. And both found constituencies among central Europeans chafing under papal and imperial strictures and who regarded the pair as liberators."[6] It certainly did not help Zwingli that Luther's introduction to him came when the Swiss theologian made friends with Andreas Carlstadt after the estrangement of the two Wittenbergers. After trying for many months, Philip finally managed to convince the two to meet on October 1 to 4, 1529, for a colloquy. Would it end in cordial compromise or in divisive inflexibility?

Luther appeared with Melanchthon, Kaspar Cruciger, and Justus Jonas, while Zwingli showed with forty Hessian cavaliers and Oecolampadius, Bucer, Andreas Osiander, Kaspar Hedio, and Stephen Agricola. Everyone appeared to sincerely desire unity. Luther seemed moody and curt. Bucer and Luther had once been quite close, but when Bucer showed himself with Zwingli's party, Luther smiled faintly and said, "As for you, you are a good-for-nothing fellow and a knave."[7] He conversed affectionately with mild Oecolampadius, and when he and his partners

---

5. Quoted by Smith and Backhouse, *The Life and Letters*, 190–1.

6. Marty, *Martin Luther*, 139.

7. d'Aubigné, *For God and His People*, 154.

greeted Zwingli, the Swiss pastor became quite emotional, stating that there were none with whom he would more happily be in accord.[8] Before the principle contest, Melanchthon engaged Zwingli in one meeting while Luther met with Oecolampadius in another.

The Sticky Communion Issue

Luther had earlier chalked on the table, *Hoc est corpus meum*, "This is my body" and covered the words with the tablecloth. At the height of the debate, he lifted the tablecloth and said, "You seek to prove that a body cannot be in two places at the same time. . . . I will not listen to proofs . . . based on arguments derived from geometry. . . . God is beyond all mathematics, and the words of God are to be revered and followed in awe. It is God who commands 'Take, eat, this is my body.' I therefore demand compelling proof from the Scriptures to the contrary."[9] It appears that he had already determined that he would not budge on the Eucharistic issue.

Zwingli contested the idea that Christ is in the communion bread. He feared that if Christians imagined that they were actually receiving Jesus Christ in the consecrated bread and wine that they would much less earnestly seek to be united with Him by faith and true repentance. Thus, he advocated that the Lord's Supper is a sacred memorial for believers. Luther rejected the strict transubstantiation[10] of the Catholic church but held that Jesus was present in the elements, and the bread and wine were a vehicle for God's grace and a means for union with Christ. That is, Christ was above, beneath, and all around the elements.

For six full hours, the debate continued. To combat the idea that Christ meant the disciples would be literally eating his flesh in the bread, Zwingli brought up many of the figures of speech Christ used, such as "I am the Vine." To further support their claim, Zwingli and Oecolampadius used Christ's words, from John 6:63, "the flesh profits nothing," which must apply to the Eucharistic phrase "this is my body."[11] To this,

8. Bainton, *Here I Stand*, 249.

9. Quoted by Kittelson, *Luther*, 223.

10. Transubstantiation is the Catholic view of the Eucharist that the bread and wine are miraculously transformed into the body and blood of Christ while keeping the appearance of the elements.

11. Kittelson, *Luther*, 223.

Luther replied, "I do not deny figurative speech [in the Scriptures], but you must prove that this is what we have here. It is not enough to say that these words . . . could be interpreted in this way. You *must* prove that they must be interpreted in this figurative sense."[12] "This is the passage that will break your neck," insisted Zwingli, to which Luther retorted, "Don't be so sure of yourself. Necks don't break so easily here. Remember you are in Germany and not in Switzerland."[13] Sensing growing tension, the Landgrave Philip interrupted and said to Luther, "Doctor Luther, do not take undue offence at this expression."[14] At this point, they broke for lunch.

The debate continued for three more days, but there was little progress. A final meeting occurred, and the Landgrave stated that the parties could not separate in such a spirit. He invited the theologians one by one into a private conference with him where he begged and cajoled. Zwingli stood before the others and said, "Let us confess our union in all things in which we agree and, as for the rest, let us remember that we are brothers. There will never be peace between churches if, while we maintain the grand doctrine of salvation by faith, we cannot agree to differ on secondary points." "Yes, Yes! You agree! Give then a testimony of your unity, and recognize one another as brothers," exclaimed Philip. Zwingli approached Luther's party and proclaimed, "There is no one upon earth with whom I more desire to be united, than with you." It appeared that the two factions were to be united. Luther, however, rejected the offer of conciliation and replied, "You have a different spirit from ours."[15]

By all accounts, the colloquy had failed, and Philip was unsuccessful in achieving a united confession. Nonetheless, so that all was not lost, he urged the theologians to compose a list of shared beliefs. Luther took on the task of drawing up what became known as the *Marburg Articles*. The two parties established commonality on fourteen articles, including Christ's work of salvation, the trinity, private confession, faith, and baptism. The fifteenth article described the Eucharist and noted that the parties were incapable of agreeing "on bodily presence of the body and blood" in the elements.[16] Interestingly, while the Landgrave and theolo-

---

12. Quoted by Kittelson, *Luther,* 224.

13. Quoted by Kittelson, *Luther,* 225.

14. Quoted by Kittelson, *Luther,* 225.

15. Quoted by d'Aubigné, *For God and His People,* 163.

16. Smith and Backhouse, *The Life and Letters,* 191.

gians involved deemed the colloquy unsuccessful, d'Aubigné notes that the Roman Catholics "were exasperated that the Lutherans and Zwinglians had agreed on all the essential points of faith. 'They have a fellow feeling against the Catholic Church.' Said they, 'as Herod and Pilate against Jesus Christ.'"[17] Perhaps the reformers had accomplished more than they foresaw at the time, and on the final day, they shook hands and departed in a friendly manner. Upon the conclusion of the symposium, Luther wrote to Katie expressing some of his thoughts on what took place in the debate:

> Dear Katie, know that our friendly conference at Marburg is now at an end and that we are in perfect union on all points except that our opponents insist that there is simply bread and wine in the Lord's Supper, and that Christ is only in it in a spiritual sense. Today the Landgrave did his best to make us united, hoping that even though we disagreed yet we should hold each other as brothers and members of Christ. He worked hard for it, but we would not call them brothers or members of Christ, although we wish them well and desire to go and see the Elector at Schleitz in Vogtland, whither he has summoned us.[18]

Martin Bucer: Bulldog for Conciliation

The impasse between Luther and Zwingli had a noticeable impact upon Bucer, who attempted to mediate between the two significant theologians—Bucer, along with Wolfgang Capito, had the reputation of being a peacemaker. In a preface to one of his commentaries less than a year later, he expressed his displeasure at the inflexible discord: "If you immediately condemn anyone who doesn't quite believe the same as you do as forsaken by Christ's Spirit and consider anyone to be the enemy of truth who holds something false to be true, who, pray tell, can you still consider a brother? I for one have never met two people who believed exactly the same thing."[19]

In negotiations among Protestant groups at this point in time, the most hotly contested doctrine was indeed that of the Lord's Supper. Bucer challenged leaders to focus more on *why* Christ instituted this sacrament

17. d'Aubigné, *For God and His People*, 163.

18. Smith and Backhouse, *The Life and Letters*, 192.

19. Quoted by Greschat, *Martin Bucer*, 93–4.

rather than on *what* they were in themselves. Luther, no doubt, found enormous comfort in the idea that sinners plagued by guilt and self-doubt could be confident that their Savior was there for them, not only in the preached Word of God but tangibly in the elements of bread and wine. Luther believed that anyone who denied this dissolved the indissoluble—in effect, denying Christ and even joining leagues with Satan. Bucer believed that it was a Lutheran weakness to claim that all who took communion indeed received Christ, irrespective of their faith. He was convinced that nonbelievers could not receive Christ but were only ingesting bread and wine; it was with distaste that he finally conceded that Christ could conceivably communicate Himself to the unworthy through the Lord's Supper.[20]

While Bucer attempted to serve as a peacemaker, he was more in Zwingli's camp and was not without his own views on the Eucharist:

> Since the Lord instituted that usage of the Eucharist which was observed in the early churches with great reverence, so that in him they were one bread and one body, likewise all those present at the Holy Supper should share in that one bread and cup of eternal salvation, the body and blood of the Lord commended and offered to the faithful through these sacraments (1 Cor 10:16–17). Surely this use of the Holy Eucharist ought with fervent zeal to be recalled to the churches: "Take and eat," says the Lord, "for this is my body." Likewise: "Take and drink of this cup all of you; this is the blood of the new covenant" (Matt 26:26–28). And how would those not commit themselves to a grave contempt of the Lord and his mysteries who refuse to take the food and drink of eternal life offered by him, when he has so lovingly and kindly invited them to partake.[21]

Zwingli, and later Bullinger, never seemed content with Bucer's efforts, and often treated him with stony silence. Luther sometimes attacked him harshly, though occasionally complimented him on his efforts. In 1531, two years after the Marburg colloquy, Luther responded to Bucer's "very conciliatory creed"[22] with a charitable response of his own: "I have received the confession sent by you, dear Bucer; I approve it and thank God that we are united in confessing, as you write, that the

---

20. Greschat, *Martin Bucer*, 103.

21. Quoted by Pauck, *Melanchthon and Bucer*, 238.

22. Smith, *The Life and Letters*, 288.

body and blood of the Lord is truly in the supper, and is dispensed by the consecrating words as food for the soul."[23]

Who exactly was this man, Martin Bucer, who pled for common ground between Roman Catholics and Protestants? Yet he also spoke out strongly against Catholicism, calling for abolishment and rejection of practices that do not bring about the restoration of the Kingdom of God: "That men so impure and profane should control the priesthood in the churches; that sacred rites should be performed for the people in a foreign language; a corrupt and perverse use of the sacraments of Christ; the addition of sacraments of human invention; invocation of the saints who have completed their pilgrimage; idolatry, and the like."[24]

Bucer was an intelligent, dominant personality who appeared enigmatic, even paradoxical at times. Reformation scholar Willhelm Paulk suggests that he deserves to be better known and considers him the most influential reformer after Luther, Melanchthon, Calvin, and Zwingli. Bucer initially was a follower of Luther but later came under the influence of Zwingli, and his views often differed from those of Luther. He was the most prominent reformer in Strassburg and much of Southern Germany, and as already noted, strove diligently to reconcile Luther and Zwingli. Some distrusted him because of his unrelenting willingness to settle disputes[25] In his lifetime, he was one of the most influential personages in continental Europe.[26] He kept most individuals at arm's length yet could win people over with charm and warmth. His moral rigidity bordered on ruthlessness if he believed people were willfully resisting divine truth, yet personal advantage and gain rarely played into his battles. Gregarious at times, he felt compelled to exchange thoughts with opposing forces in the hope of some workable compromise. His greatest enthusiasm lay in seeking to spread God's kingdom wherever he went. Instead of winning friends, occasionally, his overbearing zeal, instead, produced critics, distrustful partners, or simmering opponents. At one point a frustrated Luther wrote to Melanchthon stating, "I am not responding at all to Martin Bucer. . . . There will be no peace in the church unless we are willing to endure much from this man."[27] This is a rather interesting response

23. Quoted by Smith, *The Life and Letters,* 288.

24. Quoted by Pauck, *Melanchthon and Bucer,* 226.

25. Pauck, *Melanchthon and Bucer,* 155.

26. Steinmetz, *Reformers,* 121.

27. Quoted by Kittelson, *Luther,* 235.

from a sometimes-contentious man himself regarding an individual who persistently strove for peace. However, if Bucer was at times confrontational, it must be conceded that he was not a harborer of cynicism or bitterness.

During this entire period councils, conferences, or colloquies were numerous and elongated, and Bucer seemed to appear at most of them. He became a well-seasoned debater. He had an excellent command of both Greek and Hebrew and was a faithful biblical exegete. To build common bridges with as many groups as possible, he sprinkled Gallicisms into his Latin and would weave characters into his writings with whom diverse readers could identify. For example, one character in his books played the part of a humanistically educated adherent of the Catholic Church who was open to new ideas.

In council negotiations, Bucer rejected the sharpest theological positions from all sides as being too radical; then, he sought wordings that expressed the theological intentions of all parties with a slight compromise on the part of each. Paulk indicates that he "seemed not to take seriously the groundings of the positions that he attempted to reconcile with one another."[28] Few were the occasions when all parties were pleased with his efforts. Even his dear friend, Calvin, rebuked him in a 1538 letter, claiming he was making too many concessions to the Catholics, even to the point of abandoning justification by faith alone, and that he had made an agreement with the Bernese at the expense of Bullinger in Geneva. The accusation of slippage regarding justification by faith is surprising. In many of his negotiations with the Romanists, Bucer made concessions on what he considered peripheral matters as long as he could get them to agree to this crucial cornerstone. He believed that if justification by faith alone was explained correctly to Catholics, they would accept it, and this would form a foundation upon which all other doctrines could be discussed. In the end, of course, this is something Catholics would not tolerate.

Conclusion

In the early part of the sixteenth century, the Holy Roman Empire was in unrest. Political, religious, and social upheaval threatened the stability of what is today, central Europe. Philip, Landgrave of Hesse, was one of

28. Paulk, *Melanchthon and Bucer*, 156.

the foremost Protestant rulers of the time and advocate of the Protestant Reformation. Concerned about a possible confrontation with Roman Catholic princes, he wished to unite the Protestant factions in order to create a stable political alliance against the Catholic rulers. The eucharistic controversy was the primary obstacle to evangelical unity, and Philip invited key theologians in each camp—Luther and Zwingli the opposing principals—to resolve their theological differences at the conference at Marburg. The two factions were able to agree on fourteen articles but could not come to an accord on the doctrine of the Lord's Supper. Bucer attempted to mediate the two theologians, but with little success and the colloquy was considered by most a failure. "The result," states William Stevenson, "was a grave disservice to the Protestant cause. At a time when the best hope of success lay in a united front against the common enemy, Rome, it was tragic that the Reformers were unable to agree among themselves."[29] In chapter thirteen we continue to focus our attention on the political complexities of the Reformation, more specifically the hostile adversary of Protestantism, the Holy Roman Emperor, Charles V.

29. Stevenson, *The Story*, 46.

13

Charles V and the Complex Political and Religious Situations

"From that moment in 1521 when Luther stood before him in Worms, Emperor Charles V never wavered in his hostility to the heretics and considered it his holy duty to win them over, to force them to conform or to destroy them. To the widowed Queen Mary of Hungary, his sister, who was said to be somewhat favorably inclined toward Luther, he wrote: 'I declare to you that if I had a father, mother, brother, sister, wife or child infected with Luther's heresy, I would consider them my greatest enemies.'Not only was he thoroughly orthodox in his religious outlook, but he clung to the medieval ideal of two swords: a universal empire and a church universal."[1]

—LEWIS SPITZ

CHARLES V REIGNED AS the Holy Roman Emperor from 1519 to 1556. He also served as King of Spain (1516–1556) and Archduke of Austria (1519–1521). He toiled to keep his empire intact against the growing forces of Protestantism, increasing pressures from the Ottoman and French kingdoms, and the opposition of the pope. He was the object of hostility from his many enemies because they feared he would establish a universal monarchy. Charles was born in 1500 in Flanders to Philip the Handsome and Joana the Mad and inherited several family dynasties at a very young age—Valois-Burgundy (Netherlands), Hapsburg

1. Spitz, *The Protestant Reformation*, 115.

(The Holy Roman Empire), and Trastámara (Spain). In his later years, Charles retired to a monastery in Extremadura, where he lived alone until he died on September 21, 1558, of malaria.

As Protestantism advanced, the political situation in sixteenth-century Europe became more and more complex. The 1521 Diet of Worms (see chapter 5), presided over by Charles V, declared Martin Luther an outlaw and forbade anyone to protect him or provide him aid. The edict's implementation became increasingly unreasonable as evidenced by the first Diet of Speier (Speyer) in 1526 where the Protestant princes presumed to profess their faith. In the meantime, and shortly after the first Diet of Speier, Charles V had a falling out with Pope Clement VII, and on May 6, 1527, Charles sent 25,000 soldiers to subjugate Rome. Following the Sack of Rome, Charles V was distracted from religious issues by wars with France and the Ottoman Turks. However, he subdued these two enemies as well and subsequently turned his attention to religious issues—determined to terminate the ecclesiastical divisions in the Empire. Charles desired and fought for Catholic reform so that he could lure wayward subjects back into the fold. But Clement was not nearly as anxious to reform the abuses which had precipitated the Reformation in the first place. The pope kept putting off such a summit, and, meanwhile, at the prodding of Philip of Hesse, Luther's princes began uniting to form a resilient Protestant coalition. This chapter addresses the goals, achievements, and role Charles V played in resisting the Protestant Reformation.

The First Diet of Speier—Religious Toleration

The first Diet of Speier (Speyer) convened in the summer of 1526 in the German city of Speier under the presence of Archduke Ferdinand I who in turn was authorized by the powerful emperor of the Holy Roman Empire, his older brother Charles V. With the advancement the Protestants, implementation of the Diet of Worms and its edict against Luther became less and less practical. This was evidenced by the first Diet of Speier in 1526, where the Protestant princes had the boldness to profess their faith, and the edict called for a temporary suspension of the Edict of Worms. The diet concluded that a general council be convened to settle the question of the church division, and in the meantime, "every State shall so live, rule, and believe as it may hope and trust to answer before God and his imperial Majesty."[2] It was intended to be a temporary deferment of the Edict of Worms until a general council would assemble, but in reality, it gave considerable aid to the Protestant movement. Protestant princes took advantage of the decree to take action according to their wishes, and Luther himself interpreted the diet as giving him a temporary exoneration of heresy.[3]

The Sack of Rome—A City Laid Waste

The edict of the 1526 Diet of Speier and the clash between the emperor and the pope were advantageous to the Reformation's advancement. The diet, because it gave religious toleration to the Lutherans and German Reformed; the quarrel between the emperor and the pope, because the Catholic Church became a house divided and annulled the Edict at Worms with the Diet of Speier.[4] The 1527 Sack of Rome was a military incident carried out by the insubordinate troops of Charles V. Pope Clement and Charles had become enemies and from the pope's perspective, Charles was a growing threat to the papacy and Italy. On the other hand, Clement had allied with Charles's arch-enemy King Francis I of France.

The army of Charles, numbering twenty thousand, was a coalition of Protestant German mercenaries known as *Landsknechts*, as well as Spanish and Italian mercenaries. These unhinged killers did not merely subdue Rome; for eight days, they raped it, robbed it, and did their evil will among the citizens, about twelve thousand of which were butchered. Clement, the current pope, was a virtual prisoner in his fortified refuge until he escaped to Orvieto, Italy, in disguise. Interestingly, notes E. R. Chamberlin, the Lutheran Germans were the more humane: "In the destruction of Rome the Germans showed themselves to be bad enough, the Italians were worse, but the worst of all were the Spaniards."[5]

The emperor expressed remorse over the sacking of the city of Rome, and on November 26, 1527, released the pope from captivity. Charles finally reconciled with Clement on June 29, and crowned Clement Roman emperor on February 24, 1530. However, the city of Rome was left in

---

2. Quoted by Schaff, *History Vol. VII*, 684.

3. Schaff, *History Vol. VII*, 685.

4. Schaff, *History Vol. VII*, 686–7.

5. Chamberlin, *The Sack of Rome*, 173.

shambles, and half the population had either been killed, died of disease and famine, or fled the city.[6]

The Second Diet of Speier—Reversal of Concessions

The Second Diet of Speier in March of 1529 was convened by the Holy Roman Empire with a two-fold purpose—to take action against the threatening Turks and suppress any further advancement of the Protestant movement. The diet was attended by Catholic notables and princes and leaders of imperial cities that leaned towards Protestantism. Once again authorized by Charles V to take charge of the diet, Ferdinand attempted to reverse any concessions given to Protestants at the previous Diet of Speier, essentially declaring the decisions ineffective and requiring the Empire to return to Catholicism. Lutheran evangelicals were to be tolerated, but Zwinglians and Anabaptists were exempt even from toleration, with Anabaptists to be punished by death. The evangelicals drew up a protest against all the decrees of the diet, thus leading to the label *Protesters* or *Protestants*.[7]

The Augsburg Confession—A Superior Statement Rejected

The Augsburg Confession[8] was the first of the evangelical confessions and the pattern or model for subsequent statements. Charles V had been distracted from religious issues by a war with Francis I of France and by the Ottoman Turk, Suleiman the Magnificent. However, he subdued Francis, and Suleiman ran out of supplies and marched homeward. Now, finally, Charles tried to press the pope to attend a meeting with Reformation leaders in 1530 at Augsburg, with a resolve to bring an end to the religious division in his empire—particularly the Lutherans and the Roman Catholics. The diet was summoned to meet on April 8 but would not begin until June 20, when the tardy emperor sidled in.

The group of reformers made their way along the Magde valley to Grimma and thence to Weimar. However, as they continued southward,

6. For a detailed narrative of the ransacking of the Holy city, see Chamberlin, *The Sack of Rome*.

7. Schaff, *History Vol. VII*, 690–3.

8. This section is encapsulated from Schaff, *History Vol. VII*, 706–15, Green, *Luther*, 184–7, and Bainton, *Here I Stand*, 251–4.

they left Luther behind on April 15 as he was not permitted to attend the diet. He was smuggled into a fortress called Feste Coburg for a Wartburg-type seclusion like that after the Diet of Worms. This was done because he was still under imperial ban, and Charles had sent safe-conducts for all in the party except Luther. Thus, it was considered too dangerous for him to appear in a place where Charles V and the pope could easily arrange for his demise. The reformer spent almost six months alone with his secretary in what he called his "wilderness."[9] He chalked on his bedroom walls some of his preferred biblical texts, including a favorite from Psalm 118: "I shall not die, but live and declare the works of God."[10] Moreover, it was apparently in this place that he composed the greatest of his hymns: *A Mighty Fortress is Our God*. However, the forty-seven-year-old Luther was, if anything, less able to tolerate such loneliness than before. At times he expressed joy and lightness—at others, he seemed to fall to one of his nervous breakdowns and could not even write. It did not help that on June 5, Luther learned that his father had passed at 1:00 A.M. on a Sabbath morning. He took his psalter, retired to his quarters, and wept in seclusion for two days.

Luther wrote to Melanchthon, "This death has cast me into deep grief, not only because he was my father, but because it was through his deep love to me that my Creator endowed me with all I am and have . . . his loss has caused a deep wound in my heart."[11] Meanwhile, Luther compared the assembly in Augsburg to the jackdaws that chattered before his windows: "The daws and crows make such a racket day and night they all seem drunk, soused, and silly. I have not seen their emperor, but nobles and soldier lads fly and gadabout, all alike black, grey-eyed, the same song sung in different tones. I see by the example of the harsh-voiced daws what a profitable people they are, devouring everything on earth and chattering loud and long. I believe they are in no wise different from the sophists and papists who go for me with their sermons and books all at once."[12]

The Lutheran confession was a moderate statement emphasizing doctrines held in common with the Roman Catholic Church, avoiding controversial matters such as the power of the pope and

---

9. Bainton, *Here I Stand,* 252.

10. Spitz, *The Protestant Reformation,* 115.

11. Luther, *Letters,* 217.

12. Quoted by Smith and Backhouse, *The Life and Letters,* 196.

transubstantiation. The purpose was to present to the Catholic Church the theology of the Lutherans and to clarify misrepresentations made towards them. The final form was presented to Charles V on June 25, 1530, and accepted. The confession consisted of twenty-eight articles and became the primary confession of faith of the Lutheran Church, one of the essential documents of Reformation, and served as the model for subsequent statements of faith such as those held by the Anglicans and Methodists.

Melanchthon had finally realized he must drop plans for a basic written defense of evangelical convictions and began hammering out a comprehensive Lutheran manifesto. At first, he tried almost desperately to minimize Lutheran differences with Rome, even to the point of implying that the differences between Lutherans and Catholics were hardly more serious than the use of German in the mass. Though the Strassburgers were considered by some to be hangers-on in the Zwinglian camp, this was not true. The Strassburg group urgently sent for Martin Bucer and Wolfgang Capito to come to Augsburg and write up a separate confession that followed the general structure of Melanchthon's statement, with a long-winded article added regarding the Lord's Supper. A few cities joined Strassburg in signing the statement, and the Zwinglians submitted their own confession.

The Lutheran statement was, in essence, what Melanchthon and Luther had drawn up, but the scholar had watered down specific points, and Luther was not pleased. Not wishing to upset his friend, Luther trod softly and gently to strengthen several points he felt his friend had compromised a bit too much. Near the end of June, what was to be known as the Augsburg Confession was ready to be shown to the Catholic contingent. In the confession, Melanchthon indicated clearly that, with Luther, he considered the epistle to the Romans a key to Scripture. To love God, one must pass through the new birth and accept the benefits of Christ. Here no one can do anything for the other; everyone must hear for himself that Christ died for him. This faith alone allows humanity to become righteous before God. Out of the sinner comes a righteous individual. These are not mere words or formulas. As the sense of sin is no idle thing, so forgiveness is no weak comfort. If a share were ascribed to human achievement, it would mean laying Christ again into the grave and denying the resurrection.

On June 25, 1530, the confession was read aloud for the diet in German and read so loudly and clearly that the crowd of approximately three thousand outside the building could hear sections of it and did not complain that it took two hours. The emperor appeared bored and, by the end, had nodded off. Melanchthon was despondent much of the time initially feeling the confession was too mild and after the delivery too polemic and austere.[13] However, far off in his castle, Luther was rejoicing. On September 15, he wrote to Melanchthon: "You have confessed Christ, you have offered peace, you have obeyed the Emperor, you have endured injuries, you have been drenched in their revelings, you have not returned evil for evil. In brief, you have worthily done God's holy work as becometh saints. Be glad, then in the Lord, and exult in righteousness."[14] George Spalatin wrote, "On this day action was taken on one of the greatest works that ever took place on earth."[15]

Still hoping for some unification with the See, Melanchthon sent a note to Cardinal Campeggio in which he stated: "In doctrine we agree with the true Catholic Church. The false teachers we ourselves have fought; we are ready to obey the Roman Church, insofar as we are permitted to abolish all abuses in practice."[16] Nevertheless, the Catholics were not prepared to budge an inch. They presented grim warnings about the consequences if the reformers did not swallow their confession whole. Philip I, Landgrave of Hesse, disgustedly returned home without even telling the emperor. Some Catholics and Protestants remained until the end of August on a pretense of negotiation, but nothing came of it. Still, Luther later said that they would never again come as close to a fair compromise than they did at Augsburg.

The confession consisted of two parts. The first section consisted of twenty-one articles, most of which were not points of controversy, such as the doctrines of original sin, the nature of the Trinity, the dual nature of Jesus Christ, and infant baptism. Points of theological contention were the doctrines of justification, the Eucharist, and confession and absolution. The second part of the confession addressed what the Lutherans considered abuses of the Roman Catholic Church, such as the clergy's celibacy, the nature of the mass, confession, and power of the bishops.

It was not until August 3 that the Catholics, led by Johann Eck, offered a response entitled *Confutatio Augustana* or Catholic Confutation.

13. Schaff, *History Vol. VII*, 701.

14. Quoted by Schaff, *History Vol. VII*, 700.

15. Quoted by Stupperich, *Melanchthon*, 85.

16. Quoted by Stupperich, *Melanchthon*, 87.

Mandated by Emperor Charles, the refutation approved several of the first articles either in full but rejected some altogether (such as articles on the faith and good works, as well as veneration of the saints) or with limitations or conditions (such as the Lord's supper). The second part of the confession, which addressed abuses of the Catholic Church, was rejected entirely.

The diet officially ended on September 23 without an agreement, and Charles declared that the reformers must return to the Catholic fold by April 1531 or feel the edge of the sword. To a sometimes-despondent Melanchthon, at some point in the summer of 1531, Luther wrote, "If we fall, Christ falls with us, the Ruler of the world. I would rather fall with Christ than stand with the Emperor. Therefore I exhort you, in the name of Christ, not to despise the promises and the comfort of God, who says 'Cast all your cares upon the Lord. Be of good cheer, I have overcome the world.' I know the weakness of our faith; but all the more let us pray, 'Lord increase our faith'"[17] Furthermore, to his public, Luther stated, "wiseacres do nothing except to slander us and say, 'Luther has indeed destroyed the papacy, but he cannot build a new church,'—he cannot introduce a new form of worship and new ceremonies. They do not realize that building up the church means to lead consciences from doubt and murmuring to faith, to knowledge, and to certainty."[18]

The Schmalkaldic League—Protestant Military Alliance

Growing ever more nervous of the Holy Roman Empire, the Lutheran princes within the Empire formed a defensive military union to protect its religious and political interests, the alliance signed in Schmalkald on February 27, 1531. The two most powerful Lutheran princes Landgrave Philip I of Hesse and John Frederick I Elector of Saxony, brought the leaders into an alliance. Membership was given to states who agreed to either the Lutheran Augsburg or the Reformed Strassburg Confession (also known as the Tetrapolitan or Swabian Confession). The League was eventually expanded to include imperial city-states such as Augsburg, Frankfort, Kempten, and Hanover and in 1538 the country of Denmark aligned with the Schmalkaldic League. The members agreed that if any of the cities or states came under attack, the others would rush to their defense.

17. Quoted by Schaff, *History Vol. VII*, 727–8.
18. Luther, *Luther's Works*, 196.

The relative success of the league reinforced the Lutheran cause but was short-lived as a political force. In the Schmalkald War of 1546–1547, Charles defeated the Schmalkald League, capturing John Fredrick and securing the surrender of Philip of Hesse; both were imprisoned. Peace between the Lutherans and Catholics was finally ratified on September 15, 1655, at Augsburg, whereby the advocates of the Augsburg Confession were finally recognized by imperial rule. Various other groups, such as the Anabaptists, Zwinglians, and Calvinists, were discounted from this lawful standing.

Conclusion

In the early part of the sixteenth century, Europe was in turmoil, and at the center of much of it was Charles V, the Holy Roman Emperor from 1519 to 1556. In 1521 at the Diet of Worms, he declared Luther an outlaw. In 1527 his army of mutinous soldiers, a large number of which were Lutheran, sacked the city of Rome and essentially imprisoned Pope Clement. Several diets or religious assemblies were convened during his reign, including the already mentioned Diet at Worms, the Diet of Augsburg, and two assemblies at Speier. A major outcome of Augsburg was the Augsburg Confession, a statement that became the primary confession of faith of the Lutheran Church and one of the most significant documents of Reformation. The Lutheran princes' uneasiness towards Charles led to the formation of the Schmalkaldic League, a military alliance formed to defend their political and religious interests. The league was defeated in the Schmalkald War, but peace between Catholics and Lutherans was finally confirmed in 1555, three years before Charles died. Charles aspired to create a united empire but was thwarted by the Protestant Reformation.

14

William Tyndale

English Reformer

"Five hundred years ago, no one had a copy of the Bible in the English language. Church services in England were conducted in Latin, and English peasants, or 'ploughmen' as they were often called, had no knowledge of salvation by faith alone in Jesus Christ. But one man dreamed of spreading the gospel by putting the Bible into words the English ploughman could understand. As one of Europe's leading scholars in Greek, Hebrew, and Latin, William Tyndale was uniquely gifted to translate the Bible into English. When church officials objected to his work, Tyndale determined to continue his translation efforts no matter what the risk. Despite persecution, hunger, and hardship, Tyndale persevered with his mission, translating large parts of the Bible until he was betrayed, arrested, convicted as a heretic, and burned at the stake. Because of his sacrifice, though, the English ploughman got his Bible. And Tyndale's passion for sharing the Word of God in the language of ordinary people continues to change the world today."[1]

IN ENGLAND, HENRY VIII succeeded his father in 1491 as king and would enjoy a lengthy reign into the mid-1540s. He may have imagined himself an exceptional king, and he certainly learned quite rapidly the pomp, the political maneuverings, and cutthroat methods often equated with national leadership in his day. He went to war in splendor,

1. From the back cover of Fish and Fish, *William Tyndale*.

with thousands of attendants ensuring his constant, lavish comfort on the battlefield. When he turned against his first great administrator, Thomas Wolsey, he terrified the man to an early grave. He quickly replaced him with the wily lawyer and statesman, Sir Thomas More. More would eventually be executed in 1535 for supporting the pope, and Thomas Cromwell would succeed More. Then in March 1540—five years almost to the day after More's death—Cromwell would sway from a scaffold. In Henry's tenacious manipulations to marry multiple wives, he maintained an outlandish love-hate relationship with the pope, eventually crowning himself head of the Church in England. He proved his capricious brutality by once executing three outspoken Protestants and three Catholics on the same day.

Meanwhile, at Oxford in Magdalen College, an eighteen-year-old named William Tyndale [or Tindall] was beginning to hear of the writings of Desiderius Erasmus, the knowledge of which would result in significant angst for Henry not many years hence. Records of Tyndale's background are vague. Tyndale was born in England about 1494 somewhere between Bristol and Gloucester, but little, beyond that, is known until he appeared at Oxford. He completed his BA in July 1512, and his MA in June 1515. Magdalen College had seen many other brilliant stars pass through its halls—Greek scholars William Grocyn and Richard Croke, Thomas Wolsey (archbishop and cardinal of the Catholic Church), John Colet (theologian and educator), and Richard Fox (founder of Corpus Christi College)—Erasmus had even claimed Magdalen as a temporary home.

Tyndale Launches His Life Mission—Translation of the New Testament

As we attempt to piece together Tyndale's story, it is believed that he moved from Oxford to Cambridge for a time, somewhere between 1517 and 1521. He not only knew of Erasmus, he translated his *Obedience of a Christian Man* and his 1516 Greek New Testament into English and referred to him several times. He was surely familiar with Luther's writings, as copies of Luther's works were burned at Cambridge in 1520.

In 1521, Tyndale went to Camp Hill, England, to serve as tutor to the two sons of Sir John Walsh. In his spare time, he preached the Gospel on St. Austin's Green and in Bristol. This pure preaching did not go ignored by Catholic officials, and at one point, he was summoned before Archdeacon John Bell and accused of heresy in sophistry, logic, and divinity. He was warned that John Walsh could not protect him from the wrath of the Church. Tyndale said that they could banish him to any corner of England, give him ten pounds per year, and allow him to do nothing but teach children and preach, and he would be content. Not quite knowing how to respond, Church leaders released him with stern warnings.

As a newly ordained priest, Tyndale had already begun work on an English translation of the New Testament. Enraged by Tyndale's incessant Scripture-quoting and his logic, a Catholic acquaintance shouted, "We would better be without God's law than the pope's." Tyndale answered with the famous words, "I defy the Pope and all his laws. If God spare my life, ere many years I will cause the boy that driveth the plough to know more of the Scripture than you do."[2] In the words of one biography, "Tyndale's life-mission was declared. He would translate the New Testament into English."[3]

In July 1523, Tyndale decided that in his efforts at Bible translation, Bishop Cuthbert Tunstall might be sympathetic, so he left the Walsh's for London. Tunstall was a Greek and Hebrew scholar, a friend of Erasmus who had helped with his Greek New Testament, and an encourager of Tyndale until he [Tunstall] became a puppet of the pope through Cardinal Wolsey and the king. Thus, Tyndale found Tunstall a "still Saturn" and a "ducking hypocrite," and he was turned down coldly. In turn, Tunstall called Tyndale's work "pestiferous and pernicious poison."[4]

A merchant named Humphrey Monmouth heard Tyndale preach and took the rejected priest into his own home for six months. It was at Monmouth's dinner table that he met and befriended a merchant named Thomas Poyntz, who would play such a vital role in his future. At about this time, it is believed that Tyndale acquired Luther's German New Testament and added Luther to his shortlist of highly respected reformers. As a great admirer of Luther, Tyndale was gratified when the reformer reached out and befriended him. Some question this, but the martyrologist John Foxe affirms, "Tyndale took his journey into the furthest parts

2. Manchester, *A World Lit Only by Fire*, 203.

3. Fish and Fish, *William Tyndale*, 57.

4. Quoted by Daniell, *William Tyndale*, 190.

of Germany, as into Saxony, where he had conference with Luther and other learned men in those quarters."[5]

He only stayed at Wittenberg for nine or ten months before moving to Hamburg. The primary hypothesis for his departure from Wittenberg may be that he did not want to be labeled as fanatically supporting any particular Reformist camp. When angry contentions developed between reformers regarding doctrines such as the Lord's Supper, Tyndale pleaded, "let us close our ranks on the great issues of salvation and allow one another a free conscience on matters of secondary importance."[6] He did not wish to be thrust into peripheral wrangling.

Tyndale Becomes a Fugitive

From the beginning, Tyndale seemed to encounter rabid attacks for his translation work. Yet, the pope himself commended Erasmus' New Testament, and books such as a Gospel harmony entitled *Mirror of the Life of Christ* by Prior Nicholas Love were approved by the Archbishop of Canterbury.[7] It remains unclear why so many fellow Britishers would be so anti-Tyndale. While Tyndale had become a brilliant scholar of the Greek language, he also used Erasmus' Greek New Testament and Luther's German work as resources for his translation works. He also had assistance from several individuals at different times, including Miles Coverdale and William Roye. There is evidence that Tyndale was not very fond of Roye and of him wrote, "a man somewhat crafty when he cometh unto new acquaintance and before he be thorough known and namely when all is spent . . . his tongue is able not only to make fools stark mad, but also to deceive the wisest, that is at the first sight and acquaintance."[8] Tyndale had little respect for his translating knowledge, but he briefly worked with him on translation work in 1525 in Cologne, where he found a publisher. When John Cochlaeus learned of them and attempted to destroy Tyndale's work, the pair escaped with only scattered pages of a printed manuscript and fled to Worms, where he produced a full edition of the New Testament in 1526. From Worms, the first copies

---

5. Quoted by Daniell, *William Tyndale*, 299.

6. Quoted by Edwards, *God's Outlaw*, 81.

7. Daniell notes that nothing in the book can be considered a harmony and simply offers a mixture of paraphrase and free comment [*William Tyndale*, 98].

8. Quoted by Daniell, *William Tyndale*, 109.

were printed and must have begun trickling into England in the spring of 1526, and as many as six thousand copies of the English New Testament were in circulation. When the New Testament began spreading throughout England, it did not include Tyndale's name as translator, though it was known as his work.

When Bishop Tunstall learned of the book, he procured a copy and declared it rife with over two thousand errors. Then, in 1527 he called for a fire and unceremoniously burned all the copies he could get his hands on. When Tyndale heard of it, he said almost prophetically, "In burning the New Testament they did none other thing than I looked for; no more shall they do if they burn me also."[9] He was eventually executed at Vilvorde in 1536.

By late in 1527, Tunstall had filled his prisons to overflowing with owners of Tyndale's Testament. This included not only blacksmiths and bakers, but also brilliant young thinkers such as Robert Barnes, John Frith, and Richard Taverner. They all believed Tyndale's work to be accurate and excellently done. Of course, there were early mistakes to be corrected, but this man was a true linguist, proficient in Hebrew, Greek, Latin, Italian, Spanish, English, French, and German.

Concerning his work, Tyndale wrote John Frith in prison: "I call God to reckon, against the day we shall appear before our Lord Jesus . . . that I never altered one syllable of God's Word against my conscience, nor would this day, if all that is in the earth—whether it be pleasure, honor or riches—might be given me."[10] In April 1527, Tyndale left Worms for Marburg, where he remained until 1529. Here he labored on a translation of the Pentateuch from the Hebrew, wrote *The Parable of the Wicked Mammon*, and finished translating Erasmus's *The Obedience of the Christian Man*. In the *Parable*, he emphasized Christ's blood as overcoming all the sins and wickedness of the entire world in contrast to "a thousand holy candles, a hundred tons of holy water, a shipload of pardons, a cloth sack full of friar's coats, and all the good works and merits of humanity."[11]

In 1529, Tyndale ventured cautiously out of Marburg to Antwerp, boarding a ship bound for Hamburg. In Hamburg were friends, and he believed he could locate a printer. However, the ship wrecked on the coast of Holland, and Tyndale lost not only his belongings and money but also

9. Quoted by Schaff, *History Vol. VI,* 726.
10. Quoted by Edwards, *God's Outlaw,* 81.
11. Quoted by Daniell, *William Tyndale,* 168.

all his precious manuscripts. He ended up heartbroken, in the home of Margaret von Emmerson, where Miles Coverdale, a great encourager, met him. Coverdale helped for the next nine months as Tyndale re-translated the Pentateuch. It went to press in January 1530.

The Hounding of Tyndale

In England, some copies of the Tyndale New Testament remained in the hands of eager readers, but the authorities discovered many of them. Grave repercussions followed some such owners for their so-called heresy. A few of the more prominent leaders who suffered martyrdom through torturous burning were Thomas Bilney (burned on August 19, 1531), Thomas Benet (burned in Devonshire in January 1532), James Bainham, John Bent, and Thomas Harding (burned in the spring of 1532), Andrew Hewet and John Frith (burned on July 4, 1533), and Elizabeth Barton and several friends (burned in April 1534). All were burned alive.

More may seem an unlikely figure to enter the Tyndale drama, but he eventually became quite embroiled in it. More met Erasmus while a young man and became captivated by the humanist scholar. Their friendship flourished through the years even as More rose by 1515 to the position of Speaker of the House in English Parliament and by 1521 to Lord Chancellor to Henry VIII. One quickly sees the intimacy the two shared reflected in a description of More by Erasmus: "Nature never formed a sweeter, and happier disposition than that of Thomas More?"[12] The one thing Erasmus neglected to mention is that, to those he detested, More could be a vile enemy, full of vituperation and bile. It would be his fanatical Catholicism that would finally cause his doom, and it was that conviction that would also turn him into a sworn enemy of the Reformation.

More entered the theological fray licking his lips. Though best known as the author of *Utopia,* he also became quite well known for attacking Luther unmercifully with his pen. Perhaps the following brief excerpt from More will show the level of his bitterness: "[Luther] has nothing in his mouth but privies, filth and dung, with which he plays the buffoon. . . . If he will leave off the folly and rage . . . and will swallow down his filth and lick up the dung with which he has so foully defiled his tongue and his pen . . . he will take timely counsel."[13]

---

12. Froude, *Life and Letters,* 44.

13. More, *The Complete Works, Vol. V,* 683.

Citing the Roman Catholic party line, More claimed that he would not mind a Bible translation for the people if it were translated "by some good Catholic and learned man" and the bishops could dole out small scripture portions to trusted men from whom it would be reclaimed upon their death.[14] His diatribes against Tyndale may not have typically been quite as vindictive as those against Luther, but his three-quarters of a million words penned against the translator seem both obsessive and ultimately vague and meandering. Following is an excerpt:

> The author sheweth that the translation of Tyndall is too bad to be amended. . . . Surely, quod I, if we go thereto the faults be as ye see so many and so spread through the whole book that likewise as it were as soon done to weave a new web of cloth as to sew up every hole in a net, so were it almost as little labour and less to translate the whole book all new as to make in his translation so many changes as need must ere it were made good, besides this that there would no wise man I trow take the bread which he well wist was of his enemy's hand. . . . He is a drowsy drudge, drinking deep in the devil's dregs, a new Judas, worse than Sodom, an idolater and devil worshipper discharging a filthy foam of blasphemies out of his brutish, beastly mouth.[15]

Though the date is not certain, perhaps in 1529, Tyndale began translating the book of Genesis directly from Hebrew into English with a plan to complete the Pentateuch first and, from there, the entire Old Testament. He was elated to discover that Hebrew translates wonderfully into English, even better than Latin. It is believed that he used Johannes Reuchlin's Hebrew grammar and dictionary, Luther and Melanchthon's work from Hebrew to German, and possibly even Zwingli's commentaries.[16] He published the Pentateuch in 1530. Meanwhile, he was pursuing further publication of his New Testament.

Lurking as an observer on the outskirts of Tyndale's desperate travels and labors was a pseudo-scholar named George Joye. He was known as an expert irritant, and by the time he died in 1553, historian David Daniell claims he had likely irritated just about everyone he had ever met.[17] For the sake of financial profit, Joye oversaw the piracy of Tyndale's New Testament in 1527, 1530, and 1533–4. Besides being clunky and rife with

14. More, *The Complete Works, Vol. VI*, 341.

15. More, *The Complete Works, Vol. VI*, 292–3.

16. Daniell, *William Tyndale*, 291–308.

17. Daniell, *William Tyndale*, 322.

printing and spelling errors, the thing that irked Tyndale the most was not the fraud but Joye's theological tinkering with the text and his attachment of Tyndale's name to that tampering. This the translator attacked with the highest volume and the most force possible. Joye responded with a fourth and fifth piracy, then had the nerve to visit Tyndale and suggest they jointly publish their translation views.[18] It is probably to Tyndale's lasting credit that he did not physically assault the man. Meanwhile, in England, Tyndale was declared a felon, and sentries were posted at all English ports to seize him. At this point, it is possible that Luther intervened on Tyndale's behalf because when next we hear of him, he is under protection in the castle of Philip of Hesse.

Oliver Cromwell was born the son of a brewer and blacksmith, but he chose the profession of law, became the right-hand man of Cardinal Wolsey, and continued his upwardly mobile journey until he became Vice Regent and Vicar General for Henry VIII. At some point, the king and Cromwell seemed to reflect a softening toward Protestantism, and the king tried to send word through Cromwell that he wished an audience with the translator face to face. However, Tyndale was even more the fugitive, and for the next two years, Stephen Vaughn, Cromwell's agent, searched for him tenaciously until he finally located him in Antwerp. In a brief covert meeting, Tyndale refused to go to England, believing that even a king's promise of safe conduct could be broken by the persuasion of Tyndale's enemies. He sent a message to the king urging him to at least select someone, anyone, to translate the bare text of the Scriptures in a form that would please him so that the populace may have access to it—a humble request from a man who had devoted so many years to the work himself.

Believing himself finally to be in a safe haven, Tyndale settled in Antwerp in the home of a merchant named Thomas Poyntz. During the next year, he made minor revisions in his New Testament but worked primarily on a translation of Joshua through 2 Chronicles. However, he found time each day to visit English exiles in Antwerp, inquire of their needs, and supply some of their physical needs out of his generous allowance from Poyntz. Tyndale also wandered the alleys and slums to discover the poor and diseased, to whom he would render aid in any way possible.

Sir Thomas Elyot claimed he would locate Tyndale, kidnap him, and deliver him to the king. He freely spent the king's money on bribes and

18. Daniell, *William Tyndale*, 322–5.

expenses but finally had to resign and return in embarrassment to London. Enter Henry Phillips, a young Englishman from an affluent family. He had been given a large sum of money by his father to deliver to a party in London. Instead of delivering it, however, he gambled with it and lost it all. For the next few years, he did not dare go home, but sent fawning, self-pitying letters to family and friends, trying to clamber back into their good graces. Then, mysteriously, he appeared in Antwerp with money.

Tyndale was often invited to dinner by merchant friends and Phillips used this means to introduce himself to Tyndale. With a show of flattery and friendship, Phillips gained the full confidence of Tyndale. Tyndale invited the younger man to his lodgings and dinner several times in the Poyntz's home. He even showed Phillips his books and secret writings. Somewhat suspicious of Phillips, Poyntz asked Tyndale questions about the man but was assured of his complete trustworthiness. Then Phillips asked Poyntz to show him around the town and thereby gained his confidence as well.

Covertly, Phillips went to Brussels twenty-four miles away and brought back with him the emperor's attorney and several other officers. At that point, Poyntz journeyed to another town on business, and Phillips appeared at his home, asking if Tyndale were present. About noon, he returned, found Tyndale home, and asked if he could borrow forty shillings, having lost his purse in a journey from an adjoining town. Tyndale loaned him money, and Phillips then invited him out for dinner. Being very hospitable, Tyndale deferred, saying that he would instead treat Phillips. They went out and, on the way to the café, passed through a long, narrow alley through which Phillips insisted that Tyndale pass first. When they came upon two men seated next to a door, Phillips pointed at Tyndale from behind, and he was immediately arrested. The arrest took place on May 21, 1535, and Tyndale was imprisoned in the Castle Vilvorde, about eighteen miles from Antwerp. The castle was a massive structure, modeled after the infamous Bastille in Paris.[19]

Tyndale Demonstrates How to Die

The sale of books Tyndale owned, as well as any valuables, were used to pay for his keep during his sixteen months of imprisonment. Those who

---

19. The account of Tyndale's betrayal is taken from Foxe, *Foxe's Book of Martyrs*, 117–19.

arrested him remarked at his gentle resignation and naive shock that he had been betrayed. It is not certain who hired him, but Phillips was said to have exhibited almost psychopathic glee and pride at the successful betrayal. However, he very soon showed his cowardice when merchant friends of Tyndale vowed revenge.

Poyntz wrote letters on behalf of Tyndale, one to Cromwell himself, and replies traveled back and forth between England and Brussels until Poyntz was told that Tyndale would be released to his custody. However, Phillips, seeing his scheme go awry, immediately accused Poyntz of harboring Tyndale and believing in his innocence. He also claimed that Poyntz was alone in his appeal, having no merchants on his side and bearing false letters from England. Poyntz was immediately placed under house arrest, and it was only Providence that allowed him to escape before he was put to death.

Cromwell did not seem to try very hard to extradite Tyndale. In September 1525, Cromwell wrote again, questioning the justice of the proceedings. This slowed the process for some weeks, but the commission finally decided to move forward with the case. Cromwell's lack of tenaciousness could be partly due to his recognition of Tyndale's character. The translator was known as a man who spoke plainly, refused to compromise, and was outspoken regarding his deepest convictions—in the language of the times, he could not "hedge, or trim, or speak with double voice."[20]

Many callous and merciless individuals passed in and out of Tyndale's cell through the months, each trying his best to gain the notoriety of being the one who convinced the heretic, Tyndale, to recant. In August of 1536, seventeen commissioners, including three theologians, queried him regarding his doctrinal beliefs, writings, and general life issues. No doubt, the worst of these was Pierre Dufief, who held a reputation for his cruelty and ruthlessness towards anyone who challenged the authority of the Roman Catholic church.

The jailkeeper spoke warmly of Tyndale and told Poyntz's wife that his behavior in prison was to be compared to that of the Apostles. An agent of Cromwell wrote that "They speak much of the patient sufferance of Master Tyndale at the time of his execution."[21] Nonetheless, the favorable view of Tyndale's character did not hold back the inevitable, and in

---

20. Quoted by Mozley, *William Tyndale*, 320.
21. Quoted by Daniell, *William Tyndale*, 384.

early October 1536, Tyndale was led out at dawn to the southernmost gate of the town. He was asked one last time if he would recant. He gazed boldly into the eyes of his accusers and refused; he was then tied to a cross placed on brushwood, straw, and logs. The martyrologist William Foxe notes that "At last, after much reasoning, when no reason would serve, although he deserved no death, he was condemned by virtue of the emperor's decree . . . and, upon the same, brought forth to the place of execution, was there tied to the stake, and then strangled first by the hangman, and afterward with fire consumed, in the morning, at the town of Vilvorde, A.D. 1536: crying thus at the stake with a fervent zeal and loud voice, 'Lord, open the King of England's eyes.'"[22] A noose of hemp was placed around his neck, and when signaled, the executioner yanked upon it with all his strength. Gunpowder was added to the pile of wood, and the fire was lit. When the charred form had ceased burning, an officer broke the chain holding him up, and the body fell into the embers. It was over.

Yet in another sense it was not over. In that very year, Coverdale circulated a Bible, and John Rogers circulated another, commonly called Matthew's Bible. Both contained Tyndale's New Testament virtually unaltered and relied heavily on Tyndale's Pentateuch and other completed sections of the Old Testament. Henry VIII allowed a small phrase at the foot of the title page: "Set forth with the kinges most gracyous lycense."[23]

The Influence of the Continental Reformers on Tyndale

We have focused primarily on the continental reformers and their interaction with each other through personal interface, debates, letters, and publications. Why then do we include the Englishman Tyndale in our collation of evangelical champions of the Reformation, and what communication did he have with other reformers? To have his translation of the New Testament printed and published, Tyndale was forced to leave England for Germany sometime in the spring of 1524. It is possible he landed in Hamburg and then went on to Wittenberg for a year or so. Tyndale began work in Cologne, where he spent a short time before he was about to be arrested and his work impounded before he fled to Worms. He settled permanently in the publishing center of Antwerp until he was

22. Foxe, *Foxe's Book of Martyrs*, 120.
23. Foxe, *Foxe's Book of Martyrs*, 412.

arrested and executed in 1536. Thus, he spent about a dozen years in continental Europe.

The question as to what interaction he did have with other reformers is more difficult to ascertain. The most significant influence the continental reformers had on Tyndale was their publications—most likely Luther's German translation of the Bible, Zwingli's commentaries, and the Hebrew grammar and dictionary of the lesser-known Johannes Reuchlin. While not considered a reformer, we must include Erasmus and his Greek New Testament as an influencing effect on Tyndale as he (as well as Luther) used this in his English translation of the Bible. David Teems suggests that it was Erasmus, not Luther, who "gave Tyndale the nod" to translate the Scriptures into the vernacular.[24]

It is a possibility as well that he went to Wittenberg to study Hebrew under the university scholars. However, we can only conjecture about the personal interaction Tyndale might have had with Luther and Melanchthon during his nine or ten months spent in that university town. Daniell explores the possibility but is unwilling to state anything with certainty: "It might be tempting for a biographer to make a romantic scene in which the two great leaders of reform, Martin Luther and William Tyndale, shared their profoundest insights and enthusiasms. Calling each other 'Martin' and 'William,' and therefore necessarily using for 'you' the intimate German form '*du*' instead of '*Sie.*'"[25] Unfortunately there is no clear evidence supporting this prospect. Daniell draws a similar conclusion regarding the relationship between Tyndale and Melanchthon: "It is pleasant to think of Tyndale polishing his first New Testament in German-speaking proximity to Philip Melanchthon, though again we have no evidence at all."[26] So we must conclude that while there is a possibility Tyndale had personal conferences with Luther and Melanchthon we cannot know for certain.

Conclusion

Tyndale was a brilliant linguist—fluent in eight languages—and theologian, who holds the distinction of being the first man to translate the Bible into the English language. In so doing, he fulfilled his passion for

24. Teems, *Tyndale*, 21.

25. Daniell, *William Tyndale*, 298.

26. Daniell, *William Tyndale*, 300.

making the Word of God available to the proverbial plowboy—or the common Christian. Furthermore, a 1998 analysis of the King James Version "shows that Tyndale's words account for 84 percent of the New Testament, and 75.8 percent of the Old Testament books that he translated."[27] However, his impact goes far beyond the spiritual realm to the societal. Just as Luther played an essential role in the development of the modern German language, Tyndale did the same for the English. He is often referred to as the architect of the English language, even more so than William Shakespeare. He gave us words such as *Godspeed, network, Passover,* and *atonement,* and phrases such as *judgment seat, my brother's keeper, the powers that be,* and *seek and you shall find.* Nevertheless, history has not given him the respect due to him as one having given us the English Bible and impacting English translations to this day. Sadly, many Christians today are only vaguely aware of his story.

27. Moynahan, *God's Bestseller,* 1.

15

Reformers' Tumbles and Tests

As Desiderius Erasmus faded and weakened physically, criticisms of him began flying from all directions. Many viewed him as a sly spiritual baiter who led the masses to the edge of Church reform but would not jump while many others did take the plunge. Martin Luther, Martin Bucer, and Philip Melanchthon squirmed with embarrassment when their advice to Philip of Hesse on re-marriage became public. Luther and his wife, Katie, lost their beloved Magdalena to illness. Bucer was crushed when he lost almost his entire large family to the plague. Melanchthon was reaching the raw edges of resignation as another colloquy in Regensburg ended with no gains and no compromises. Finally, to the grief of many, that great heart of a worn out, used up, Luther gave out. In this chapter we address the struggles of some of the key players in the Reformation—Erasmus, Bucer, Luther, and Melanchthon.

Last Days of a Theological Eel—Erasmus

Through all the rage and tumult of the times, Erasmus appeared to remain unscathed. However, rather lengthy excerpts from one of his letters to an anonymous recipient spelled out more clearly what sort of peaceful co-existent Reformation he preferred:

> Indulgences, with which the monks so long fooled the world with
> theologians' connivance, are now exploded. But the reformers

turn the images out of the churches, which originally were useful and ornamental. They might have been content to forbid the
worship of images and to have removed only the superfluous.
They will have no more priests: It would be better to have priests
of learning—better three good than three hundred bad. *They do
not like so much ritual:* True, but it would be enough to abolish
the absurd. Let those who have no faith in Saint's merits pray to
Father, Son and Holy Ghost, imitate Christ in their lives, and
leave those alone who do believe in vain. If the Saints do not
hear them, Christ may hear them. *Confession is an ancient custom:* Let those who deny that it is a sacrament observe it till the
Church decide otherwise. *Purgatory is not scriptural:* Let men
think as they please about purgatory without quarreling with
those who do not believe as they do. Theologians may argue
about free will in the Sorbonne; laymen need not puzzle with
conundrums. Whether works justify or faith justifies matters
little since all allow that faith will not save without works.[1]

Rarely does one see an individual so conflicted with feelings both
for and against an individual as Erasmus toward Luther, and this to the
very end. In his lectures at Oxford (1893–1894) James Froude addresses
this struggle:

But what was Erasmus to do in the new element which had
sprung out so suddenly? Turn against Luther, he would not, for
he knew that Luther's denunciation of the indulgences had been
as right as it was brave. Declare for him he would not. He could
not commit himself to a movement which he could not control,
and which for all he could see might become an unguided insurrection. Like all men of his temperament, he disbelieved that no
good could be done except through established authorities. He
determined therefore to stand aside, stick to his own work, and
watch how things went. He held aloof. He purposely abstained
from reading Luther's books that he might be able to deny that
he had been in communication with him. Not wishing to write
to Luther himself, yet not wishing to seem to be without sympathy for him.[2]

Excerpts taken from letters as late as 1528–1530 show strong support for the German reformer: "The theologians curse Luther and in
cursing him curse the truth delivered by Christ and the Apostles and,

1. Quoted by Froude, *Life and Letters,* 344.
2. Quoted by Froude, *Life and Letters,* 214.

idiots that they are, alienate with their foul speeches many who would have returned to the Church."[3] "Luther's books were burnt when they ought to have been read and studied by earnest and serious persons. There was too much haste to persecute."[4] Elsewhere he tempers his support for Luther and makes it clear he sides with the Church: "Many great persons have entreated me to support Luther. I have answered always that I will support him when he is on the Catholic side. They have asked me to draw up a formula of faith. I reply that I know of none save the creed of the Catholic Church, and I advise everyone who consults me to submit to the Pope. I was the first to oppose the publication of Luther's books. I recommended Luther himself to publish nothing revolutionary."[5] One of the issues Erasmus had with Luther was not so much regarding theology, but to his conduct: "Luther has said many things excellently well. I could wish, however, that he would be less rude in his manner. He would have stronger support behind him, and might do real good."[6]

Erasmus often seemed too delicate to be one to take action. While he was invaluable to the Protestant movement through his edition of the Greek New Testament, he was, notes Philip Schaff, a scholar and "not a man of action or of deep fervor of conviction. At best, he was a moralist. . . . His piety was not deep enough to brave a rupture with the old order. He courted the flattery of the pope, though his pen poured forth ridicule against him. . . . He did not see that something more was needed than literature and satire to work a change. . . . He lacked both the candor and the courage to be a religious hero."[7] These are harsh words from the historian. Luther himself was a little kinder to Erasmus, in attempting to make a similar point: "Erasmus has done what he was ordained to do. He has introduced the ancient languages in place of the pernicious scholastic studies. He will probably die like Moses in the land of Moab. . . . He has done enough to overcome the evil, but to lead to the land of promise is not, in my judgment, his business."[8]

Some reformers charged Erasmus with leading them to the brink, inspiring them to jump, and then taking to his heels. Horace Walpole

3. Quoted by Froude, *Life and Letters,* 359.
4. Quoted by Froude, *Life and Letters,* 385.
5. Quoted by Froude, *Life and Letters,* 263.
6. Quoted by Froude, *Life and Letters,* 215.
7. Schaff, *History Vol. VI,* 640.
8. Quoted by Schaff, *History Vol. VI,* 642.

later called him "a begging parasite, who had parts enough to discover the truth, and not courage enough to profess it."[9] The year before Erasmus' death, a friend wrote to him of the great spiritual posterity he would leave behind. Erasmus replied, "I care nothing for fame and nothing for posterity. I desire only to go home and to find favor with Christ."[10] Erasmus died of a sudden attack of dysentery in 1536 in Basel and was buried in the cathedral there. "He died in isolation, without a party. The Catholics would not claim him; the Protestants could not."[11]

A Bigamy Embarrassment—Bucer, Luther, and Melanchthon

In 1539 Bucer, along with Luther, lost some credibility because of a situation that was handled in a manner inconsistent with the Scriptures. Philip of Hesse claimed to be an evangelical, but after his conversion continued to live a somewhat promiscuous life. At nineteen, he had been married to Christina, daughter of Duke George. The couple bore seven children, but they were unhappy together, and Philip asked Luther and other reformers how he could either divorce his wife or simply add another in Old Testament fashion. It seems they would have learned from Henry VIII's fiasco eight years earlier in which he wished to annul his marriage and wed someone else. Luther had pronounced a resounding disapproval to such a union, but initially, Bucer seemed disposed to approve of it. But then, step by step, he retreated from the position to one similar to the Wittenbergers.

In the new case, Philip had consorted with a woman who then demanded marriage, and he was so troubled with the relationship his conscience prevented him from being present at the Lord's Supper. When Bucer learned of it on November 4, he was appalled. However, driven into a corner, he believed, along with many others of his time, that marrying a mistress was undoubtedly better than having assorted extramarital affairs. At the request of Philip, Bucer drafted a detailed pro and con treatise regarding bigamy, then traveled to Wittenberg for an emergency conference with Luther and Melanchthon. Luther interpreted the Gospels accurately and held to the notion that divorce was permitted only

9. Walpole, *The Letters*, 184.

10. Quoted by Froude, *Life and Letters,* 428.

11. Schaff, *History Vol. VI,* 632.

in adultery. Looking for a remedy to the situation, he oddly appealed to the "Old Testament patriarchs, who had practiced bigamy and even polygamy without any manifestation of divine displeasure."[12] They ended up telling Philip that marrying another woman *legally* would be bigamy, and that it was illicit. However, perhaps it could be arranged *pastorally*; that is, the second marriage would take place secretly, and the woman would technically be a concubine. Since it would be against the law of the land, it would have to be done in secret—but that was not how the scenario unfolded.

In March of 1540, Melanchthon and Bucer happened to be in the prince's region and were invited to the castle. They suddenly found themselves unwitting wedding guests. Philip had decided to go public with it, and he claimed, moreover, that any children the two bore would have equal inheritance rights with his first brood. The consequences for all the parties were grievous. The episode had disastrous aftereffects for the evangelical movement because Philip—the leader of the Protestant political movement—was forced to detach himself from a military coalition with the Protestants. Bainton maintains that Luther's solution to the problematic situation was a "pitiable subterfuge."[13] Luther was furious, and Melanchthon was so disturbed that, on a journey to Hagenau, he became gravely ill.

The resulting ramifications for Bucer were similarly distressing. A long-winded anonymous dialogue defending Philip's bigamy appeared in the summer of 1541. It turned out the author was Pastor Johannes Lening, but many people, even in Strassburg, spread the word that Bucer wrote it. Ugly rumors and jeering rhymes sprang up, ridiculing the theologian. As if this was only a mild prelude to trials, in 1541 the plague struck Strassburg and wiped out over three thousand people, at least nine in Bucer's home alone: two servants, a foreign boarding student, Bucer's wife, three of his children on November 16 and, at the turn of the year, two more infant daughters. His grief at the phenomenal loss was almost immeasurable. He remarried the next year to Wibrandis nee Rosenblatt, the widow of two of his dearest friends—Oecolampadius, who had died in November of 1531 and Wolfgang Capito, dead the previous year, both victims of the plague. [14]

12. Bainton, *Here I Stand*, 293.

13. Bainton, *Here I Stand*, 293.

14. Greschat, *Martin Bucer*, 201.

Luther's Humanness

Looking back, Luther could hardly believe that his life had turned out as it had. "Who would have divined," he said, "that I would receive a Bachelor's and then a Master of Arts, then lay aside my [law] student's cap and leave it to others in order to become a monk . . . and that despite all I would get in the pope's hair—and he in mine, and I would take a runaway nun for my wife. Who would have predicted this for me?"[15] It seemed that Luther's private life was almost as busy as his public life. He read through the Bible twice a year, studied it regularly, and taught it to his children when he was home. He conversed for hours with multiple guests around his dinner table each evening. However, with all the positives Luther experienced, came much strife and distress. Luther battled against bouts of depression, no doubt augmented by conflict with his adversaries and personal crises such as the loss of two of his children. In his latter years Luther suffered much from various maladies, consequently struggled with his temper, and became increasingly bitter towards the Jews.

Melancholy Fight for Faith

He advised young men candidly about his weaknesses and how they could manage theirs: "I advise you young fellows . . . beware of melancholy for it is forbidden by God because it's so destructive to the body. My temptation is this, that I don't think I have a gracious God. God comforts us by saying, 'I am your God. . . . I'm not going to devour you, I'm not going to be poison to you.' But I preach to others what I don't do myself."[16] He could not always practice what he preached, as his whole life was a struggle against depression, "a fight for faith."[17]

Luther fought deep melancholy with humor. For example, at home, his servant Wolfgang Sieberger was trapping birds on the property to sell to people for caging or eating. Instead of confronting him directly, Luther sent him a letter as if written by the birds themselves:

> We, the plaintiffs: blackbirds, thrushes, finches . . . and other good and honorable birds who must travel this fall via Wittenberg—want your Kindness to know that one called Wolfgang

15. Quoted by Nichols, *The Reformation*, 26.

16. Quoted by Wilson, *Out of the Storm*, 274.

17. Bainton, *Here I Stand*, 283.

Sieberger, your servant, as has been credibly reported to us, is guilty of a vagrant crime. Motivated by great anger and hatred against us, he has purchased some old worn-out and damaged nets at an expensive price in order to build a trap. . . . [He] deprives us of the God-given right to fly and collect some grain. . . . If he does [not] stop, but continues to threaten our lives, we shall plead with God that He might make him catch frogs, grasshoppers, and gnats during the day and that he be covered with lice, fleas, and bedbugs at night so that he forgets about us and no longer impedes our free flight.[18]

Apparently, his servant caught the hint and quit trapping birds.

Loss of Children

Despite his hectic schedule, Luther always was thoughtful of his six children. The following is a brief excerpt of a warm and affectionate letter to Hans, his eldest, at four years of age: "My dearest son: I am glad to know that you learn well and pray hard. Keep on, my lad, and when I come home, I'll bring you a whole fair. . . . So my darling son, study and pray hard and tell Lippus and Jost to do this to, so that you may all come together into the garden. May the dear God take care of you. Give my best to Auntie Lena and give her a kiss for me."[19]

Luther's daughter, Elizabeth, died at only eight months of age, and he said that he had never imagined that a father's heart could be so broken for his child's sake. Then in 1542, Luther lost another daughter, Magdalena, to illness in her fourteenth year. At the bedside, he turned away from her and said softly, "I love her very much; if my flesh is so strong, what can my spirit do? God has given no bishop so great a gift in a thousand years as he has given me in her. I am angry with myself that I cannot rejoice in heart and be thankful as I ought."[20] As his daughter began to falter, he fell to his knees and wept unashamed, praying that God might free her. She then lost consciousness and departed in her father's arms. At her coffin, he said, "*Du liebes Lenchen*, you will rise and shine like the stars and the sun. How strange it is to know that she is at peace and all is well, and yet to be sorrowful!"[21]

18. Gritsch, *The Wit*, 61.
19. Quoted by Bainton, *Here I Stand*, 236–7.
20. Smith, *Life and Letters*, 354.
21. Quoted by Bainton, *Here I Stand*, 237.

Luther never got over this daughter's death, and some believe it has-tened his own. He wrote to his friend, Justus Jonas, noting that neither he nor his beloved Katie was able to thank God even though Magdalene was free from both the flesh and the devil: "The force of our natural love is so great that we are unable to do this without crying and grieving in our hearts . . . [and] experiencing death ourselves. . . . The features, the words, and the movement of our living and dying daughter, who was so very obedient and respectful, remain engraved in our hearts; even the death of Christ . . . is unable to take all this away as it should. You, therefore, please give thanks to God in our stead."[22] Little more than a year later, it ap-peared that Luther might also lose his one remaining daughter, Margaret. She contracted the measles, and it left her with a severe fever, which clung for ten weeks. By this point, Luther had steeled himself against falling apart emotionally, and he only commented that should she die he would, "not be angry with God" as he had been with the loss of Magdalene.[23] Soon afterward, she overcame the fever and survived.

Attitude Towards the Jews

Luther had wrestled with the Jewish issue for many years, though he wrote little about it. In a brief early work of 1523, *That Jesus Christ was Born a Jew*, he advocated compassion and kindness toward the Jews and encouraged Christians to lead them to salvation in Christ. Of the Catho-lic treatment of the Jews, he wrote, "They have dealt with the Jews as if they were dogs rather than human beings; they have done little else than deride them and seize their property . . . if we really want to help them, we must be guided in our dealings with them not by papal law but by the law of Christian love. We must receive them cordially and permit them to trade and work with us . . . hear our Christian teaching and witness our Christian life."[24]

However, when all Luther's efforts to evangelize the Jews were rebuffed, he became increasingly bitter. In 1543, a few years before his death, he wrote a vicious work about the Jews, *On the Jews and Their Lies*, in which he argued that they were no longer the chosen people but "the devil's people," adding that the synagogue was a defiled bride and

22. Quoted by Ozment, *Protestants*, 167.
23. Quoted by Ozment, *Protestants*, 168.
24. Quoted by Michael, *Holy Hatred*, 109.

that their boast of lineage, circumcision, and Law must be accounted as filth.[25] He also wished that Saxon rulers would exile the Jews to Palestine. And if that were not possible, "they should be forbidden to practice usury, should be compelled to earn their living on the land, their synagogues should be burned, and their books including the Bible should be taken away from them."[26] Following is an excerpt from his book, which unmistakably unveils his loathing for the Jews:

> They are the real liars and bloodhounds, who have not only per-
> verted and falsified the entire Scriptures from beginning to end
> and without ceasing with their interpretations. And all of the
> anxious sighing, longing and hope of their hearts is directed to
> the time when some day they would like to deal with us heathen
> as they dealt with the heathen in Persia at the time of Esther.
> Oh how they love that book Esther, which so nicely agrees with
> their bloodthirsty, revengeful and murderous desire and hope!
> The sun never did shine on a more bloodthirsty and revengeful
> people as they who imagine to be the people of God who desire
> to and think they must murder and crush the heathen.[27]

It is puzzling as to how Luther's attitude toward the Jews took on such conflicting forms during his lifespan—from empathy and a desire to see them converted to Christianity, to a vulgar abhorrence for God's chosen people. Perhaps it was merely an emotional over-reaction to the rebuff of his evangelistic efforts. Bainton suggests, "Luther justified himself by appealing to the ire of Jehovah against those who go awhoring after other Gods."[28] In an apparent effort to make the best of Luther and his views, Bainton writes, "One could only wish that Luther died before ever this tract was written. Yet one must be clear as to what he was recommending and why. His position was entirely religious and in no respects racial. The supreme sin for him was the persistent rejection of God's revelation of himself in Christ."[29] James Kittelson echoed these thoughts several years later: "There was no anti-Semitism in this response. Moreover, Luther never became an anti-Semite in the modern, racial sense of the term. . . . Luther was anti-Jewish in the sense that he opposed anyone who taught contrary to his doctrine. . . . But, as with so many of his other

---

25. Michael, *Holy Hatred*, 111.

26. Bainton, *Luther*, 297.

27. Luther, *On the Jews*, 16.

28. Bainton, *Here I Stand*, 298.

29. Bainton, *Here I Stand*, 297.

opponents, he could never let the issue go. . . . The pity remains that he simply repeated the prejudices of his age in proposing specific policies for them."[30] Luther was not a blind racist and to individual Jews, he was open and generous. For years he supported Jacob Gipher, a converted Jew, and when Gipher had to leave Wittenberg in search of work, it was Luther and Melanchthon who tenderly looked after his children.

Failing Health

Though Luther was kind to Katie and his children, nothing, including marriage, thoroughly mellowed Luther's fiery temper, which increased in his later years. By the 1540s, Luther's health was beginning to fail. As he grew older, he continued to suffer from a variety of ailments, including kidney and bladder stones, gout, sciatica, ulcers, abscesses in the ears, toothache, heart palpitations, and arthritis. By 1544 he was feeling the effects of angina. As his blood pressure increased, he became more short-tempered and easily angered. He grew increasingly pessimistic and foreboding. To his old friend Jacob Probst he disclosed, "I am exhausted with age and work—old, cold, and all out of shape—and yet I am not allowed to rest, but daily tormented with all manner of business and the toil of scribbling."[31] He grew out of compassion and understanding of the times, especially with the people. In 1543 he objected that "Everywhere the licence and impudence of the people increase. The magistrates are to blame, for they do nothing except exact taxes. The governments have become institutions for the gathering of treasures and taxes. Therefore, the Lord will destroy us in His anger. Would that the day of our redemption would quickly come!"[32] Once again, Luther wrote to Probst, bemoaning his state: "Old, decrepit, bereft of energy, weary, cold, and now one-eyed I had hope that now at least peace would be vouchsafed to me as to a dead man. And yet, as if I had never done anything, never spoken, written, achieving anything, I must still be overwhelmed with such toils. But Christ is all in all, both to do and to finish, blessed forever!"[33]

Luther's life was finally grinding to a halt. In January 1545, he lost his old comrade, Spalatin. Luther regretted that his temper now sometimes

30. Kittelson, *Luther*, 274.
31. Quoted by Green, *Luther*, 201.
32. Quoted by Green, *Luther*, 202.
33. Quoted by Green, *Luther*, 202.

got the best of him. V. H. H. Green writes, "The long procession of ill-nesses weakened his constitution; nervous depression lowered his spirits. As his blood-pressure increased, his temper became more frayed. He was more and more irascible, not merely in controversy but in his ordinary day-to-day relations."[34] During his final summer of life, Luther became utterly disgusted with the moral corruption he saw and the sexual dis-plays within Wittenberg. A woman of questionable standards, and preg-nant with an illegitimate child, had also infiltrated his home and been hired as chief maid. He finally left home near the end of June 1545 with his son Hans and a lodger, and on the way, attempted to settle a dispute between two clergymen at Naumburg. He wrote a letter to Katie, claim-ing he did not wish to return to "this Sodom."[35] Katie and others were so alarmed that Melanchthon, Bugenhagen, the town burgomaster, and his physician converged to talk him out of it. In a milder mood, he listened to reason and was home again by August 16.

Nonetheless, in recent months Melanchthon had found Luther milder in spirit, and the tender side of their friendship was again evident. They started out together in December 1546, to seek to reconcile quarrel-ing counts in Mansfeld, but they turned back when Melanchthon became ill. When Luther tried again in January, Melanchthon remained behind in Wittenberg. Though his three sons accompanied him, Katie worried much about him on this trip because his health was so poor. Even though Luther was feeling very weak, he somehow found it in him to write her letters, some of which were light-hearted: "I thank you very kindly for your great worry which robs you of sleep. Since the date you began wor-rying about me, the fire in my quarters tried to devour me . . . a stone almost fell on my head and nearly squashed me as in a mouse trap. For in our secret chamber [the toilet] mortar has been falling down for about two days . . . and it fell down . . . it intended to repay you for your holy worries, had the dear angels not protected [me]. I worry that if you do not stop worrying the earth will finally swallow us up and all the elements will chase us."[36]

Luther worked out a signed agreement between the two counts and on his way home he stayed over at Eisleben. That evening, February 17, 1546, his heartbeat grew wild and erratic. At approximately 2:00 A.M.,

---

34. Green, *Luther,* 202.

35. Smith and Backhouse, *The Life and Letters,* 249.

36. Quoted by Gritsch, *The Wit,* 64.

feeling ill, he went to his temporary study and lay down on a couch. Medication seemed to calm him down, but he woke again and shouted, "Oh, dear God, my pain is so great!"[37] A group rushed to Luther's bedside. He said, "God of all comfort, I thank you that you have given for me your dear Son Jesus Christ, in whom I believe, whom I have preached and confessed, loved and praised. . . . O heavenly Father, if I leave this terrestrial body and depart I am certain I will be with you for ever and can never, never tear myself out of your hands."[38] As he faded, Dr. Jonas asked, "Do you want to die standing firm on Christ and the doctrine you have taught?"[39] Luther's body moved, and he murmured, "*Ja*." At about 3:00 A.M., that mighty heart beat its last.

Melanchthon had written a letter to Luther after he reached Eisleben in which he once again expressed his gratitude and respect, calling Luther the restorer of true doctrine and his dearest father in the faith. However, Luther died before he received it. Upon hearing of his death, Melanchthon, reflecting rare emotion, announced to his students, "Ah! The Charioteer and the Chariot of Israel is gone; he who guided the Church in those last days."[40]

Melanchthon's Life Without Luther

"The friendship of these two great and good men," writes Philip Schaff, "is one of the most delightful chapters in the religious drama of the sixteenth century. It rested on mutual personal esteem and hearty German affection, but especially on the consciousness of a providential mission entrusted to their united labors."[41] Luther's death on February 18, 1546, was among the saddest days of Melanchthon's life. Moreover, it is upon the death of his good friend that Melanchthon's toughest trials began. James Richard writes,

> Hitherto he had looked to the great Reformer for guidance and solace. Now by force of circumstance, he himself had become the theological head of the Reformation. He was born to teach, to write, to dispute, to negotiate, not to control the passions of

37. Quoted by Kittelson, *Luther*, 297.
38. Quoted by Smith and Backhouse, *The Life and Letters*, 256.
39. Quoted by Kittelson, *Luther*, 297.
40. Quoted by Richard, *Philip Melanchthon*, 309.
41. Schaff, *History Vol. VII*, 192–3.

men, and to direct them in time of excitement. By his powerful
personality Luther had kept the refractory elements at bay, and
had held his followers well in line; but no sooner was he gone
than disputes and parties arose in the Lutheran Church, which
live to disturb its peace to the present day. That Melanchthon
did not settle these, and could not control them, was his misfortune, not his fault.[42]

In November 1546, when hostile forces entered Wittenberg, Melanchthon escaped to Zerbst. Amid all the turmoil, grief was added when
he heard that his daughter Anna had died in Konigsberg. He wrote a
brief tract entitled *Loci consolationis* and dedicated it to the principle that
the Christian must bow under God's hand and accept both success and
tragedy. Feeling unsafe in Zerbst, he moved on to Brunswick, then to
Nordhausen. Peace came, and the new Elector invited all professors back
to Wittenberg University, stating that they could continue teaching as
before.

However, things would never be as before in Germany. Melanchthon
was aging and feeling the effects of years of conflict and struggle. In years
past, a much tougher Luther had absorbed much of the impact of both
internal strife and assaults from external sources. Now, however, he was
alone, and the attacks were coming from unexpected places. A former
pupil, Matthew Vlacich (Flacius) of Illyria, turned against Melanchthon,
accusing him of falsifying the truth, thus deviating not only on issues
of church practice but in tenets of the faith. A 1548 publication titled
Leipzig Interim[43] essentially rejected the notion of adiaphora—the idea
that some Christian teachings are neutral—by suggesting that followers
of Christ should submit to the longstanding teachings of the Church that
were neither forbidden nor commanded in Scripture, such as the use of
candles, confirmation, and vestments. The Lutherans led by Melanchthon had attempted a compromise for political reasons by agreeing to
adiaphora as long as nothing was changed concerning the pure doctrines
of Christ (something he later regretted). He was met with opposition by
some reformers on the grounds that under no condition or political pressure should Lutherans accept adiaphora. Flacius was the most vehement

---

42. Schaff, *History Vol. VII*, 313.

43. The *Leipzig Interim* attempted to settle disputes between Emperor Charles V
and Saxon Lutherans. The Lutherans attempted to explain their stand on doctrines of
indifference—indifferent because they are neither commanded nor prohibited in the
Scriptures.

opponent of the *Interim* and Melanchthon. Indeed, Melanchthon had reluctantly contributed to the pamphlet, but Flacius poured out his wrath against the document and Melanchthon as if Melanchthon were the author: "You will learn that the occasion was in part the desire of the wicked to betray and to crucify Christ, and to set the Roman Barabbas free; in part it was the false faith, the fear and carnal wisdom of weak Christians . . . the end is the restoration of the papacy, the setting up of Antichrist in the temple of Christ, the confirmation of the wicked, that they may triumph over the Church and Christ, the distress of the pious, weakness, the leading into doubt, unnumbered offences."[44]

Then the mystic, Andreas Osiander, viciously attacked Melanchthon regarding the balance of Christ's human and divine character as well as matters of imputed righteousness versus substantial righteousness in justification. Osiander believed that justification for the Christian was the result of Christ indwelling a person, rather than the commonly held view of the reformers that God's grace imputed justification. He declared Melanchthon and his followers to be ministers of Satan, knowing nothing of the doctrines of Christianity. He then wrote, "I will open a vein in him, and will spill his blood all over Germany."[45]

Though Melanchthon had to endure much hostility from both Romanists and Evangelicals during this period, his reputation and authority were still powerful, and he was very frequently asked for counsel and clarification from nations and territories both near and far. Nonetheless in a letter to the chancellor of Saxony in April 1548, Melanchthon admitted in discouragement that he had "an unseemly servitude" in character."[46] On October 11, 1557, his wife died. Upon hearing the news, he looked up to heaven and exclaimed, "Fare thee well I shall soon follow thee."[47] He joined her on April 19, 1560, at the age of sixty-three.

Conclusion

The Reformation took its toll on many of the leaders of the movement. The humanist Erasmus, who paved the way for the reformers, died alone revered by neither Catholics nor Protestants. Bucer, along with Luther

---

44. Quoted by Richard, *Philip Melanchthon*, 340.

45. Quoted by Richard, *Philip Melanchthon*, 358.

46. Schaff, *History Vol. VII,* 311.

47. Quoted by Richard, *Philip Melanchthon* 372.

and Melanchthon, took on fierce criticism over his mishandling of Philip of Hesse's bigamous affair. In his later years, and as his health began to fail, Luther became increasingly irritable and ill-tempered. His gravest error during this point in his life came when he viciously attacked the Jewish people. Life for Melanchthon became more difficult after the loss of his good friend and colleague Luther; he came under fierce attack of fellow Lutherans for some of his doctrinal beliefs. We now turn our attention to John Calvin, one of the great second-generation reformers.

16

John Calvin

Second Generation Reformer

*"Calvin was twenty-five years younger than Luther and Zwingli and
had the great advantage of building on their foundation. He had less
genius but more talent. He was inferior to them as a man of action but
superior as a thinker and organizer. They cut the stone in the quarries,
he polished them in the workshop. They produced the new ideas, he
constructed them into a system. His was the work of Apollos rather
than of Paul; to water rather than to plant, God giving the increase."*[1]

—PHILIP SCHAFF

ONE OF THE REFORMATION giants, John Calvin, was among the second
generation of reformers—at the time of his birth, Martin Luther and
Ulrich Zwingli were already twenty-five years old. A theologian, author,
and pastor, he was the primary figure in the development of the systematic theology, which came to be known as Calvinism, and included the
doctrines of the sovereignty of God and predestination in the salvation
of humanity. His elucidation of the Christian faith was expounded in his
Institutio Christianae Religionis (*Institutes of the Christian Religion*) in
1536 and elaborated upon in subsequent editions. Raised as a Catholic,
he broke ranks with the Roman Catholic church somewhere between
1529 and 1533. He was a prolific writer, and in addition to *Institutes*,

1. Schaff, *History Vol. VIII*, 257–8.

he wrote commentaries on most of the books of the Bible, some thirteen hundred letters, as well as other theological works. While born in
France, he fled to Basel Switzerland as a young man to escape violence
against the Protestant Christians in that country. In 1536 he was invited
to join the Reformation movement in Geneva.

His Early Years

Calvin was born July 10, 1509, in Noyon, a town in Picardy, northern
France, where he spent the first fourteen years of his life. His parents, Gérard and Jeanne Cauvin, who had five children who grew to maturity—
three sons and two daughters—were of middle-class standing. Gérard,
who was employed by the Noyan cathedral, had ambitions for his three
sons to enter the priesthood. We know little of John's childhood, save the
fact that he was given an ecclesiastical charge in the cathedral of Noyon
when he was about twelve years old. He also benefited from a wealthy and
influential family, the Montmors, who made it possible for him to attend
the Collège de la Marche.

At age fourteen, John, the third son, attended the Collège de la
Marche of the University of Paris for the priesthood. Here he learned
Latin from one of the great teachers of the time, Mathurin Cordier. In
John's first class with him, Cordier stated to his students that the first
lesson they must learn is to love Jesus Christ. John was surprised, as most
academics frowned on such sentimentalism. He was to learn that Cordier
meant what he said and was reformation-minded, though not a reformer.
Much later in a book dedication, Calvin would write of Cordier, "I was so
helped by you that whatever progress I have since made I gladly ascribe
to you."[2] Upon completing his course there, he studied philosophy at
the Collège de Mantaigu, also part of the University of Paris. He received
his Master of Arts in 1528.

His father had a change of heart regarding his desire for John to become a theologian and in 1528, enrolled him at the University of Orléans,
where he engaged in the study of law. Later in life Calvin writes, "When I
was as yet a very little boy, my father had destined me to be for the study
of theology. But afterward, when he considered that the legal profession
commonly raised those who followed it to wealth, this prospect induced

---

2. Quoted by Parker, *John Calvin*, 23.

him suddenly to change his purpose."[3] After Orléans, he enrolled in the University of Bourges in 1529. By the time he completed his study of law, he was bright enough to stand in at times for the doctor professors themselves. Upon earning his licentiate in law by 1532, he returned to Paris and subsequently authored his first book, a commentary on Seneca's *De Clementia*, a work that garnered relatively little attention from other scholars.

His Conversion and Growth as a Christian

Sometime around 1532–1534, Calvin converted to the evangelical faith and shortly thereafter surrendered his clerical benefices and the income that helped him carry out his studies. It is not precisely certain when he began hearing of Luther's convictions, but he was surely thinking about them from the time they became public. Indeed, he would later come out with his own reformed views on the church. Calvin had made friends with reform-minded individuals such as Sucquet (a protégé of Erasmus), Melchior Wolmar, Nicolas Cop, and Pierre Robert and studied Greek with them. During this period, Calvin was not only powerfully influenced by ideas of church reform, but he would himself be converted, possibly under the influence of Robert. Calvin held that, generally, individuals are "converted little by little to God, and by stages."[4] However, his personal conversion seemed to be more of a crisis than of gradation as noted many years later in his *Commentary on the Psalms* (1557): "And first, since I was too obstinately devoted to the superstitions of Popery to be easily extricated from so profound an abyss of mire, God by a sudden conversion subdued and brought my mind to a teachable frame which was more hardened in such matters than might have been expected from one at my early period of life."[5] Elsewhere, he retrospectively describes his crisis experience as follows: "My mind being now prepared for serious attention, I at length perceived, as if light had broken in upon me, in what a stye [sic] of error I had wallowed, and how much pollution and impurity I had thereby contracted. Being exceedingly alarmed at the misery into which I had fallen, and much more at that which threatened me in the view of eternal death, I, as in duty bound, made it my first business to

---

3. Quoted by Gordon, *Calvin*, 1.

4. Collinson, *The Reformation*, 88.

5. Calvin, *Writings on Pastoral Piety*, 59.

betake myself to Thy way, condemning my past life, not without groans and tears."[6]

Calvin began to grow as a Christian straightaway:

> Having thus received some taste and knowledge of true god-
> liness, I was immediately inflamed with so intense a desire to
> make progress therein, that although I did not altogether leave
> off other studies, I yet pursued them with less ardour. I was quite
> surprised that before a year had elapsed, all who had any desire
> after purer doctrine were continually coming to me to learn,
> although I myself was as yet but a mere novice . . . whilst my one
> great object was to live in seclusion without being known, God
> so led me about through different turnings and changes, that
> he never permitted me to rest in any place, until, in spite of my
> natural disposition, he brought me forth to public notice.[7]

Though brought to conversion directly or indirectly through Luther's writings, Calvin was not destined to meet him face to face. One senses in a later letter Calvin's wistful desire: "Would that I could fly to you, that I might even for a few hours enjoy the happiness of your society . . . but seeing that it is not granted to us on earth, I hope that shortly it will come to pass in the kingdom of God. Adieu, most renowned sir, most distinguished minister of Christ, and my ever-honored father."[8]

Calvin Becomes a Fugitive

Calvin returned to Paris from Orléans in 1533, where religious tensions emerged. Nicolas Cop, the rector of College Royal, preached against the Roman Catholic Church, provoking a strong reaction from the faculty. Being a close friend of Cop, Calvin was implicated in the umbrage and was driven into hiding. In the following year, some ill-advised Lutherans posted vitriolic attacks on placards in major French cities, including the Cathedral of Notre Dame in Paris. They condemned the Catholic mass as an abuse of the Holy Supper of our Lord. Two hundred arrests were made, and at least thirty-five executions were carried out. Etienne la Forge, a merchant with whom Calvin had lodged temporarily, was among those martyred, as well as one of Calvin's brothers.

6. Calvin, *John Calvin*, 114.

7. Calvin, *John Calvin*, 26–7.

8. Calvin, *Letters*, 442.

This was likely one of the low points in Calvin's life. His father had died in disgrace, suspected of mismanaging church funds, and his brother Charles was excommunicated from the Catholic church. His publication on Seneca caused no sensation at all. By 1533 he was a fugitive, suspected of being a heretic, and Queen Marguerite of Navarre warned him to stay away from her court. In 1534, using the alias Martianus Lucianius, he fled France on horseback with friend Louis du Tillet and his two servants. They stopped for the night at Metz near the German border. One of the servants realized that neither Calvin nor du Tillet would be willing to backtrack into France, so in the night, he stole their money and fled on one of the horses back to France.

Now Calvin, at age twenty-five, had no country, no job, and no money. He continued his rather aimless wanderings and arrived sometime in January of 1535 in Basel, Switzerland, a city won to the Reformation by Oecolampadius, Zwingli's friend and Erasmus' collaborator. An elderly Erasmus also lived here, plus reformers Wolfgang Capito, Sebastian Munster, Guillaume Farel, and Robert. Here Robert worked on a new French translation of the Bible for the Waldensian Christians, for which Calvin wrote the preface.

Calvin's Institutes of the Christian Religion

In March 1536, Calvin completed his first draft of the *Christian Institutes* in Latin and had it published by Platter and Lasius, printers in Basel. The *Institutes* were an *apologia pro fide*, a clear statement of the doctrinal position of the evangelicals, "A plea for the new views as well as their elaboration in the form of what is believed, and what is to be believed."[9] The purpose for the *Institutes* is expressed in his French edition of 1541 as follows: "Although the teaching contained in holy Scripture is perfect and cannot be added to, since there our Lord has chosen to display the infinite treasures of his wisdom, nevertheless someone who is not well trained in it needs a certain amount of guidance and direction in order to know what to look for, what mistakes to avoid and what path he may safely keep to; that way he will be sure of attaining the goal to which the Holy Spirit is calling him."[10] Opinions differ as for whom the *Institutes* were written. Philip Schaff, for example, argues that it "is not a book for

9. Dillenberger, from "An Introduction to John Calvin," in Calvin, *John Calvin*, 3.
10. Quoted by Rich, "Calvin's Theology."

the people . . . but it is a book for scholars of all nations, and had a deeper and more lasting effect upon them than any work of the Reformers."[11] Perhaps it depends on which edition one is referring to. The 1541 edition was clearly written for the common people in everyday French as Calvin distinctly indicates, whereas the final version swelled to four books and eighty chapters and became a more complex theological text of the Reformation.

In 1521 Melanchthon published his *Loci communes,* treatises on cardinal doctrines threaded through the overarching doctrine of salvation by faith in Christ alone. Zwingli wrote a concise statement in his *Commentarius de vera et falsa religione* in 1525, and in 1534 Farel wrote an even briefer work for French speakers in his *Sommaire.* Thus, Calvin's work was not the first such statement, but it was by far the most thorough. In the *Institutes,* Calvin wished to present the true way to religion and godliness in the most straightforward language he could muster, the sum of doctrine being contained almost entirely in two parts: 1) the knowledge of God and, 2) knowledge of ourselves. Regarding the volatile matter of the Sacraments, Calvin saw them as an outward sign by which the Lord represents His goodwill toward us, that is, a testimony of God's grace, declared to us by an outward symbol, the sole office of the Sacraments being to turn our eyes to behold God's promises, as perceptible to more senses than our ears alone.

Calvin claimed that the Church of the Middle Ages, for all its supposed orthodoxy, represented a grave departure from biblical theology's spirit and truth in the first centuries of the Church. Roman Catholic leaders said that the Church must have a visible form and supreme hierarchy from the pope, down. Calvin insisted that the Church could lack a visible form and, when visible, could be known by the holy activity growing out of its holy being. Though Calvin wrote a theology that covered every doctrine and church practice, he is often best known for his teachings regarding salvation and predestination. He agreed wholeheartedly that it was a horrible decree. However, He believed that since God foreknew the final fate of humanity when he created them, the fate of each was also decreed by Him: "Again I ask: whence does it happen that Adam's fall irremediably involved so many peoples, together with their infant offspring, in eternal death unless because it so pleased God? Here their

11. Schaff, *History Vol. VIII,* 330.

tongues, otherwise so loquacious, must become mute. The decree is dreadful indeed, I confess."[12]

Augustine had developed this general idea centuries before. Calvin would not be pressed to hypothesize regarding exact percentages of humankind who are elect; he varied his estimates from a habitual estimate of one in a hundred to one in twenty, or even one in five (after a fine dinner with no indigestion). He was also wary of claiming that people could be sure of their own election, much less of anyone else's. Calvin relentlessly skewered, albeit namelessly, those who disagreed with him on such doctrines.

It is likely a moot subject whether Luther's theology of predestination was as radical as was Calvin's or whether he perhaps softened a little during his later years. However, there is an interesting letter Luther wrote to a stranger on July 20, 1528. This stranger apparently had grave fears regarding God's sovereignty, and if God was totally sovereign, whether he would be elected to salvation. Luther wrote,

> Although the Almighty knows everything, and no one can go against the decrees of His will, still it is His earnest desire, nay command, decreed from all eternity that all men should be partakers of everlasting joy, as is clearly seen from Ezekiel 28:23. Seeing He desires the salvation of sinners who swarm beneath heaven's lofty vault, why will you with your foolish thoughts prompted by Satan separate yourself from them, thereby cutting yourself off from the grace of God? And consider that God Almighty created and elected us, not to damnation but to everlasting life, even as the angels in the first sermon proclaimed to the shepherds on the field. . . . Hence one can see from the Scriptures how great is God's mercy and these and such like thoughts can enable him to form an opinion as to God's foreseeing, and then there is no occasion for a man to torture himself, nor would it avail even were he to worry his flesh from his bones.[13]

In his later years, Luther rebelled against even discussing predestination's confusing arguments. He stated, "When a man begins to discuss predestination, the temptation is like an inextinguishable fire; the more he disputes, the more he despairs. . . . The discussion of predestination should be wholly avoided. . . . I forget all that Christ and God are when I

12. Calvin, *Institutes*, 955–6.
13. Luther, *Letters of Martin Luther*, 177.

get to thinking about this matter and come to believe that God is a villain
... we scrutinize mysteries which ought to be adored."[14]

Farel Invites Calvin to Geneva

After about a year in Basel and after his publication of *Institutes*, Calvin set out with his friend du Tillet for Italy (1536). At this time, Calvin
appeared to have no thoughts of being a pastor or spiritual leader. He
seemed to see himself as a scholar and writer, but he needed sponsorship
to survive. Princess Renée, Duchess of Ferrara, gave him asylum in Italy
and he, "made a deep and permanent impression on her."[15] After two
months, Calvin was back in France. He went to Noyon, his hometown,
and from there he headed to Strassburg with a few family members. His
apparent plan was to partner with Martin Bucer, whom he respected as
a mentor. The presence of French troops forced them to detour, and they
had to pass through Geneva, considered a medium-sized city at this time
but very small by today's standards.

Calvin arrived in Geneva in July 1536, only two months after the
city council had taken an oath to live "by the holy law of the gospel."
But by no means did the city come to this conclusion easily or quickly.[16] Guillaume (William) Farel, a fanatical evangelical, had entered this
Roman Catholic city and began preaching in the homes of the few who
embraced Reformation teachings. On October 3, 1532, Farel was arrested
and brought before the city council. One council cleric shouted, "Come
thou, filthy devil, art thou baptized? Who invited you hither? Who gave
you authority to preach?" Farel denied all charges, and boldly replied,
"I have been baptized in the name of the Father, the Son, and the Holy
Ghost, and I am not a devil. I go about preaching Christ, who died for our
sins and rose for our justification." One of the councilors shouted, "He
has blasphemed; we need no further evidence; He deserves to die." Upon
this, the assembly shouted, "Away with him to the Rhone: Kill the Lutheran dog."[17] Club wielding attackers chased him out of town, but he sent
other reformers covertly into the city. Antoine Froment, a preacher from
the Dauphine arrived on November 3 and began gathering evangelicals

---

14. Luther, *Table Talk: Conversations with Luther*, 135–7.
15. Schaff, *History Vol. III*, 343.
16. Steinmetz, *Calvin*, 9–10.
17. Quoted by Schaff, *History Vol. VIII*, 243–4.

around him. On New Year's Day of 1533, he preached against the pope, priests, and monks, accusing them of being false prophets. The bishop's council commanded him to cease immediately and he was forced by the police to flee. He eventually left but returned time and again aided by his colleagues Farel, Pierre Viret, and Calvin.[18]

Realizing the opposition to Roman Catholicism was proliferating, in July 1533, Catholic bishop Pierre de la Baume appealed to Duke Charles III of Savoy, pleading for military intervention. The Duke intended to take over Geneva completely, but Geneva declared a state of siege and razed all buildings outside city walls to eliminate military shelters and covert military approaches. Intense battles took place between October 1535 and March 1536, but Geneva stood firm. Finally, the army of Bern again came to the rescue in January 1536, and by the end of March, Savoy fortresses surrendered.[19]

By this time, new syndics had been voted into the Geneva city council, which gave the evangelicals a clear majority. Farel and Viret engaged in debates with the Catholics and were declared victorious in August of 1535. On May 24, 1536, all Genevan citizens were assembled and required to swear to live "according to the new reformation of the faith as it is preached."[20] Canons, nuns, Dominicans, and Franciscans were given the choice of either evacuating the city or attending the evangelical services.

At this precise time, the evangelical du Tillet shared with Farel the presence of a brilliant twenty-seven-year-old theologian who happened to be passing through Geneva for Strassburg. Calvin had intended to stay overnight, but, notes Calvin, "Providence had decreed otherwise."[21] Farel rushed down to Calvin's lodgings at the Hotel De'Ours bound and determined that Calvin would not escape. Farel was a stumpy little man, weak in constitution but mighty in voice; his pale face brightened by flashing eyes and a beard of fiery crimson. Thus, under these circumstances, Calvin returned in 1536 to Geneva and emerged as the new leader in the Reformation movement.

In later writings, Calvin stated that when he first refused his request, Farel threatened him. He puts it this way:

18. Schaff, *History Vol. VIII*, 253.

19. Spitz, *The Protestant Reformation*, 206.

20. Spitz, *The Protestant Reformation*, 207.

21. Schaff, *History Vol. III*, 347.

Farel, who burned with an extraordinary zeal to advance the gospel, immediately strained every nerve to detain me. And after learning that my heart was set upon devoting myself to private studies, for which I wished to keep myself free from other pursuits, and finding that he gained nothing by entreaties, he proceeded to utter the imprecation that God would curse my retirement and the tranquility of the studies which I sought if I should withdraw and refuse to help when the necessity was so urgent. By this imprecation I was so terror-struck that I gave up the journey I had undertaken; but sensible of my natural shyness and timidity, I would not tie myself to any particular office.[22]

Consequently, a cause finally arose to tie Calvin down to one location, and through him, the reformers were eventually to gain a strong foothold in Geneva. He began his labors on September 5, 1536, by advancing a course of lectures on the Epistles of Paul as well as other New Testament books, delivered in the Church of St. Peter. About a year later, in 1537, he was elected a pastor and doctor in the church. Geneva, the city where Calvin was obliged to settle, was on a lake—a fair-sized city in those days with ten thousand inhabitants and walls like a fortress. It was primarily a middle-class society. The government was rather complex. First, there was a quadrumvirate, the four Syndics elected each year by the commune, the general assembly of male citizens. The Syndics led the Petit Conseil, made up of twenty-five members, and this was the central administrative body. The Deux Cents—the Council of Two Hundred— was a lesser administrative body which met monthly to discuss relevant legislation. The government would eventually have implications upon the efforts of Calvin and his company of evangelicals.[23]

Calvin's First Geneva Period

In 1536, then, Calvin took up residence in Geneva and along with Farel set course to reorient the Swiss city to the Protestant movement. And Geneva was indeed in need of a moral compass and government based on the evangelical Reformation. Schaff describes the people of Geneva as follows: "The Genevese were a lighthearted joyous people, fond of public amusements, dancing, singing, masquerades, and revelries. Reckless gambling, drunkenness, adultery, blasphemy, and all sorts of vice

22. Quoted by Parker, *John Calvin*, 53.
23. Schaff, *History Vol. VIII*, 426.

abounded. Prostitution was sanctioned by the authority of the State and superintended by a woman called the *Reine du bordel*. The people were ignorant. The priests had taken no pains to instruct them and had set them a bad example."[24]

To resolve the people's evil activities, the Reformers drew up a Confession of Faith and Discipline to be adhered to by members of all the churches. The City Council approved the Confession, but a crisis emerged when the ministers prohibited those who did not sign it from coming to the Lord's Table for communion. Furthermore, members who performed open and noticeable sins were excluded from the church. The best method of disciplining and excommunicating, if needed, was thought to be the appointment of overseers in various quarters of the city who should report faults to the ministers.

Ambiguity arose in the enforcement of punishments. The reformers presented their items of polity to the Genevan government and told the Council that, "it will be your duty to consider if you must for long tolerate and leave unpunished such contempt and mockery of God and His Gospel."[25] Thus it was not expressly stated by whom the sinner was to be sentenced. The civil authority was undoubtedly involved in that it had a duty of enforcing punishment, not just for civil crimes but for perceived biblical disobedience.[26]

Submission by the people of Geneva to the church ministers and city council was temporary. The crisis came to a head when the ministers denied communion to those who did not sign the Confession. On Easter Day, 1538, the ministers preached in their churches but refused to serve communion. A mob rioted against the reformers, and the Council ordered them to leave the city within three days. Calvin and Farel rushed to Bern, then Zürich pleading for intervention. The Bern Council tried to intercede urging the magistrates of Geneva to administer less harsh discipline. While admitting that some of the blame may rest with Calvin for misplaced energy and a lack of tenderheartedness towards the unmanageable people, they believed his presence was still significant in the city. However, Geneva refused forgiveness, and the pair departed the city—sent into exile—on April 23, 1538. Calvin ended up in Basel before moving on to Strassburg, where he stayed for three years.

24. Schaff, *History Vol. VIII*, 353.

25. Reid, *Calvin: Theological Treatises*, 52-53.

26. Parker, *John Calvin*, 64.

Conclusion

No person, save Martin Luther, contributed more to the Protestant Reformation's advancement than Calvin. And while Luther is credited with
igniting the Reformation and is, along with Melanchthon, the founder
of a denomination, Calvin is the primary expounder of the Reformed
theological system—commonly known as Calvinism. Melanchthon
called him "the theologian." However, notes Richard Stauffer, among the
reformers, "there is not one who has been more bitterly discussed than
Calvin,"[27] often disdained as a theologian sans humanity. To a degree,
his austerity was evidenced during his first Genevan period. While this
chapter summarized Calvin's early life and contributions as theologian
and pastor up to his first residence in Geneva (1536–1538), the subsequent chapter focuses on his time spent in Strassburg and his second stay
in Geneva.

27. Stauffer, *The Humanness*, 19.

17

Calvin

Strassburg and Return to Geneva

"I always loved retirement and peace and I began to look for some hideout where I could be away from people; but far from gaining my desire, every retreat and hideaway became like a public school to me. In short, although my aim was always to live a private life without being known, God has so taken me about and whirled me around by various vicissitudes that He has never let me rest anywhere, but in spite of my natural inclination, has thrust me into the limelight and made me 'get into the game' as they say."[1]

— JOHN CALVIN

"Calvin was foreordained for Geneva, and Geneva for Calvin. Both have made 'their calling and election sure.' He found the city on Lake Leman 'a tottering republic, a wavering faith, a nascent Church.' He left it a Gibraltar of Protestantism, a school of nations and churches."[2]

— PHILIP SCHAFF

IN 1541 JOHN CALVIN returned to Geneva, as recently elected officials sought him out as the only man who could restore order to the church and troubled city. The city leaders responsible for his expulsion were all gone, and two of the new preachers could not deal with Geneva and

1. Quoted by Harbison, *The Christian Scholar*, 142.
2. Quoted by Schaff, *History Vol. VIII*, 348–9.

left. His friends Heinrich Bullinger and Guillaume Farel encouraged him to return to the city that had driven him out. Nevertheless, before he settled in Geneva, he spent three positive and fruitful years in Strassburg. Perhaps the happiest years of his life, it was here that he experienced the camaraderie of fellow reformers such as Martin Bucer, wrote his outstanding commentary on the book of Romans, and married a member of his congregation Idelette de Bure.

Calvin's Satisfying Stay in Strassburg (1538–1541)

Bucer and Wolfgang Capito dearly wanted Calvin to come to Strassburg as minister of the French Church and theology lecturer. He journeyed to confer with them but refused the initial invitation because his friend Farel was not included. However, Farel departed to lead a church in Neuchâtel and gave his assent to Calvin to go to Strassburg. As did Farel earlier, Bucer accused Calvin of possibly rejecting God's call and threatened him with God's wrath if he did not come. In early September 1538, he was welcomed to Strassburg with open arms by the leading church leaders.

Pastor and Professor

As he had done in Geneva, Calvin held the dual offices of pastor and professor of the Scriptures. He organized and pastored a Protestant congregation of French refugees, which numbered in excess of four hundred members. As their pastor, Calvin preached four times a week, held Bible classes, and equipped deacons to assist him in caring for the poor. Furthermore, summarizes Schaff, "He converted many Anabaptists. . . . He was consulted by magistrates on all important questions touching religion. He conscientiously attended to pastoral care, and took a kindly interest in every member of his flock. In this way he built up in a short time a prosperous church, which commanded the respect and admiration of the community of Strassburg."[3] In addition to his pastoral duties, Capito made it possible for Calvin to give public lectures, and Johann Sturm appointed him as a professor of the Scriptures at his Protestant college. The college had a theology department, and Calvin, in 1539, was appointed assistant professor of theology, lecturing on books of the Bible, including the Gospel of John and the Epistle to the Romans.

3. Schaff, *History Vol. VIII*, 369.

In his desire to pursue church unity and as an employed commissioner of the city and pastor of the Church of Strassburg, Calvin attended several public colloquies, conferences convened to heal the split between Catholics and Protestants caused by the Reformation. In 1539 he attended the first Colloquy at Frankfurt in a personal role to meet with Philip Melanchthon and pleaded the case for the persecuted Christians in France. In that same year, he attended a Colloquy at Worms, where he played a prominent part in the discussions and earned from Melanchthon and other Lutheran leaders the distinguished title of "the theologian." In 1541 Calvin attended the conference at Regensburg at the invitation of Melanchthon but was unhappy with Bucer and Melanchthon's passivity and left as soon as he had the chance—much to the dismay of both Bucer and Melanchthon.[4]

The Special Friendship of Calvin and Bucer

Reformers have been exposed to severe criticism over the centuries; however, notes Richard Stauffer, not one has been disparaged as much as Calvin.[5] Part of the criticism is pointed towards his personality, whereby he is branded as a markedly austere and judgmental individual—an assumption based not so much on the accounts of others as on his theology. Calvin himself admits he was shy and timid, perhaps what we would today call an introvert. However, in contrast to what Calvin's critics say, Stauffer suggests "that there were few men who developed as many friendships as he and who knew how to retain not only the admiration but also the personal affection of these friends."[6] Among his many friends was Bucer, with whom he nurtured a special relationship during his three years at Strassburg. It was Bucer who urged Calvin to perform his ministry in Strassburg in a manner similar to what Farel had done previously in Geneva. In Calvin's words, "I had decided to live in solitude without taking a public post until the fine servant of Jesus Christ, Martin Bucer, using a similar argument to that employed by Farel earlier, called me to another position."[7]

---

4. Schaff, *History Vol. VIII*, 381–4.

5. Stauffer, *The Humanness*, 19.

6. Stauffer, *The Humanness*, 47–8.

7. Quoted by Stauffer, *The Humanness*, 63.

Calvin lived first in the home of pastor Matthew Zell and his wife Katharina on his return to Geneva but also spent much time with the Bucers. At this time, he was only twenty-nine years old, and Bucer—eighteen years his senior—took on the role of mentor to him, almost a father figure. A sign of Bucer's high esteem for Calvin is reflected in this statement: "Calvin is a truly learned and singularly eloquent man, an illustrious restorer of a purer Christianity."[8] Perhaps it is going too far to attribute most of Calvin's later ideas of church structure to Bucer, but there can be no doubt that Bucer shared with Calvin his rich and interactive doctrine of the Church, his emphasis on love to one's neighbor, and belief that discipline was one of the central marks of a healthy church.

Calvin and the Lutheran Reformers

Calvin was very much aware of the Reformation movement transpiring in other parts of Europe through Martin Luther, Bucer, Melanchthon, Ulrich Zwingli, Oecolampadius, Bullinger, and others. He had close relationships with Melanchthon, Bucer, and Bullinger and, though he perhaps had less esteem for Oecolampadius and the now-deceased Zwingli, he read their writings. Calvin never met Luther in person but was in friendly contact with him through his works. Luther was near the end of his life and, notes Paul Henry, that he "was of one faith and of one mind with Calvin. He regarded him as a brother and viewed his doctrine as fitted to restore union to the distracted church. And as Luther inclined to Calvin, so did Calvin to Luther."[9] Like Zwingli, he did not consider Luther the only early reformer, nor the only one in God's church to be granted particular respect. However, it was unquestionable for Calvin that Luther was superior to Zwingli, against whom Calvin at first directed a sharp critique. Luther most likely read the 1539 edition of Calvin's *Institutes* and sent warm greetings to Calvin through Bucer: "Present my respectful greetings to Sturm and Calvin, whose books I have perused with singular pleasure."[10]

In the interest of helping resolve the Eucharistic controversy, Calvin wrote his *Little Treatise on the Lord's Supper* in 1540. When Luther read it, he stated, "If my opponents had done the like, we should soon have

8. Quoted by Schaff, *History Vol. VIII*, 272.

9. Henry, *The Life and Times*, 98–9.

10. Quoted by Schaff, *History Vol. VIII*, 272.

been reconciled, since it only needed that Oecolampadius and Zwinglius should have thus explained themselves, to prevent the [Lord's supper] controversy from proceeding to such lengths."[11] On Calvin's part, he wrote "I am so far from repudiating the Augsburg Confession, that I have willingly and gladly subscribed it, interpreting it as I am authorized to do. . . . Hence, if I do not greatly err, we are agreed, that the Supper of the Lord is no vain, dramatic representation of a spiritual feast, but that it truly imparts to us what it presents, and that holy hearts are nourished therein by the body and blood of Christ."[12]

Melanchthon was only twelve years older than Calvin and the two reformers had many points of contact; over time they developed an authentic and enduring relationship. Philip Schaff remarks that "Melanchthon, in sincere humility and utter freedom from jealousy even acknowledged the superiority of his younger friend as a theologian and disciplinarian."[13] During his stay at Strassburg, Melanchthon and Calvin had extensive conversations at multiple councils. Their first encounter was at Frankfurt in 1539, where they freely debated many of the urgent topics of the time, including worship, doctrine, and discipline. At one of the colloquies, Calvin expressed concern that Melanchthon was too quick to make concessions to opponents regarding matters of truth.[14] Following the colloquy at Regensburg, Calvin responded to Melanchthon's message with words of warm affirmation: "Would, indeed, as you observe, that we could oftener converse together were it only by letters. To you that would be no advantage; but to me, nothing in this world could be more desirable than to take solace in the mild and gentle spirit of your correspondence."[15] The friendship that these two leaders initiated during Calvin's brief stay at Strassburg extended for years beyond that time.

---

11. Quoted by Henry, *The Life and Times*, 98.

12. Quoted by Henry, *The Life and Times*, 99.

13. Schaff, *History Vol. VIII*, 386.

14. Schaff, *History Vol. VIII*, 388; Dillenberger in the "Introduction" in Calvin, *John Calvin*, 5.

15. Quoted by Schaff, *History Vol. VIII*, 390.

Calvin's Marriage

Perhaps it was the stress of life and his worsening health that motivated some of Calvin's friends—more specifically Farel and Bucer—to encourage him to consider marriage. He was willing, but in a May 1539 letter to his good friend Farel he wrote, "I am not of that crazy breed of lovers, who, stricken by the beauty of a woman, love even her faults. The only beauty which captivates me is that of a chaste, kind, modest, thrifty, patient woman, who I might finally hope would be attentive to my health."[16] He was not to be rushed into marriage and waited until he was over thirty before marrying.

Calvin had no idea that searching for a wife would be so problematic, taking almost two years. His first candidate, a woman of noble background, did not speak French, though she said she would learn a little. Calvin was also concerned about her wealth. He was a poor minister and felt she would be more accustomed to a lavish lifestyle. On February 6, 1540, he wrote to a pastor friend and stated, "A certain damsel of noble rank has been proposed to me, and with a fortune above my condition. Two considerations deterred me from that connection—because she did not understand our language, and because I feared she might be too mindful of her family and education."[17] Calvin commissioned his brother to ask the hand of another lady. March 10, 1540, was set as a possible wedding date, but this endeavor failed as well.

Then he recalled a widow named Idelette de Bure Stordeur, who was 31—about his age. She had attended his congregation and impressed Calvin with her attentive nursing of her dying husband and her care for her two children. Around August 10, he married de Bure, the widow of a former Anabaptist who had changed his views to the Reformed position before his death. Calvin found in her what he desired in a wife and called her "the excellent companion of my life . . . the ever-faithful assistant of my ministry . . . a rare woman."[18] Idelette gave birth to one child, Jacques, who did not live. While Calvin and his wife experienced a happy marriage, it was short-lived. After nine years of wedlock, his wife was taken from him in early March 29, 1549, after a prolonged illness. Calvin never remarried, remaining a widower for the final fifteen years of his life.

---

16. Quoted by Stauffer, *The Humanness*, 35.

17. Quoted by Schaff, *History Vol. VIII*, 415.

18. Quoted by Schaff, *History Vol. VIII*, 416.

Calvin's Return to Geneva

While Calvin's brief stay in Strassburg was satisfying and decidedly beneficial to the Kingdom, he never forgot Geneva—and Geneva never forgot Calvin. However, like a spurned lover, he had no proclivity to return
to the city and church he loved so dearly, and only by the identifiable
indications of God's sovereign will would he do so. He refused call after
call, even from his dearest of friends and associates—Bucer, Farel, and
Bullinger all pleaded with him.

His eventual return and his influence in Geneva may very well have
been instigated in 1539 when he was invited to respond to Cardinal Jaco-
po Sadoleto, a reform-minded Catholic who glimpsed a possible opportunity to return Geneva to the Catholic fold. Sadoleto invited himself to
visit the city and addressed a letter to the people of Geneva, urging them
to return to the faith of their fathers—Roman Catholicism. The Genevans
could think of no one who could adequately respond to Sadoleto, so they
called upon Calvin to compose a rejoinder. He responded with a public
letter, *Reply to Sadoleto*, which opposed the historic Catholic church and
defended the reformed beliefs and principles. It was considered an apologetic masterpiece, and the respect for Calvin in the city was intensified.

Later, in 1540, two deputies were sent to Strassburg to retrieve Calvin, and upon learning he was attending a colloquy between the Romanists and evangelicals at Worms, Louis Dufour followed him there. When
Dufour finally contacted him, he delivered a formal letter of invitation.
The letter read, in part, "On the part of our lesser, great and general councils, (which hereupon have strongly admonished us,) we pray you very
earnestly that you would transfer yourself hitherward to us, and return to
your old place and former ministry; and we hope, with the help of God,
that this shall be a great benefit, and fruitful for the increase of the holy
Evangel, seeing that our people greatly desire you among us, and will
conduct themselves toward you in such sort, that you shall have occasion
to rest content."[19] Calvin gave the suitors only a little hope, though he
was moved to tears by the displays of esteem and loyalty. In a lengthy letter of response, he included the statement, "I can neither relinquish nor
delegate such a vocation, but am constrained to await the issue, and see
what success the Lord will give. For although of myself I can do nothing,
it ought to suffice me that I am set here in this place [Strassburg] by the

19. Calvin, *Letters of John Calvin*, 214.

will of the Lord, on purpose to employ me in whatsoever he would have me to apply myself."[20]

But by the summer of 1541, it was agreed that Strassburg should lend Calvin to Geneva on the condition of his return, though the Senate of Geneva "expressed the determination to keep Calvin permanently in their city, where he could be as useful to the Church universal as at Strassburg."[21] On these terms, he returned on September 13, and, this time, he had a full escort and a wagon in which to transport his family and possessions. One of the better houses available was loaned to him furnished, and he was offered an adequate stipend, plus twelve strikes of corn and two casks of wine. Calvin was glad to learn that Peter Viret, a valued colleague, would be assisting him for a period of time in restoring the church.

Upon his return to Geneva, Calvin was determined to be more conciliatory and less churlish. He wrote to Oswald Myconius in Basel: "Indeed I value the public peace and cordial agreement among ourselves so highly, that I lay restraint upon myself: those who are opposed to us are themselves compelled to award this praise to me. This feeling prevails to such an extent, that, from day to day, those who were once open enemies have become friends; others I conciliate by courtesy, and I feel that I have been some measure successful, although not everywhere and on all occasions."[22]

Calvin's Activities During His Return to Geneva

In the years to follow, Calvin seemed to struggle with workaholism, and no doubt, his health problems—headaches, fevers and chills, indigestion, to name a few—were partly due to this, leading to premature death. He held the multiple offices and activities of professor, preacher, pastor, school superintendent, writer, church administrator, and leader of the Reformation movement in Western Europe. He had, notes Schaff, "an amazing power for work notwithstanding his feeble health."[23] Furthermore, "He indulged in no recreation except a quarter or half an hour's walk in his room or garden after meals, and an occasional game of quoits

20. Calvin, *Letters of John Calvin*, 215.
21. Schaff, *History Vol. VIII*, 434.
22. Calvin, *Letters of John Calvin*, 315.
23. Schaff, *History Vol. VIII*, 444.

or *la clef* with intimate friends. He allowed himself very little sleep, and for at least ten years he took but one meal a day, alleging his bad digestion."[24]

Debates will continue regarding whether Calvin was an obsessive controller, a spiritual dictator, or a narrow-minded leader—but the benefits his presence brought to Geneva should not be ignored. He supported a smarter and more effective infrastructure, including building quality hospitals and an efficient sewage system. He supported new industries in the city and was a powerful advocate of a universal education system for children and adults. The sick and poor were cared for; in fact, Calvin cared so much he had to be restrained by the Council from visiting plague victims because the church needed him so.

Calvin also continued to edit and polish his *Institutes,* publishing his Latin version in 1559 and his final French text in 1560. His last edition consisted of eighty chapters divided into four books, as opposed to twenty-four chapters of the 1550 version. He preached daily through both Old and New Testaments and, based on his exegetical studies, authored commentaries on almost every book of the Bible. In addition, he taught theology three days per week. Though he prepared carefully, he preached extemporaneously directly from the Hebrew and Greek Testaments. Preaching the Word of God was considered a wondrously sacred task. He felt so strongly that a preacher must be an example to the flock that he wrote, "It would be better for him to break his neck going up into the pulpit, if he does not take pains to be the first to follow God."[25]

The society of refugees in Geneva seemed to value his sermons more than native Genevans. It was this group that hired a professional scribe to transcribe the sermons for publication. They located a French refugee named Denis Reguenier, who had evolved a remarkable form of shorthand, which enabled him to record the sermons of approximately six thousand words in an hour while Calvin delivered them. He faithfully did this year-round in both freezing and steaming hot sanctuaries. When the sermon was completed in shorthand, he transcribed them into a longhand manuscript with other scribes' help.[26]

Like other reformers, Calvin recognized the importance of education. Consequently, the most enduring and crowning achievement of Calvin—beyond his *Institutes*—was his reform of the educational system

---

24. Schaff, *History Vol. VIII,* 444.

25. Quoted by Parker, *Calvin's Preaching,* 40.

26. Parker, *Calvin's Preaching,* 65–6.

in Geneva and the founding of the Geneva Academy. He patterned the
school after Sturm's *gymnasium* or academy of Strassburg. The school
had two parts. The *Schola privata* was for children up to about age sixteen. Subjects included French, Latin, writing, Greek, history, grammar,
the classics, and dialectic. The *Schola publica* served as the university
(known today as the University of Geneva) and offered subjects such as
theology, Hebrew, Greek, and the liberal arts. Faculty members included
Theodore Beza, Viret, and Calvin himself. The Geneva Academy became
a bastion for Calvinist theology as well as a training institute for countless
reformed pastors and missionaries to other parts of Europe.

His close companion and biographer Theodore Beza describes
more specifically what he calls the "ordinary labors" of Calvin: "During
the week he preached every alternate and lectured every third day, on
Thursday he met with the Presbytery, and on Friday attended the ordinary Scripture meeting, called 'The Congregation.' Where he had his full
share of the duty. He also wrote most learned Commentaries on several
books of Scripture, besides answering the enemies of religion, and maintaining an extensive correspondence on matters of importance."[27] Beza
concludes that "Any one who reads these attentively, will be astonished
how one man could be fit for labors so numerous and so great."[28]

Calvin and the Civil Government

While Calvin was often consulted on Geneva's affairs and his advice usually followed, he never occupied a civil office of the city-state; nor was
he a citizen of Geneva until 1559. Geneva had a tumultuous history of
conflict, especially the years preceding Calvin's return to the city. Three
parties vied for control of the city—the bishop, the House of Savoy, and
the citizens themselves.[29] There are, of course, widely varying opinions
regarding blame for the conflicts involving the governing bodies, Calvin,
and dissenting individuals or groups. No matter the explanations, let it
be said that no blame falls wholly on any one party. The governing bodies
had much more authority indeed over church matters than do governments in the West today. As for Calvin, he was very zealous, excitable,
and determined that if God's Word enjoined some principle, everyone

27. Beza, *The Life of John Calvin*, 28–9.

28. Beza, *The Life of John Calvin*, 29.

29. Walker, *A History*, 469.

claiming Christian faith must obey it. The dissenters disliked and feared such authority, claiming it denied them their liberties and pleasure.

The Genevan government, under the influence of Calvin, controlled the personal lives of the citizens and was extremely zealous in keeping them in line morally and ethically by the use of tortures, excommunications, banishments, and executions. Between 1542 and 1546 alone, fifty-eight citizens were executed for crimes such as heresy, adultery, blasphemy, and witchcraft, and seventy-six were banished from the city. It should be noted that while Calvin cannot be personally blamed for all these judgments, he did not, in most cases, use vigorous means to prevent them. However, it is also true that, at the time, similar punishments for such offenses were not unknown in other parts of Europe.

There were two parties among Calvin's enemies that detested his system of discipline. The Patriots belonged to longstanding families of Geneva who opposed the new discipline and sought liberty without law. The Libertines formed the contrasting—indeed extreme—opposite of the austere strictness of Calvin. Both factions contested the infringement on personal freedom and fondness for pleasures and licentiousness; many followers of both parties held significant administrative and leadership positions in Geneva. Confrontations between Calvin and these parties took many forms—from verbal abuse, libel, and threats on the part of the insubordinate factions to excommunication, execution, and torture on behalf of Calvin and the church authorities.

A key example of Calvin's influence in the city was the instance of Pierre Ameaux, a member of the Council of Two Hundred and one who hated Calvin and his theology. At one point, he indulged in too much alcohol and accused Calvin of teaching false doctrine and being a very bad man. The Little Council tried him and sentenced him to pay a fine of sixty crowns and make public acknowledgment of his fault. When the case was then referred to the Two Hundred, they reduced the sentence to merely making an apology to Calvin in their presence. Calvin immediately was up in arms and demanded a harsher sentence, claiming that he must make reparations because his attack was really against the Word of God. Calvin refused to ascend the pulpit again until he did so. A near-riot ensued, and the Two Hundred finally caved in somewhat by sentencing the man to parade through Genevan streets in his shirt, carrying a torch, kneeling at specific locations, and begging God's pardon.

While Ameaux's punishment amounted to mere humiliation, other transgressors were committed to much harsher treatment. On June 27,

1547, a threatening letter was found on Calvin's pulpit. It read, "Gross hypocrite, thou and thy companions will gain little by your pains if you do not save yourselves by flight, nobody shall prevent your overthrow, and you will curse the hour when you left your monkery. Warning has already given that the devil and his renegade priests were come hither to ruin everything. But after people have suffered long they avenge themselves. . . . We will not have so many masters. Mark well what I say."[30] The Libertine Jacques Gruet was arrested for the action, and several incriminating writings were located in his home, including letters critical of Calvin as well as pages in his handwriting that ridiculed the Scriptures and blasphemed Christ. Under prolonged torture, Gruet confessed that he had declared the Mosaic Law to possess only human and relative power, not divine, that he had declared that laws were made at man's whim, that he had been in contact with a foreign power, that he had endeavored to subvert Church order, that he had written in a counterfeit hand the letter in the pulpit, and that he had written letters persuading others to lewdness. The court condemned him to death, and he was beheaded on July 26 of the same year. It was only later that a workman allegedly found in Gruet's former home pathological and blasphemous ravings written against both Christ and the Virgin Mary, the Prophets, the Apostles, and all the Scriptures.[31]

Ami Perrin was a military chief, a prominent member of the Patriotic faction, and at one point, one of the most influential figures in Geneva. Perrin, his wife Francesco, and other family members shared an intense hatred for Calvin and his influence. They were cited for dancing and revelry at a party attended by many Genevan notables, and subsequently, Perrin, his wife, and her father were imprisoned for the offenses. Initially, Perrin refused to appear before the Consistory,[32] pretending that the story was fanciful. Calvin sent Perrin a letter stating that the only reason he pursues such issues is that he held the Law of his Master so much at heart that he would not be moved from it with a good conscience for any human in existence. This missive may have convinced Perrin because eventually, he made an apology to the Consistory.

---

30. Quoted by Schaff, *History Vol. VIII*, 502.

31. Schaff, *History Vol. VIII*, 502–3.

32. The Consistory was an ecclesiastical tribunal that exercised church discipline over Genevans by summoning and rebuking them for sins such as adultery, gambling, blasphemy, and cursing.

The most notable incident is that of Michael Servetus, the brilliant Spanish physician. Servetus had been a secretary to Emperor Charles' chaplain, but when he fled France for his evangelical convictions, he became a medical doctor. During this period, he developed anti-trinitarian views and was condemned to death by the Roman Catholic Church in Vienne, France. Escaping execution in that country, he eventually appeared in Geneva, where by now he was considered a heretic by Catholics and Protestants alike. He was eventually arrested and interrogated for his false beliefs. The Council of Two Hundred sentenced Servetus to be burned for his heresies, but Calvin and the other ministers petitioned the court to choose the less painful sentence of beheading. The plea was refused, and on October 27, 1533, Servetus was put to death by burning.

The execution drew controversy in Protestantism for imposing the death sentence for heresy and, notes Bruce Shelley, later generations sometimes remembered Calvin as "the man who burned Servetus."[33] Calvin defended the death penalty for heresy and wrote, "Whoever shall now contend that it is unjust to put heretics and blasphemers to death will knowingly and willingly incur their very guilt. This is not laid down on human authority; it is God who speaks and prescribes a perpetual rule for his church."[34] Calvin's petition for the Christian's duty to punish heresy by death is drawn primarily from the laws of Moses against blasphemy and idolatry. Furthermore, the prevailing philosophy of the day stated that God ordains laws and those who administer them; rulers were ministers and servants of God and, as such, purportedly bore the authority not only of an earthly office but of the Lord by whom and for whom they execute their office.[35]

Calvin's Impact on Geneva

By 1555 the Libertines were defeated, and Calvin's position in Geneva was secure. His influence was increased, and his work progressed until he died in 1564: "The churches were well filled; the Word of God was preached daily; family worship was the rule; prayer and singing of Psalms never ceased; the whole city seemed to present the aspect of a community

---

33. Shelley, *Church History*, 278.
34. Quoted by Schaff, *History Vol. VIII*, 791.
35. Parker, *John Calvin*, 153.

of sincere, earnest Christians who practiced what they believed."[36] Geneva owes its moral genuineness to the discipline and Reformation of Calvin.[37] Drunkenness was outlawed, and taverns were closed for a period and converted into non-profit religious public houses where people had to bless the food before they ate. Among the banned activities were gambling, dancing, indecent songs, extravagance, immodest dress, jewelry and lace, and secular plays.

Almost fifty years after Calvin's death a German Lutheran by the name of Valentine Andreæ visited Geneva and reported finding a city closer to the ideals of a theocracy than he had seen anywhere in his travels: "I observed something great which I shall remember and desire as long as I live. There is in that place not only the perfect institute of a perfect republic, but, as a special ornament, a moral discipline, which makes weekly investigations into the conduct, and even the smallest transgressions of the citizens. . . . All cursing and swearing, gambling, luxury, strife, hatred, fraud, etc. are forbidden; while greater sins are hardly heard of. What a glorious ornament of the Christian religion is such a purity of morals!"[38]

Despite the Christian ideals evidenced by the citizens of Geneva, historians have not been able to deny the severity—indeed the brutality—of Calvin and the city he so influenced. A summary of some of the most conspicuous instances of discipline includes imprisonment of three men for laughing during a sermon, children punished for remaining outside the church during a sermon, men and women burned for doing witchcraft, and a young girl beheaded for striking her parents. Schaff notes that "this kind of legislation savors more of the austerity of old heathen Rome and the Levitical code than of the gospel of Christ, and that the actual exercise of discipline was often petty, pedantic, and unnecessarily severe."[39]

Conclusion

When Calvin died on May 27, 1564, he left a transformed Geneva and passed on a theological movement that helped shape the modern world. Calvinism eventually spread throughout continental Europe, to England

36. Schaff, *History Vol. VIII*, 516.
37. Schaff, *History Vol. VIII*, 517.
38. Quoted by Schaff, *History Vol. VIII*, 519.
39. Schaff, *History Vol. VIII*, 493.

and Scotland, and finally to North America. This chapter focused on his three-year stay in Strassburg and his return to Geneva, where he not only continued to refine and sharpen his theology but where he established his notion of a reformed church order that he had begun to develop in Strassburg. The final chapter highlights the final years of key reformers as they are removed from the scene and elucidates how Reformation leadership was passed on from one reformer to another.

18

The Close of an Era

"Few periods in the long history of Europe have had such a momentous impact upon the western world as the four decades lying between the years 1517 and 1559. It began when a very personal matter, Luther's struggle for a right relationship to God, became a popular cause. Its end was marked by an auspicious public event [Treaty of Cateau-Cambrésis], for Europe entered one of its rare interludes of peace."[1]

—LEWIS SPITZ

ACCORDING TO MOST HISTORIANS, the Protestant Reformation began in 1517 with the publication of Luther's *Ninety-five Theses* and ended anywhere between the Peace of Augsburg in 1555 to the Treaty of Westphalia in 1648. The Peace of Augsburg, also called the Augsburg Settlement, ended the struggle between the Protestants and Catholics and made for a legal division of Christianity in the Holy Roman Empire, giving rulers the privilege of choosing the official confession of their state. The Treaty of Westphalia ended the European religious conflicts, including the Thirty Years War. Philip Schaff identifies six great Continental Reformers who changed the world as Martin Luther, Philip Melanchthon, Ulrich Zwingli, Heinrich Bullinger, John Calvin, and Theodore Beza.[2] To this group, we add Martin Bucer and Guillaume Farel. In this chapter, we highlight the latter years of the key reformers

---

1. Spitz, *The Rise of Modern Europe*, 1.
2. Schaff, *History Vol. VIII*, 870.

as the age of the Reformation draws to a close, and they are removed from the scene. More specifically, we explain how leadership was passed on from one to another. For example, in Zürich, Bullinger succeeded Zwingli; Melanchthon continued the Lutheran movement after Luther passed; Beza followed Calvin in Geneva.

Zwingli Succeeded by Bullinger

Sometimes referred to as the third great reformer (after Luther and Calvin), Zwingli's impact on history is not quite as profound as that of the other two significant reformers. A central leader of the Reformation in German-speaking Switzerland and founder of the Swiss Reformed Church, Zwingli's legacy lives on in confessions of Reformed churches. Outside of Switzerland, however, no church claims him as a founder, and church historians have difficulties in assessing or even determining if there is such a thing as "Zwingliansm." Perhaps this is because it evolved under the leadership of Zwingli's successor Heinrich Bullinger, who adopted most of his theological premises and also in part to his premature death at age forty-seven. Ulrich Gäbler proposes that "Calvinism is inconceivable without the Zürich Reformation. Zwingli affected Calvinism through Bullinger and Calvin, and therefore he can be counted as one of the founders of Reformed Reformation."[3] Zwingli was killed in battle in 1531, part of an army that intended to defend Zürich against a coalition of Swiss Catholic forces. The council unanimously elected Bullinger as the preacher of the Great Minster, possibly at Zwingli's prior recommendation.[4]

However, while Bullinger succeeded Zwingli as chief pastor of the church in Zürich it was Calvin who became the primary leader of the Swiss Reformation after Zwingli's death.

Luther's Declining Years

As we have already noted, Martin Luther suffered ill health for years, and from around 1530 to his death in 1546, his health deteriorated even further. By the 1540s, his powers and constitution had diminished, and his failing health caused him to be more cantankerous in both his public

3. Gäbler, *Huldrych Zwingli*, 159.
4. Schaff, *History Vol. VIII*, 206.

discourse and his daily interactions. While his mind remained clear as ever, "his attacks on his critics were even more abusive, vulgar and hysterical than they had been."[5] He was short-tempered and harsh in his publications and public comments. His wife Katie, at one point, said, "Dear husband you are too rude," to which he replied, "They are making me to be rude."[6] Luther did not quietly fade into oblivion as he continued to be productive until his final days taking care of the affairs of the church, writing, preaching, teaching, and counseling. A third of his letters were written in his final years and in 1545 wrote his final polemic attack on the pope, a pamphlet titled *Against the Papacy at Rome, Founded by the Devil*. Luther preached his final sermon at Eisleben on February 15, 1546, three days before his death in the same town. Philip Melanchthon carried the Lutheran torch for another sixteen years after the passing of Luther.

James Kittelson concludes his biography of Luther by declaring that Luther was just as convicted in his beliefs in his latter days, as he was in his earlier years: "The words and deeds of the older Luther reflected his most deeply grounded convictions just as surely as did those of the young man. Building and defending the church—and doing so in the teeth of 'false brethren,' ignorant peasants, grasping politicians, and bitter enemies—was just as perilous an undertaking as defying pope and emperor. Whether rightly or wrongly, Luther kept to it. It is therefore not possible to speak well of the young man and cringe at the old man."[7]

Bucer's Difficult Years in England

Bucer was a leader in the Reformation movement and passionate about reconciling disagreements between reformers. He also envisioned healing the Catholic-Protestant division. Sadly, he was a victim of the type of conflict he sought to eradicate. In March 1547, his adopted city of Strassburg surrendered to the imperial forces of Charles V, who subsequently enforced Catholic rites and ceremonies throughout the empire. Bucer fought for concessions to the Protestants with little success, and on March 1, 1549, he was officially dismissed from the city. After twenty-five years of sacrificial service to the city, Bucer had to depart under cover of darkness. Melanchthon and Calvin offered Bucer sanctuary, but he chose

5. Green, *Luther*, 201.

6. Quoted by Smith, *The Life and Letters*, 407.

7. Kittelson, *Luther*, 300.

to accept an invitation from England. Thomas Cranmer welcomed Bucer and his friend Paul Fagius with full honors and was introduced to King Edward VI and the entire court.

It was a promising beginning as he took on the position of Professor of Divinity at the University of Cambridge. Unfortunately, his new colleagues tried to drag him into theological controversies, the very thing he tried to avoid. About the time the semester was to begin, Bucer's young protégé, Fagius, died unexpectedly. This was apparently a blow from which Bucer never fully recovered. He not only felt isolated from former friends but fell sick himself. He dragged himself to class for several months, then collapsed. His time in England was beset with illnesses including rheumatism, intestinal disorders, and quite likely tuberculosis.

Consequently, his years in England were unfulfilling for the most part. While his influence on the Church of England is minimal, his most significant impact was on the revision of the *Book of Common Prayer*. He died in 1551 at fifty-nine years of age. Six years after his death, Queen Mary had his body dug up along with his colleague Fagius and burned them along with their books.

Melanchthon—Final Years Without Luther

Melanchthon had never been quite the same after Luther, the backbone to which he had lent his brilliance, passed on. In the years following, he had developed close friendships with both Bucer and Calvin. Melanchthon was essentially a man of patience, compromise, gentleness, and humility. He eventually wearied of the incessant bitter wranglings and infighting of diets and synods. He tried desperately and wisely to establish a *corpus doctrinae*, an official body of doctrine—that is, a standing authority similar to a consistory. Years earlier, Luther had observed what a toll controversy took on his colleague and friend: "Melanchthon is lighter than I and therefore more easily moved if things don't go his way. I am heavier and stupider and am not so much affected by things I cannot remedy . . . I rough hew and Melanchthon planes."[8]

Melanchthon had worked himself almost to death. In early April 1560, he went to Leipzig to verify the recipients of stipends. On the return journey, he grew very sick with a severe cold that worsened into a raging fever which lingered. Though extremely weak, he continued to

---

8. Luther, *Table Talk: Conversations*, 200–1.

teach at the university until Easter, and even labored at home, attended an academic senate, and wrote letters. On Good Friday, he led devotions for foreign students and planned to do so again on Easter morning but could not. As his condition worsened, his one focused prayer was for the unity of the Church. His favorite Scripture passages were read to him. As his breathing grew labored, he was asked if he needed anything; he answered in a whisper: "Nothing but heaven." With hundreds of his students holding a vigil outside his home, he died on the evening of April 19, 1560.[9]

Before Melanchthon passed away, some Lutherans were condemning him as having besmirched the pure theology of Luther. Melanchthon's final years were likely not very satisfying or fulfilling ones. He did enjoy a fairly close friendship with Calvin, which may be another reason some Lutherans turned against him. Lutherans and those of Calvin's Reformed faith were to stand at loggerheads on several critical issues for many decades to come, and it would be a costly schism. Catholics would use it to make inroads and gain back ground as these two groups struggled for supremacy.

Calvin's Farewell

Calvin toiled for twenty-three years after his second advent in Geneva. Life in Geneva continued to be a virtual rollercoaster of controversy and struggle for the reformer. In 1555, the Perrinists, avowed foes of Calvin in Geneva, overplayed their hand and provoked a riot, which was interpreted as a coup attempt. They were executed or exiled, and their confiscated property was used to fund the spiritual Academy. Two events occurred in 1558-1559 that no doubt took their toll on Calvin. His friend, Guillaume (William) Farel, who had initially called him to Geneva, announced that he was to marry. At this point, he was sixty-nine years of age, and it turned out he wished to marry the daughter of his refugee housekeeper, a mere girl who was already living in his home. When Farel asked Calvin to officiate the wedding, Calvin refused and would have nothing to do with the event. Their relationship became quite strained, and though Calvin's letters became less frequent and briefer, he never wholly disregarded him.

The other trauma was Calvin's contraction of the quartan fever (1558-1559). He no sooner recovered from the fever than he overstressed

---

9. Stupperich, *Melanchthon*, 150.

his voice preaching and brought on a violent fit of coughing—so violent that he broke a blood vessel in his lungs and experienced a severe hemorrhage. From this point, his delicate health declined. He already suffered from arthritis, nephritis, pulmonary tuberculosis, gall stones, hemorrhoids, and gout. Despite the severe health problems, he continued to preach. When he was unable to walk to church, he had himself carried in a chair. He preached his final sermon on February 6, 1564.

Finally, it came time for his last words to the city council, Geneva's ministers, and Farel. There is only space for brief excerpts from these farewells. He thanked the council for their kindnesses to him. He asked pardon for not doing all he should have done and apologized for his impatience and bad temper, for which he was ashamed. He stated that he had lived in a Geneva of continual strife:

> I have been saluted in derision before my door with forty or fifty arquebus [musket] shots. Just imagine how that frightened a poor scholar, timid as I am, and as I confess I have always been. Then I was expelled from this city and went to Strasbourg; and when I had lived there some time was called back here. But I had no less trouble when I tried to do my duty than previously. They set the dogs at my heels, calling out "Wretch! Wretch!", and they snapped at my gown and my legs. . . . I have willed what is good, that my vices have always displeased me, and the root of the fear of God has been in my heart. . . . As to my doctrine, I have taught faithfully, and God has given me grace to write what I have written as faithfully as it was in my power. I have not falsified a single passage of Scripture nor given it a wrong interpretation to the best of my knowledge.[10]

As death drew near, he penned a letter to his old friend Farel: "I draw my breath with difficulty and expect each moment to be my last. It is enough that I live and die for Christ, who is to all His followers a gain both in life and in death."[11] He was only fifty-four years old when he passed. Morally, his life had been circumspect. He had no sexual affairs, lived simply, ate sparingly, fasted without public show, slept only six hours per night, never took a holiday, refused increases in salary, and raised funds to aid the poor. Theodore Beza, a disciple of Calvin, succeeded him as the Republic of Geneva's spiritual leader.

10. Quoted by Parker, *John Calvin*, 188-9.
11. Quoted by Parker, *John Calvin*, 190.

Farel—Elijah of the Alps

It was Farel who was responsible for introducing the Reformation to the
French-speaking cantons of Switzerland—thus known as the Elijah of the
Alps. Moreover, as noted elsewhere, it was Farel who encouraged Calvin
to come to Geneva. He labored in that city for a brief time alongside Calvin, until they were both banished from the city. While Calvin returned
to Geneva, Farel accepted a call to the church in Neuchâtel in 1538, where
he had previously served. Here he faithfully served as chief pastor for
twenty-seven years and as a preaching evangelist and ambassador to
other parts of Switzerland, Alsace and Lorraine, and Germany. He died
in 1565 at the age of seventy-six.

Bullinger—Zwingli's Successor

Bullinger, Zwingli's able successor, wrote many theological works and
sent out some 12,000 letters during his ministry. He continued to minister
faithfully in Zürich, but strife with the Zürich city council grew instead of
lessening. Indeed, with his writings and correspondence blanketing the
continent, he was undoubtedly far more prevalent in other places than
in Switzerland. "His last days were clouded," notes Schaff, "like those of
many faithful servants of God. The excess of work and care undermined
his health. In 1562 he wrote to Fabricus at Coire: 'I almost sink under the
load of business and care, and feel so tired that I would ask the Lord to
give me rest if it were not against his will.'"[12] To add to his burdens, the
plague of 1564–1565 took his wife, three daughters, and his brother-in-
law. Nevertheless, he recovered from his stressful years and served Christ
and the church for another decade. He preached his last sermon on the
day of Pentecost, 1575, and in late August assembled the pastors and
theology professors of the city and exhorted them, among other things,
towards perseverance, purity of life, harmony, and obedience to the officials. He passed into eternity on September 17, 1575. Among Bullinger's
successors who were trained under his pastoral leadership were Rudolph
Gwalter, Zwingli's son-in-law, and his own adopted son.[13]

12. Schaff, *History Vol. VIII*, 213.
13. Schaff, *History Vol. VIII*, 213.

Beza—Last of the Continental Reformers

Following Calvin's death, Theodore de Bèze, known to us as Beza, a forty-year professor of the Geneva Academy, became Calvin's recognized successor and the one who saved Calvinism from the internal disputes that tore Lutheranism apart after Luther's departure. His style was to crystallize and deepen rather than break any new ground. Schaff describes his role in Geneva as follows: "He continued Calvin's leadership in city and church affairs. He preached and lectured to the students. He received the fugitives from France and the visitors from other lands. He gave his voice and opinion upon the innumerable things which turned up daily. He conducted an enormous correspondence. And every now and then he had to enter the field of controversy and repel 'heretics.'"[14] However, as it was with many of the reformers, the weight of the years and responsibilities took their toll on him as he lost both his hearing and short-term memory in his later years. After Calvin's passing, Beza had become the chief theologian of the Reformed Church, advancing reformed doctrine in his many scholarly works. Beza died in 1605, the last of the great Continental Reformers.

Conclusion

Though the passing of Beza marks the end of the time for the great reformers, the movement continued well into the 1600s. Historians suggest the ending be placed somewhere between 1555 (The Peace of Augsburg) and 1648 (The Treaty of Westphalia). The work of the great reformers continued through lesser-known ministers. For example, in Zürich, Bullinger personally equipped younger men to carry on the work in that city after he died.

---

14. Schaff, *History Vol. VIII*, 863.

Epilogue

WE THE AUTHORS ANTICIPATE that this book will spark interest and further discussion regarding what the Christian Church can learn from the character, ideals, and inter-relationships of the reformers presented here. Hopefully, the following comments can serve as an impetus toward constructive personal reflection and dialogue between readers.

The Counter-Reformation

The Protestant Reformation and the Catholic Counter-Reformation continued well into the 1600s. We have noted earlier that the end of the Reformation came somewhere between the Peace of Augsburg in 1555 and the Treaty of Westphalia in 1648. Of course, its reverberations are still being felt today in the Christian Church worldwide. Perhaps the closest the Catholics and Protestants came to reaching a compromise was in 1541 at the Colloquy of Regensburg, an attempt to restore unity between Catholics and Protestants in the Holy Roman Empire. At the summit, a consensual doctrine of justification was conceivable. The two factions were able to agree on some articles such as free will and original sin but stumbled on justification. In 1542 the Catholic Church launched the Inquisition and expelled Italy's would-be reformers when the Catholic Reformation turned into the Counter-Reformation.

Ulrich Zwingli, Oecolampadius, Conrad Grebel, and Wolfgang Capito had long passed from the scene, and the other primary reformers began to leave this world—Martin Luther in 1546, Martin Bucer in 1551, Philip Melanchthon in 1560, and John Calvin in 1564. Pope Paul III (1534-1548) commissioned an analysis of the Roman Church, and the report was a stinging indictment of the corruption and malfeasance of the institution. The pope called the Council of Trent in December 1545, and it would convene off and on over the next eighteen years. In the end, this council would play an extremely significant role in what is now known as the Counter-Reformation. The pope who would follow through most thoroughly with true reform was Pope Paul IV (1555-1559), though his reign was relatively brief. He transformed all the brothels into convents, and monks who did not make themselves accountable to reforms were offered the choice of imprisonment or the galleys. He sent all the non-resident bishops in Rome back to their dioceses to serve, and he exhorted the bishops to preach regularly.

What was the single most powerful impetus for the Counter-Reformation? Many believe it was the Jesuit movement. The Society of Jesus (Jesuits) was formed by Ignatius Loyola, a young soldier who began studying religious books in 1521 while his leg healed from a severe battle-field wound. He lived as a hermit for a time in contemplation and prayer, then went on to receive schooling at several universities. His humble piety attracted some fellow students, and they formed a group devoted to serving the Roman See. In 1534 they took monastic vows, which speci-fied absolute obedience directly to the pope. They ended up in Rome and requested to be received as a new religious order, their application finally accepted in 1540. The Jesuits were an intensely disciplined order with rigorous spiritual exercises, advanced education, unquestioned and total loyalty to the pope, and a wartime casuistry of "the end justifies the means." This meant that they could even use deception and trickery to lure people back to Roman Catholicism.

Interestingly, though they brought many individuals back into the Roman fold, obliterating Protestantism was not their primary goal. From Loyola's position as superior general of the Society of Jesus, there are al-most seven thousand letters extant, and they mention Luther only two or three times. Just the same, due to massive Church reform and orders such as the Jesuits, by shortly after 1600, the remarkable Protestant advances had been largely rolled back. Catholics set up some of the finest schools to teach the higher classes, and they also infiltrated the courts of kings and princes. That gave them an excellent position from which to recap-ture Catholic influence in places such as Poland, Hungary, and portions of Bohemia.

However, violence did materialize as some Catholics attempted to eradicate Protestantism. There had been small military clashes between

Catholics and Protestants for some years. However, on March 1, 1562, in Champagne, a leading Catholic prince, Francois de Guise personally engineered an attack upon a Protestant congregation meeting that was held legally under an edict of peace; at least fifty worshippers were slaughtered in what became known as the Massacre of Vassy. This violent action kindled open military conflict in the French Wars of Religion. A month later, Louis, Prince of Conde, a Protestant leader, issued a declaration for a defense that began over forty years of intermittent religious wars—eight wars in all, according to the figuring of historians.

The Counter-Reformation also included the Roman Inquisition that began in 1542 as well as the Catholic Index of prohibited books in 1559. As mentioned Jesuits began an aggressive mission to recover various parts of Europe for the Roman Church and suppress the Reformation in Bohemia, the Silesia region of Central Europe, and the Pilatinate region of Southwest Germany. There were attempts at new conquests for the Church in such places as the Americas, China, and Japan.

Surely Luther, as well as some other reformers, would have groaned in their graves, as many Protestants turned back to the scholastic, Aristotelian approach of reason-centered analysis and means of categorizing theology. Calvin had characterized scholastic theology as slimy and frivolous word battles. Luther claimed he had shown from their own writings that scholastic theology is nothing else than ignorance of the truth and a stumbling block in comparison with Scripture.

However, when the Jesuits and others took the offensive using scholastic methods of reasoning, Protestants felt they must also take up again the sword of scholasticism to do battle with them. Thus, at least through the end of the seventeenth century, the strict logic and objectification of scholasticism ruled. In the very simplest terms, the emphasis changed from *whom* we know and believe to *what* we know and believe. This makes a great deal of difference in the personal versus the impersonal nature of the Christian faith. It was too easy under scholasticism to depersonalize Scripture and, in essence, silence the intimate connection essential to revelation. For example, to the reformers, sin was unfaithfulness toward God and estrangement from him—it was grievously failing to respond appropriately to Him. For the later Protestant scholastics, sin was a technical violation of divine law, rendering the offending individual guilty. Both concepts are correct, but one is more personal and connected to daily reality than the other.[1]

There has been a tempering of the tension between Catholics and Protestants in recent decades, especially following the Second Vatican Council of the early 1960s. In the mindset of Vatican II there has been an effort to more openly embrace Protestantism (as well as Eastern Orthodoxy) in an effort to move towards Christian unity. Nonetheless many Protestant Christians and indeed whole movements, especially in Canada and the United States, remain distrustful at the least and antagonistic at worst towards Roman Catholicism. Roman Catholic layman Karl Keating laments the attacks by fundamentalist Christians on Romanists, resulting in many Catholics joining fundamentalist Churches: "In fact," he proposes, "in many fundamentalist churches, more than half the members converted from Catholicism." He goes on to suggest "The reasons for the conversions are many, but most converts have been influenced by arguments attacking 'Romanism.' Some fundamentalists who seek out Catholics as converts are not merely profundamentalist; they are also decidedly anti-Catholic. They expend more effort abusing the Catholic religion than on justifying their own. They are more interested in showing Catholicism is wrong, no matter what it takes to 'prove' that, than they are in showing their position is right."[2]

In the same era as Vatican II some Catholic leaders in the West adopted a theology that was much more compatible with historic Protestantism than with orthodox Catholicism. "The new theology," notes Reformed theologian R. C. Sproul, "made great inroads in Germany, Holland, and the United States. As a result, Roman Catholic priests in these countries began to sound like Protestants in the things they taught." Consequently, he goes on to say, "These changes have led many Protestants to join the Roman Catholic Church. I suspect there are vastly greater numbers leaving Rome for evangelicalism than the other way around, but a number of leading evangelicals have embraced Rome, the most high profile of whom was probably Francis Beckwith, who resigned as president of the Evangelical Theological Society in 2007 when he decided to convert to Roman Catholicism."[3]

---

1. Payton, *Getting,* 208.

2. Keating, *Catholicism and Fundamentalism,* 27–8.

3. Sproul, *Are We Together,* 7–8.

In 1994 leading Catholic and Evangelical scholars signed a document called *Evangelicals and Catholics Together* (ECT). The accord, drafted by participants led by evangelical Charles Colson and Catholic Richard Neuhaus came about over concern for common social and ethical issues such as family values, abortion, and moral relativism. Also included was a statement of affirmation by both parties of the doctrine of justification by grace through faith in Christ. This was followed by ECT II (1997) which continued to address theological concerns while encouraging continuation of dialogue regarding differences and disagreements in doctrine, worship, and practice.

A Central Theme of the Reformation: Church and State

Two crucial questions related to Church and State lie at the very core of the Reformation: 1) *How did the reforming groups relate to the Roman Catholic papacy as a governing power?* and 2) *How did they relate to the State?* Luther gained much of his early following because princes and nobles in Germany were disgruntled with Roman Catholic demands—both ecclesiastical and financial. Melanchthon and Luther knew that some princes cared not in the least about religion. They were only anxious to gain dominion over the people, plunder the churches, and be free from the bishops' control. Nevertheless, especially in his early years, Luther had a close relationship with individual state leaders, and they sought and often followed his counsel. He may have imagined that any reform-minded leaders would have the same relationship with secular nobles. Derek Wilson writes that,

> The Wittenberg theologians were determined that warlords should not hijack the Reformation. It was a religious movement, and Luther, more vehemently than his colleagues, insisted that it should not be tainted by politics. This was naïve. In their conflict with Rome the preachers had already placed dependence upon secular power for support and protection and their developing vision was for State churches in which the clergy defined Christian belief and practice and the magistracy framed and enforced the laws which enshrined this belief and practice. Such collaboration was an unrealistic ideal, depending as it did, on the goodwill and, ultimately, on the righteousness of the prince or civic authority.[4]

4. Wilson, *Out of the Storm*, 251.

Thus, Luther was to unwittingly place himself in an impossible position. He declined to sever Church from State totally; he rejected theocracy and therefore left the way open for caesaropapism, that is, a leader or emperor who, in effect, has power over the Church. Though he did not realistically contemplate a Christianized society, he was also not resigned to a thoroughly secularized culture. The Church must run the risk of dilution rather than leave the State to the cold light of judgment, unwarmed by tenderness. He did believe that the social fabric could be "darned and patched," and he labored strenuously to rebuke and instruct the State through pamphlets, tracts, and over one thousand letters written to political leaders at all levels.[5]

Nonetheless, Luther spoke of two necessary kingdoms: the kingdom of God's right hand (the Church) and the kingdom of his left hand (the State). The State must not be forced to live by the gospel but by natural law (which comes from God apart from Scripture) and the civil law (enacted by governmental decree). According to Luther, if God's laws governed the State, it would suggest that the scriptures could be fulfilled by what even an unbeliever does as a law-abiding citizen. Luther tried to place the Church and State in two separate spheres, corresponding roughly to dualisms in God's nature and humanity. As summarized by Roland Bainton, "God is wrath and mercy. The State is the instrument of His wrath, the Church of His mercy. Man is divided into an outward and inward. Crime is outward and belongs to the State, and sin is inward and belongs to the Church. Goods are external and belong to the State. Faith is inward and falls to the Church."[6]

Luther believed that in most cases, Christians must obey the State, even if they disagree. However, there were two general situations in which Christians could disobey: 1) if the State transgressed one of the first three of the Ten Commandments; for example, if they commanded Christians to stop reading the Bible, Christians would be justified in resisting, and 2) if the State required service in a war "manifestly unjust" Christians could refuse to fight.[7]

Luther expressed the notion that secular authorities had to keep societal order because true Christians were so few. He even lacked trust in the goodness of certain professing Christian citizens. He identified

5. Ozment, *Protestantism,* 129.

6. Bainton, *Here I Stand,* 187.

7. Bainton, *Here I Stand,* 189.

Augustine's *City of God* as the Church and distinguished it from the temporal or earthly city. Yet, he believed the temporal city was not necessarily hopelessly profane—never beyond the scope of God's activity. Christians were to be subject to earthly authority, yet speak publicly, boldly, and honestly to authorities lest they be ruled as if they were mere pigs or dogs. Both believers and unbelievers could cooperate with God in matters related to civil obedience, but none could cooperate with God to achieve personal Christian righteousness without Christ.

Though peasant unrest had been building long before Luther, the population took Luther's writings of religious freedom and mistranslated them into a declaration of the right to demand change at all costs. The revolt, as noted earlier, was one of the darkest moments in Luther's career. He struggled mightily over the issue of civil obedience and war. In simplest terms, Luther believed in the hierarchies of authority from the king and subject, down to the master and servant. The magistrate, and only the magistrate, had full right to use the sword, the father the fist, the pastor the tongue, and the slave could appeal gross abuse of the sword.

For Zwingli (in Zürich), Bucer (in Strassburg), and Oecolampadius (in Basel), Luther's two-kingdom approach did not resonate. They had serious concerns for the improvement of society, the development of responsible participation in government by its citizens, and the improvement of social life and ethics. They believed citizens could practice secular vocations for the glory of God. Leaving urban life in the secular realm, unshaped by God's Word, seemed to them no true solution. They eventually formulated directives regarding education, care for the poor, health matters, oversight of guilds, as well as fair prices and wages.[8]

Calvin's ultimate goal appeared to be the establishment of a *City of God* in Europe. In his remarkably dynamic view of history, God was a very busy, active, all-encompassing deity whose elect were an army on the march to build His kingdom now. Calvin held that the real law of a Christian state must be the Bible, and the clergy are the proper interpreters of that law. Civil governments are subject to this law and are thus constrained to enforce it. He longed so much for a Christian society that he was willing to work very closely with the governing body of a city—so close that at times it seemed that the Church and the State almost stood as one. It may be that Calvin wanted total Christian unity so earnestly that he was willing to push for the next best thing to full-blown theocracy. He

8. Payton, *Getting,* 104–5.

believed that the government could and should have a prominent role in protecting the church and regulating the lives of people according to the moral law laid out in Scripture. He did not seem to realize that, invariably, when Church and State are allied, one tends to dominate, and that is a harbinger of grave trouble.

Returning to Luther's perspective, it is evident that he did not adopt Augustine's dream of the *City of God* or Calvin's Genevan concept of a Christianized city. He wrote, "a man who would venture to govern an entire community or the world with the gospel would be like a shepherd who should place in one fold wolves, lions, eagles, and sheep. The sheep could be said to keep the peace, but they would not last long. The world cannot be ruled with a rosary."[9]

Anabaptists believed that secular governments are manifestly evil if left to themselves, and the "Church, is a voluntary society of convinced believers, that it should be separate from the State, and that where religion is concerned no man's assent should be won by force."[10] In a general sense, many Anabaptist groups wanted a Church independent of civic control and free to govern itself, much like the pre-Constantine Church.

The Reformers as Communicators

As public speakers or preachers, Calvin and Luther may have been the most welcome to both the ears and mind. Erasmus was known as a writer, not an orator, though his speech could be both charming and brilliant. Melanchthon's content was incomparable, and he drew overflowing crowds to his classrooms, though he had a stammer, and his voice was shrill and harsh sounding. Luther's voice was clear and strong, and he showed a sophisticated understanding of theology when teaching at university or debating with theologians. However, in his sermons, he tried to present Scripture in a manner that even his young children could understand. Zwingli's sermons were quite articulate, though his style was a bit more informal and extemporaneous than some. His voice was not strong, and his delivery, quite rapid. He heightened listener interest by use of occasional anecdotes and humor. Calvin was generally easy to follow, using short, clear sentences. He used no gimmicks, merely moving expositorily

9. Quoted by Bainton, *Here I Stand,* 184–5.
10. Bainton, *Christianity,* 263.

from one scripture passage to the next. One of his strengths was his succinct application of the text to the situations of listeners.

Of the Strassburgers, Matthew Zell may have been the most popular preacher. He was dynamic, warm, and wise, and hundreds flocked to his services. Bucer and Capito were both capable in the pulpit, though Bucer had a reputation of being a bit long-winded.

William Tyndale was known far more as a translator than a preacher, but there exists one interesting event related to his discoursing. While he served as a tutor to two young boys, he began preaching in the open air in the town of Bristol and the College Green outside the Augustinian priory. Apparently, his preaching drew enough public attention that he was commanded to quit.

As writers, the reformers displayed varying levels of ability and success. History has proven Erasmus, Luther, Melanchthon, Calvin, and Tyndale were all undoubtedly talented with the pen, though some a bit more prolific than others. It is interesting to note that many of the best-known reformers were expert linguists: Erasmus for the Netherlands, Luther for Germany, Tyndale for England, and Calvin for Switzerland and France. Erasmus translated the Latin Vulgate from the Greek and consequently provided the example and inspiration for the others. Tyndale, an expert in eight languages, translated the New Testament brilliantly into English. With assistance, Luther translated the entire Bible into German. Luther did not profit from his many books, and he did not even possess copies of some of them in later life. Nevertheless, he did take pride in his translation of the Bible, and he spent close to twenty-five years revising and improving it. It was his greatest scholarly achievement.

Melanchthon, Luther's ingenious partner, artfully articulated many of the tenets of the Reformation in writings such as his famous *Loci Communes* and, in some ways, was a better writer than Luther. As for Calvin, it should not be surprising that Melanchthon called him "the theologian." Calvin is famous for his *Institutes of the Christian Religion*, which constitute within a thousand pages, a masterful catechetical handbook *Protestant Apologia,* a Reformation manifesto, and a guide to Christian practice. Zwingli's fundamental theological beliefs were well thought out, but unfortunately were the writings of a hurried, harried leader. Thus, they betrayed some weaknesses—weaknesses that his successor, Heinrich Bullinger, attempted to rectify. It might be hypothesized that if Erasmus was too little focused upon himself as a sinner, Luther might have been too despairing. Melanchthon and Calvin seemed to strike a healthy balance between personal concern and a focus on objectively verifiable truth. Erasmus continually pointed out how revolutionary the *Philosophy of Christ* could be if taken seriously. Melanchthon subjected philosophy to rhetoric and claimed that wisdom is useless if merely enjoyed in contemplation. Luther and Calvin attempted to write with deep insight and substance, yet on a level that even the commoner could grasp. Regarding the Reformation, Erasmus is likely best known for his work, the *Praise of Folly*, a light but barbed satire of Roman Catholic abuses, though some argue other writings were more brilliant.

It may be interesting to note the ages of reformers when their masterpieces were published. Erasmus was almost fifty when he published his Greek New Testament; Luther was nearly forty when his translation of the New Testament appeared and almost fifty when he finished translating the whole Bible. In contrast, Calvin was twenty-six when he wrote his *Institutes*, and Melanchthon was twenty-four when he wrote *Loci Communes*.

How vital was the printing press to the Reformation? The vast majority of people in the sixteenth century were illiterate, unable even to read simple pamphlets written for the masses. Just the same, a great deal was learned through spoken words, acted-out truths, pictures, and, above all, word of mouth. Throughout Europe, peasant crowds gathered around the rare readers in their midst, even in pubs, and listened for hours to the writings of such men as Luther and Erasmus. Vivid language and figures of speech were immediately committed to memory and repeated endlessly to neighbors. However, it is sad to realize that whole generations were denied many of the writings we now value so highly. For decades public book burnings were frequent, and in 1557, Pope Paul IV's Roman Inquisition banned the writings of individuals such as Erasmus and Luther, and many thousands of precious manuscripts were burned in public bonfires.

The Dark Side of Reformation Leadership

Gary McIntosh and Samuel Rima discovered in their research on leadership in Christian organizations that "a paradox of sorts existed in the lives of most of the leaders who had experienced significant failures: the personal insecurities, feelings of inferiority, and need for parental approval (among other dysfunctions) that compelled these people to become successful leaders were very often the same issues that precipitated their failure."[11] They go on to suggest that this paradox can be seen in other leaders such as Adolph Hitler, Douglas MacArthur, and Richard Nixon, as well as some of the leaders we find in the Bible. We would add that the same enigma can be found in the lives of some of the great leaders of the Reformation, including Luther and Zwingli. "In almost every case" conclude McIntosh and Rima, "the factors that eventually undermine us are shadows of the ones that contribute to our success."[12] This is clearly evidenced in the leadership of many of the reformers.

Coarse Behavior and Violence

In any review of the sometimes–ugly competition between reformers, the culture of the time must be taken into consideration. Even in "enlightened" Europe, life could be vulgar and brutal. It was often cut short by disease, violence, or accident, and a stoic acceptance of this inevitability made life seem cheaper. Conversation, at least among the general population, was frequently coarse and earthy. The display of crass emotion was sometimes even admired. Rome's harsh, violent defense of their medieval theology and practices made reformers think it a shame for "Christ's magistrates" to show themselves less ardent in defense of the certain truth.

However, can the reformers be excused for exhibiting these traits as they pushed for a purer, more biblical church? Though we may soften our judgment based on the times and our knowledge of human weakness, we must not merely overlook or minimize these failings. These individuals were very fallible. The reformers were great heroes of the faith. They were wise, courageous, hard-working, godly, and tenacious. They saw a wayward Church far off her moorings and led thousands back to orthodox biblical truth. Most of them were good to great communicators.

Nonetheless, it must also be admitted that these individuals were far from perfect. They exhibited, at times, personal faults and a lack of self-control over their emotions and actions. Luther frequently lost his temper and the words that flowed out of his mouth could be both vulgar and loathsome. His private conversations, table talk, and even a few of his lectures and sermons were laced with words, expressions, and stories

11. McIntosh and Rima, *Overcoming*, 13.

12. McIntosh and Rima, *Overcoming*, 28.

that we might today characterize as gutter talk. Though in our day we might recoil from such language, it was a practically universal custom of that era. Not only was popular literature often vulgar, the conversation of high society often included quite shocking examples of vulgar or ribald language.

It seems that Luther was cognizant of his behavior and, though many observants today may disapprove of his coarseness and temper, in his mind, there was a purpose for it. In a letter to a friend in Nuremberg in August 1519, he wrote, "I see that whatever is treated mildly in our age soon falls into oblivion, for no one minds it. Even Paul calls his adversaries 'dogs, babblers . . . and ministers of Satan,' and what prophet does not use the bitterest invective? Such [mild] language becomes so trite it ceases to move."[13]

Furthermore, Luther's sometimes unrestrained language can, to some degree, be explained by his writing habits. He claimed to write best when impassioned by some harsh attack or some new doctrinal challenge. He did not have time to edit his work and did not desire anyone else to do so. Illness, arrest, or even assassination could occur any day; there was no time to belabor over fifth and sixth drafts. It is also a fact that, when Luther devoted himself, heart and soul, to convincing individuals or groups of his teachings or of what he considered right behavior and those parties rudely rejected him, he sometimes reacted somewhat bitterly. These individuals included theologians such as Erasmus and Zwingli, the peasants participating in the tragic rebellion, and the Jewish people. Luther could not seem to graciously accept those who abruptly rejected him or refused in the end to follow his advice and opinion.

Calvin bemoaned his "wild animal of a temper." But he was able in most cases to lay aside the temptation towards bitterness and revenge for the sake of his mission. He could be cantankerous and agreed to forms of church discipline through the state, including the death penalty. Much worse, Zwingli approved of the death sentence for Christian Anabaptists, and his railroading of Conrad Grebel's father to execution reflected a spirit of vengeance against Conrad. Thomas Müntzer, a conservative in many ways, adopted a policy of violence and murder, and, through that violence, over a hundred thousand German peasants were slaughtered. Grebel, in the immaturity of youth, was not willing to wait for various reforms to be adopted. He did not appear to work gently and wisely to

13. Quoted by Smith, *The Life and Letters*, 87.

wrest control of the church out of the hands of the state; instead, he tried
to force immediate action and suffered for it.

Mishandling of Conflict

Christian leaders should be messengers of grace, rather than harbingers
of dissension. Good leaders understand the values of being approachable
and able to handle conflict. Kenn Gangel and Samuel Canine identify
common myths adhered to regarding conflict. One myth holds that conflict is abnormal; in reality, it is a normal part of daily life. A second myth
is that conflict and disagreement are synonymous; the truth is that while
individuals can agree to disagree, conflict is a clash of wills on an issue. A
third myth is that conflict is pathological in nature or reflects a personality disorder. This is occasionally the case but holding to the notion that
conflict is always dysfunctional short-circuits a resolution process that
can lead to mutual understanding of issues. A fourth myth maintains
that conflict must be avoided; however peace at all costs can result in
deep, long-term resentments and leave issues unresolved. A final myth is
that conflict is an admission of failure; in actuality, only if handled in an
unscriptural manner can it result in failure.[14]

Principles on conflict management are invaluable for Christian
leaders. One important principle is that conflict must be dealt with in its
earliest stages. If Luther or even Grebel had talked through the issues with
Müntzer early on, perhaps they could have softened his position regarding violence and religious rights, and thousands of lives might have been
spared. A second principle is that adversarial parties must remain focused on the issue at hand rather than veering off into peripheral disputes
and waging personal attacks on each other. Though Luther and Zwingli
never became friends, they did agree to an open forum and, through this,
learned that they only disagreed substantively on one or two issues.

Third, conflict must be monitored so as to make sure parties are
1) allowed to disagree without feeling guilty, 2) state their position with
energy and precision, 3) be protected from attack, and 4) be optimistic
even when minimal progress is made. In the conflict between Zwingli
and Grebel, there seems to have been the dangerous combination of
Zwingli's greater biblical knowledge and desire for unquestioned preemi-
nence and Grebel's youthful idealism and rash impatience. Consequently,

14. Gangel and Canine, *Communication*, 129–31.

disagreements escalated into anger, verbal attack, and finally, physical violence and martyrdom.

Fourth, parties must be cognizant of the fact that their conflict represents a problem to be solved instead of a battle to be waged or a position to be doggedly defended. They must gather all the information possible, verify that it is accurate and relevant, and then find creative options for solution or compromise.[15] Some of the reformers clearly did not persist in investigating issues in-depth in an unbiased, un-manipulative manner, so as to hammer out positions upon which they might agree.

Warning for Spiritual Leaders

Some biographies, textbooks, and articles make the reformers out to be faultless spiritual giants. In our society, Christians often set charismatic pastors, scholars, or radio/television preachers on a pedestal. Their mass following is not surprising, in view of the fact that some of these leaders have the financial empires to churn out advertising, books, videos, and DVD series *ad infinitum*. The naive image of these leaders is that they can do no wrong and everything they teach is without error. "But the myth that a leader is an answer man . . . creates an impossible burden that God neither intends nor supports. Arrogance says, 'I like people needing my strength (or wisdom, etc.) but I don't like needing someone else's strength.' This is arrogance, not leadership."[16]

One glance at the list of Christian leaders who have fallen in recent decades to such wrongs as financial impropriety, sexual immorality, and unconventional teaching should convince us that every leader has faults. It is also true that in matters of faith and practice, a leader may preach one lifestyle while he or she is living another. Leaders should be respected but never idolized. Great disillusionment and bitterness have resulted when an idolized leader falls. Moreover, like the Berean saints, we should diligently search the Scriptures ourselves to confirm that preachers and teachers we hear are rightly interpreting the Word. Whatever Luther's human weaknesses, Preserved Smith does not believe one of them was rank arrogance. He writes, "It is characteristic of Luther that all of his bravest and best acts seemed to be done in the simple course of everyday duty. He

---

15. Gangel and Canine, *Communication*, 260–3.

16. Susek, *Firestorm*, 168.

never seems to have had the exclusive goal of achieving fame, which has inspired so many others. He simply saw the duty before him and did it."[17]

Christian leaders should indispensably seek personal accountability. Moreover, those looked to for accountability should not merely be *yes* people who rubber stamp everything a leader says, plans, or does. They should ideally be friends who hone their brother or sister as iron sharpens iron. Errant leaders are not victims of social circumstance and should not be granted that excuse. "You buy that," states Tom Robbins, "and you pay with your soul. What limits people is lack of character."[18] This means that when a leader is sliding into sin, is treating others improperly, is ignoring critical issues, or is not searching out the will of God, his or her peers must be willing to confront gently and firmly. They also must be willing to follow through in helping an individual change, repent, or make restitution when a serious mistake or transgression has been committed.

Doing the work of God in the world is not a competition. It is evident among the reformers that they occasionally viewed one another not so much as beloved Christian brothers but as competitors for the ears of the public, for the prestige of their ministries, and for their place in history. However, notes John White, the elite of God's leaders are different: "They are the meek who inherit the earth (Matt 5:5). They weep and pray in secret, and defy earth and hell in public. They tremble when faced with danger, but die in their tracks sooner than turn back. They are like a shepherd defending his sheep or a mother protecting her young. They sacrifice without grumbling, give without calculation, suffer without groaning. To those in their charge, they say, 'We live well if you do well.' Their price is above riches. They are the salt of the earth. For the cause of the kingdom, we need more of them."[19]

Because influential administrators often have powerful, driven personalities, it is easy for them to be competitive with others and view fellow leaders as enemies or at least opponents. They feel they must have the larger audience, the higher salary, the greater fame, or the greater respect. This is a subtle pitfall. Leaders may not recognize it in themselves until another leader is chosen above them, is drawing away radio listeners or church parishioners, expresses a conviction different from theirs. Then

17. Smith, *The Life and Letters*, 417.

18. Quoted by Maxwell, *Developing*, 30.

19. White, *Excellence*, 89.

jealousy, that old green-eyed monster, rears her head and unleashes an offspring of pride, covetousness, slander, greed, anger, and bitterness.

It is evident that, in some cases, the reformers held tenaciously to points of doctrine (especially in relation to other reformers) about which they could have legitimately negotiated. The Protestant Reformation would have been a much less violent and vitriolic process if leaders had compromised graciously in cases where the Scripture allows for it. By all means, Christians should hold firmly to their most fundamental doctrines of faith. However, we should reach out in love toward those saints who believe differently and should not let differences in peripheral doctrines cause us to stubbornly isolate ourselves from them. Also, there are aspects of doctrine about which the scriptures are not adamant or specific; on these, there may be opportunities for compromise.

Bibliography

Aland, Kurt. *Four Reformers: Luther, Melanchthon, Calvin, Zwingli*. Minneapolis: Augsburg, 1979.

Atkinson, James. *Martin Luther and the Birth of Protestantism*. London, UK: Pelican, 1968.

Bainton, Roland. *Christianity*. Boston: Houghton-Mifflin, 1992.

———. *Here I Stand: A Life of Martin Luther*. Nashville: Abingdon, 1950.

———. *Women of the Reformation in Germany and Italy*. Minneapolis: Augsburg, 1971.

Bax, E. Belfort. *Rise and Fall of the Anabaptists*. New York: American Scholar, 1903/1966.

Beard, Charles. *Martin Luther and the Reformation in Germany*. London: UK: Kegan Paul, Trench, & Co., 1889.

Bender, Harold. *Conrad Grebel*. Scottdale, PA: Herald, 1950.

Beza, Theodore. *The Life of Calvin*. Translated by Henry Beveridge. Lindenhurst, NY: Rotolo Media, 2012.

Boehmer, Heinrich. *Road to Reformation: Martin Luther to the Year 1521*. Translated by John Doberstein and Theodore Tappert. Philadelphia: Muhlenberg, 1946.

Bonar, Horatius. *Words Old and New*. Edinburgh, UK: Banner of Truth Trust, 1994.

Bornkamm, Heinrich. *Luther in Mid-Career*. Philadelphia: Fortress, 1983.

Bouwsma, William J. *John Calvin: A Sixteenth Century Portrait*. New York: Oxford University Press, 1988.

Brecht, Martin. *Martin Luther: The Preservation of the Church 1532–1546*. Translated by James L. Schaaf. Minneapolis: Fortress, 1999.

Bromily, G. W. *Zwingli and Bullinger*. Philadelphia: Westminster, 1953.

Breen, Quirinus. *John Calvin: A Study in French Humanism*, 2nd ed., N.c: Archon, 1968

Calvin, John. *John Calvin: Selections from His Writing*. Oxford, UK: Oxford University Press, 1975.

———. *Letters of John Calvin, Vol. 1*. Translated by Jules Bonnet. Eugene, OR: Wipf and Stock, 2007 reprint.

———. *Writings on Pastoral Piety*. Translated by Elsie Anne McKee. Mahwah, NJ: Paulist, 2001.

———. *Instruction in Faith*. Translated by Paul T. Fuhrman. Louisville: Westminster/John Knox, 1977.

———. *Institutes of the Christian Religion*. Translated by Ford Lewis Battles. Louisville: Westminster/John Knox, 1960.

Carlyle, Thomas. *The Selected Works of Thomas Carlyle*. Morrisville, NC: Lulu, 2014.

Chamberlin, E. R. *The Sack of Rome*. New York: Dorset, 1985.

Christoffel, Raget. *Zwingli: Or, The Rise of the Reformation in Switzerland*. Translated by John Cochran. Edinburgh, UK: T & T. Clark, 1858.

Clouse, R. G. "Erasmus, Desiderius." In *Evangelical Dictionary of Theology*, edited by Walter A. Elwell, 361. Grand Rapids, MI: Baker, 1984.

Cohn, Norman. *The Pursuit of the Millennium Revolutionary Millenarians and Mystical Anarchists of the Middle Age*. New York: Oxford University Press, 1970.

Collinson, Patrick. *The Reformation: A History*. New York: The Modern Library, 2003

Daniell, David. *William Tyndale: A Biography*. New Haven, CT: Yale University Press, 1994.

d'Aubigné, Jean Henri Merle. *For God and His People: Ulrich Zwingli and the Swiss Reformation*. Greenville, SC: BJU Press, 2000.

———. *History of the Reformation of the Sixteenth Century Vol. I*. Translated by H. White. New York: American Tract Society, N.d.

———. *History of the Reformation of the Sixteenth Century Vol. II*. Translated by H. White. New York: American Tract Society, N.d.

———. *History of the Reformation of the Sixteenth Century Vol. III*. Translated by H. White. New York: American Tract Society, N.d.

Davies, James A. "Calvin, John." In *Evangelical Dictionary of Christian Education*, edited by Michael J. Anthony, 103. Grand Rapids, MI: Baker Academic, 2001.

Durant, Will. *Heroes of History: A Brief History of Civilization from Ancient Times to the Dawn of the Modern Age*. New York: Simon & Schuster, 2001.

Durant, Will and Ariel Durant. *The Reformation: A History of European Civilization from Wyclif to Calvin, 1300-1564*. New York: Simon & Schuster, 1957.

Edwards, Brian. *God's Outlaw*. Darlington, UK: Evangelical, 1976.

Edwards, Mark U. Printing, Propaganda, and Martin Luther. Minneapolis: Fortress, 2005.

Erasmus, Desiderius. *In Praise of Folly*. Translated by John Wilson. Grand Rapids, MI: University of Michigan Press, 2000.

Estep, William R. *The Anabaptist Story*. Grand Rapids, MI: Eerdmans, 1975.

Farner, Oskar. *Zwingli the Reformer: His Life and Work*. Translated by D. G. Sear. N.c.: Archon, 1968.

Fish, Bruce and Becky Dorost Fish. *William Tyndale: Bible Translator and Martyr*. Uhrichsville, OH: Barbour, 2000.

Foxe, John. *Foxe's Book of Martyrs*. Newberry, FL: Bridge-Logos, 1563/2001.

Friedenthal, Richard. *Luther: His Life and Times*. Translated by John Nowell. New York: Harcourt Brace Jovnanovich, 1970.

Froude, J. A. *Life and Letters of Erasmus*. New York: Scribner's and Sons, 1894.

Gäbler, Ulrich. *Huldrych Zwingli: His Life and Work*. Philadelphia: Fortress, 1986.

Gangel, Kenn and Warren Benson. *Christian Education: Its History and Philosophy*. Chicago: Moody, 1983.

Gangel, Kenn and Samuel Canine, *Communication and Conflict Management*. Nashville: Broadman, 1992.

Gordon, Bruce. *Calvin*. New Haven, CT: Yale University Press, 2009.

Green, V. H. H. *Luther and the Reformation*. London, UK: New English Library, 1964.

Greschat, Martin. *Martin Bucer: A Reformer and His Times*. Translated by Stephen Buckwalter. Louisville: Westminster/John Knox, 2004.

Gritsch, Eric W. *Martin: God's Court Jester, Luther in Retrospect.* Philadelphia: Fortress, 1983.

———. *The Wit of Martin Luther.* Minneapolis: Fortress, 2006.

Harbison, Harris E. *The Christian Scholar in the Age of the Reformation.* Philadelphia: Porcupine, 1956.

Henry, Paul. *The Life and Times of John Calvin Vol. 2.* Translated by Henry Stebbing. London, UK: Whitaker and Co., 1849.

Heraud, John Abraham. *The Life and Times of Girolamo Savonarola.* London, UK: Whitaker and Co., 1843.

Keating, Karl. *Catholicism and Fundamentalism.* San Francisco: Ignatius, 1988.

Kittelson, James. *Wolfgang Capito: From Humanist to Reformer.* Leiden, NL: E.J. Brill Academic, 1975.

———. *Luther: The Reformer.* Minneapolis: Augsburg, 1986.

Luther, Martin. *The Bondage of the Will.* Translated by J. I. Packer and O. R. Johnston. Grand Rapids, MI: Baker Academic, 2012.

———. *Luther's Works Vol. 10.* Edited by Hilton C. Oswald. St. Louis: Concordia, 1974.

———. *Luther's Works Vol. 25.* Edited by Hilton C. Oswald St. Louis: Concordia, 1972.

———. *Luther's Works Vol. 29.* Edited by Jaroslav Pelikan and Walter A. Hansen. St. Louis: Concordia, 1968.

———. *Luther's Works Vol. 31.* Edited by Harold John Grimm and Helmut T. Lehmann. Philadelphia: Fortress, 1957.

———. *Luther's Works Vol. 34.* Edited by Lewis William Spitz and Helmut T. Lehmann. Philadelphia: Fortress, 1960.

———. *Luther's Works Vol. 42.* Edited by Helmut T. Lehmann and Martin O. Dietrich. Philadelphia: Fortress, 1969.

———. *Luther's Works Vol. 47.* Edited by Franklin Sherman and Helmut T. Lehmann. Philadelphia: Fortress, 1971.

———. *Luther's Works Vol. 48.* Edited by Franklin Sherman and Helmut T. Lehmann. Philadelphia: Fortress, 1963.

———. *Luther's Works Vol 54.* Translated and edited by Gottfried G. Krodel. Philadelphia: Fortress, 1963.

———. *The Table Talk of Martin Luther.* Edited by William Hazlitt and Alexander Chalmers. London, UK. 1884.

———. *Table Talk: Conversations with Martin Luther.* Translated and edited by Preserved Smith and Herbert Percival Gallinger. New Canaan, CT: Keats Publishing, 1979.

———. *Letters of Martin Luther.* Translated by Margaret A. Currie. London, UK: MacMillan, 1908.

MacCulloch, Diarmaid. *The Reformation.* New York: Viking, 2004.

Manchester, William. *A World Lit Only by Fire: The Medieval Mind and the Renaissance.* Boston: Little, Brown, and Company, 1993.

Manschreck, Clyde Leonard. *Melanchthon: The Quiet Reformer.* New York: Abingdon, 1958.

Marty, Martin. *Martin Luther.* New York: Viking Penguin, 2004.

Mathison, Keith A. *The Shape of Sola Scriptura.* Moscow, ID: Canon, 2001.

Maxwell, John. *Developing the Leader Within You.* Nashville: Thomas Nelson, 1993.

McIntosh, Gary L. and Samuel D. Rima. *Overcoming the Dark Side of Leadership.* Grand Rapids, MI: Baker, 2007.

McClintock, John. *Cyclopaedia of Biblical Theological and Ecclesiastical Literature Vol. 3*. New York: Harper & Brothers, 1891.

Melanchthon, Philip. *Commonplaces: Loci Communes*. Translated by Christian Preus. St. Louis: Concordia, 1521/2014.

———. *Selected Writings*. Translated by Charles Leander Hill. Westport, CT: Greenwood, 1978.

More, Thomas. *The Complete Works of Thomas More Vol. V*. New Haven, CT: Yale University Press, 1969.

———. *The Complete Works of Thomas More Vol. VI*. New Haven, CT: Yale University Press, 1969.

Moynahan, Brian. *God's Bestseller*. New York: St. Martin's, 2002.

Mozley, James F. *William Tyndale*. Westport, CT: Greenwood, 1937.

Naphy William G. *Documents on the Continental Reformation*. Translated by W. G. Naphy. London, UK: Palgrave Macmillan, 1996.

Neff, Christian. "Wolfgang Capito," *Mennonite Encyclopedia Vol 1*, edited by Harold S. Bender and Cornelius Krahn, 512–16. Scottdale, PA: Herald, 1955.

Nichols Stephen J. *Martin Luther: A Guided Tour of His Life and Thought*. Phillipsburg, NJ: P&R, 2002.

———. *The Reformation: How a Monk and Mallet Changed the World*. Wheaton, IL: Crossway, 2007.

Noll, M. "Zwingli, Ulrich." In *Evangelical Dictionary of Theology*, edited by Walter A. Elwell, 1203–4. Grand Rapids, MI: Baker, 1984.

Ozment, Steven E. *Protestants: The Birth of a Revolution*. New York: Image, 1991.

Parker, T. H. L. *Calvin's Preaching*. Louisville: Westminster/John Knox, 1992.

———. *John Calvin—A Biography*. Louisville: Westminster/John Knox, 2006.

Pauck, Wilhelm. *Melanchthon and Bucer*. Philadelphia: Westminster, 1959.

Payton, James. *Getting the Reformation Wrong*. Downer's Grove, IL: InterVarsity, 2010.

Pollock, Constance and Daniel Pollock, *Book of Uncommon Prayer*. Nashville: Thomas Nelson, 1996.

Potter, G. R. *Zwingli*, Cambridge, UK: Cambridge University Press, 1976.

Putnam, George Haven. *Anecdotes of Luther and the Reformation*. London, UK: Hodder and Stoughton, 1883.

Reid, W. S. "Calvin, John." In *Evangelical Dictionary of Theology*, edited by Walter A. Elwell, 185–6. Grand Rapids, MI: Baker, 1984.

Reid, J. K. S. *Calvin, Theological Treatises*. Louisville: Westminster/John Knox, 1954.

Rich, James. "Calvin's Theology: The Aim and Purpose of the Institutes." https://www.placefortruth.org/blog/calvins-theology-aim-purpose-institutes.

Richard, James William. *Philip Melanchthon: The Protestant Preceptor of Germany*. New York: G. P. Putnam's Sons, 1898.

Rupp, E. Gordon. *The Righteousness of God: Luther Studies*. London, UK: Hodder and Stoughton, 1953

Rupp, Gordon and Philip Watson. *Luther and Erasmus: Free Will and Salvation*. Translated by Gordon Rupp and Philip Watson. Philadelphia: Westminster, 1969.

Ruth, John L. *Conrad Grebel: Son of Zürich*. Scottdale, PA: Herald, 1975.

Sattler, Michael and John H. Yoder, *The Legacy of Michael Sattler*. Translated and edited by John H. Yoder. Walden, NY: Plough, 2019.

Schaff, Philip. *History of the Christian Church Vol. VII*. New York: Charles Scribner's Sons, 1910.

———. *History of the Christian Church Vol. VI.* New York: Charles Scribner's Sons, 1910.

———. *History of the Christian Church Vol. VIII.* New York: Charles Scribner's Sons, 1910.

Shelley, Bruce. *Church History in Plain Language.* Waco, TX: Word, 1982.

Schilling, Heintz. *Martin Luther: Rebel in an Age of Upheaval.* Translated by Rona Johnston. Oxford, UK: Oxford University Press, 2017.

Schnucker, R. V. "Melanchthon, Philip." In *Evangelical Dictionary of Theology*, edited by Walter A. Elwell, 702–3. Grand Rapids, MI: Baker, 1984.

Simon, Edith. *Luther Alive.* Garden City, NY: Doubleday, 1968.

Smith, Preserved and Robert Backhouse. *The Life and Letters of Martin Luther.* London, UK: Hodder and Stoughton, 1911/1993.

Smith, Preserved. *The Life and Letters of Martin Luther.* Boston: Houghton Mifflin Company, 1911.

Spitz, Lewis. *The Protestant Reformation: 1517–1559.* New York: Harper & Row, 1985.

Sproul, R. C. *Are We Together?* Sanford, FL: Reformation Trust Publishing, 2012.

Stauffer, Richard. *The Humanness of John Calvin.* Translated by George Shriver. Nashville: Abingdon, 1971.

Steinmetz, David C. *Reformers in the Wings.* Grand Rapids, MI: Baker, 1971.

———. *Calvin in Context.* New York: Oxford University Press, 1995.

Stevenson, William. *The Story of the Reformation.* Richmond, VA: John Knox, 1959.

Stork, Theophilus. *Martin Luther and Reformation in Germany.* Philadelphia: Lindsay & Blakiston, 1857.

Stupperich, Robert. *Melanchthon.* Translated by Robert H. Fischer. Philadelphia: Westminster, 1965.

Susek, Ron. *Firestorm: Preventing and Overcoming Church Conflicts.* Grand Rapids, MI: Baker, 1999.

von Ranke, Leopold. "The Beginning of the Reformation." In *Luther: A Profile*, edited by H. G. Koenigsberger, 3–45. New York: Hill and Wang, 1973.

———. *History of the Reformation in Germany.* Translated by Sarah Austin. London, UK: George Rutledge and Sons, 1905.

Vedder, Henry C. *Balthasar Hübmaier: The Leader of the Anabaptists.* New York: Ames, 1905/1917.

Walker, Williston. *A History of the Christian Church,* 4th ed. New York: Scribner, 1985.

Walpole, Horace. *Letters.* London: H.G. Bohn, 1880.

Wenger, John Christian. *Even Unto Death.* Richmond, VA: John Knox, 1961.

Wengert, Timothy J. "Introducing the Pastoral Leader." In *The Pastoral Luther: Essays on Martin Luther's Practical Theology*, edited by Timothy J. Wengert, 1–32. Minneapolis: Fortress, 2017.

White, John. *Excellence in Leadership.* Downer's Grove, IL: InterVarsity, 1992.

Williams, Donald T. *Ninety-Five Theses for a New Reformation: A Road Map for Post-Evangelical Christianity.* Toccoa, GA: *Semper Reformanda* Publications, 2021.

Williams, George Hunston. *The Radical Reformation.* Philadelphia: Westminster, 1962.

Wilson, Derek. *Out of the Storm: The Life and Legacy of Martin Luther.* New York: St. Martin's, 2007.

Index of Names and Places

Vadian, Joachim, 91, 109
Valla, Lorenzo, 7
Vaughn, Stephen, 174
Venice, 138
Vienne, 219
Vilvorde, 171, 175, 177
Viret, Pierre, 203, 214, 216
Vitrier, Jean, 16
Vlacich, Matthew, 192
Volta, Gabriel della, 42

Waldo, Peter, 6
Waldshut, 114–5, 128
Walsh John, 168–9
Wartburg, 62, 67, 69–70, 72, 146
Westphalia, Treaty of, 222, 229–30
Wildhaus, 18, 90, 94
William of Braunschweig, 64
William of Henneberg, 64
Wittembach, Thomas, 90–1
Wittenberg, 27, 29–32, 40, 42, 45–7,
    50, 53, 60–2, 64, 67, 69–71, 73–6,
    80–3, 85, 127, 133, 137, 139,
    144–5, 170, 177–8, 183, 185,
    189–90, 192
  Concord, 84
  Confession, 83

Wolfflin, Henry, 18, 90
Wolmar, Melchior, 197
Wolsey, Thomas, 168–9, 174
Word of God (see God, Word of)
Worms, 43, 54, 62–4, 67, 74, 85–6,
    158, 170–1, 177, 209, 213
  Diet at (of), 60, 62, 76, 136, 146,
    159, 162, 166
  Edict of, 63, 73, 159–60,
Württemberg, 114–5
Wycliff, John, 4–5, 51

Zell, Katharina, ix, 119, 210
Zell, Matthew, ix, 119, 122, 210, 238
Zerbst, 192
Zollikon, 108
Zürich, 58–9, 75, 92, 94–102, 105–8,
    110–2, 115–6, 205, 223, 228–9,
    236, 250
  Council, 108, 112
Zwingli, Huldrych, vii, viii, ix, 8, 15,
    18–9, 21, 36–7, 58–60, 75, 84,
    88–113, 116, 122, 141, 148–57,
    195, 200, 210, 222–3, 230, 236,
    240–2, 247–8, 250
Zwickau, 47, 71, 75, 132

Index of Subjects